D0872430

The Frost Weeds
Vietnam: 1964–1965
©2014 James Oliveri

Published by Hellgate Press
(An imprint of L&R Publishing, LLC)

Hellgate Press
PO Box 3531
Ashland, OR 97520
email: sales@hellgatepress.com

Editor: Harley B. Patrick
Interior design: Michael Campbell
Cover design: L. Redding

Library of Congress Cataloging-in-Publication Data
Oliveri, James.
The frost weeds : Vietnam: 1964-1965 / James Oliveri. -- First edition.
    pages cm
  ISBN 978-1-55571-760-5
1. Oliveri, James. 2. Vietnam War, 1961-1975--Personal narratives, American. 3. Soldiers--United States--Biography. 4. United States. Army--Military life--History--20th century. 5. Vietnam War, 1961-1975--Campaigns. 6. United States--Relations-- Vietnam. 7. Vietnam--Relations--United States. I. Title.
  DS559.5.O44 2014
  959.704'342092--dc23
      2014008739

Printed and bound in the United States of America
First edition 10 9 8 7 6 5 4 3 2 1

THE FROST WEEDS

VIETNAM: 1964–1965

•

JAMES OLIVERI

CONTENTS

PREFACE

It hardly seems possible that so many years have elapsed since I returned home from Vietnam in the spring of 1965. The public attitude then toward veterans of that growing war was not yet hostile, as it was soon destined to become. People still tended to react with apathy rather than with anger toward our military. It was more a case of, "So you're back from Vietnam, huh? That's good. Say, did you see the Yankee game last night?" But that changed quickly, and not for the better.

Truthfully, no one ever spat on me or called me a "baby-killer" while I was in uniform, something many returning soldiers experienced later. In fact, the only "baby-killers" I ever saw were on the other side, and they were devastatingly efficient at it as I learned for myself. But when it comes to wars, some people can be quite irrational and deeply mean-spirited in their misguided opposition to those who must fight them.

Going off to the military is something of a tradition in my family. I was born while my father was in the Army Air Corps Band during WWII, based in Malden, Missouri. He served his entire enlistment without ever leaving the States. My father-in-law, Tom Ford, flew fifty missions as a B-17 tail gunner over Europe and North Africa. Uncle Ralph Bevilacqua, my mother's brother, was wounded at the "Battle of the Bulge." My son Jimmy Jr. was in the Army Military Police during "Operation Desert Storm." In fact, most of my male relatives served "Uncle Sam" at one time or another in various corners of the globe.

We weren't always good soldiers either. During World War I another of my uncles was slapped into a ball and chain for desertion from the Navy. We weren't necessarily expected to volunteer for combat, but the unspoken rule was that, if called, we had to show up.

As an adolescent I was fascinated by all things military. Memorial Day was one of my favorite holidays, as it still is. My friends and I had the usual complement of toy guns and lead soldiers. We played war games in our back yards. Our favorite movies were "Sergeant York," "They Died With Their Boots On," and "The Sands of Iwo Jima." War seemed glorious then. In retrospect, I realize that I still had much to learn.

War is many things, but glorious is not one of them. War is frightening, painful, exhausting, ugly, revolting, uncomfortable, depressing, and even boring. Yet I have to admit that it can also be exhilarating. I have never felt so intensely alive as I did during my experiences in battle. Nothing I've done since can compare to that.

I was about ten years old when I first saw "High Noon." Gary Cooper's portrayal of a less-than-perfect lawman who stood up for his beliefs when it would have been much easier and safer to just run away made a lasting impression on me. The fact that he did it for unappreciative and non-supportive townspeople merely served as an eerie parallel to what I would experience some ten years later. Of such things are tender young psyches sometimes molded.

So when the growing conflict in Southeast Asia drew me in during the mid-sixties, I grudgingly shouldered my share of the burden in keeping with the family custom. While I wasn't particularly anxious to march off to the sound of the guns, neither was I capable of avoiding it. Running off to Canada was not an option. Idealism like that can bring you much grief, as I was soon to learn.

In 1964, the Vietnam conflict was still a "comfortable" war. I like to think of it as the "campaign" period before massive numbers of American troops were unleashed on the Indo-Chinese mainland. I arrived in the Republic of Vietnam in the spring of 1964 as an apprehensive twenty-year-old Army private. There were just 16,000 Americans in-country at the time, the vanguard of a force that would soon grow to more than half a million men. I was not particularly enthusiastic about being one of them. That May, a one year tour of duty seemed like an eternity, with the end a lifetime away.

The Army immediately assigned me to an advisory team located in the I Corps tactical area, which comprised the provinces lying directly below the Demilitarized Zone separating North and South Vietnam. I was based in the peaceful and beautiful city of Hue, but spent relatively little time there. My primary duty was to serve as a radio operator at the remote outposts along the Laotian border manned by the Army of the Republic of Vietnam (ARVN). Most of them had little-known and exotic names. But vicious conflict in the coming years would soon make Khe Sanh, Lang Vei, and the A Shau Valley practically household words.

I was fortunate to have missed most of the heaviest fighting. Much of my combat experience consisted of brief sniping engagements or small unit actions. However, I was part of the relief force sent to secure the shattered Special Forces camp at Nam Dong after an eerie night attack by 1,000 Viet Cong. It was at the battle for Nam Dong that Captain Roger Donlon won the first Medal of Honor awarded in Vietnam.

I also helped to build sandbag emplacements after North Vietnamese patrol boats attacked American destroyers at sea, precipitating the now-controversial Tonkin Gulf incident that led to a widened war. I was there when the first Allied aircraft flew low overhead on their way to bomb North Vietnam. And I saw the initial U.S. Marine combat units arrive, blissfully unaware of the fate awaiting them in the bloody days ahead.

Many have questioned the value of what we did in Vietnam. For me, there was never any doubt. I saw the relief etched on the faces of simple people who appreciated the security our presence provided. I delighted in the laughing children who followed the Americans everywhere, begging for money, food, and cigarettes. I watched groups of primitive Montagnards wait patiently in remote villages to be examined by teams of Green Beret medics. For most of them this was the first and only medical treatment they would ever receive. As a result, I've always taken special pride in my Vietnam service, even when it wasn't fashionable to do so.

But during the late 1960s, public opinion of the military plummeted to such a shameful level that returning soldiers were cautioned to travel in civilian clothes instead of uniforms rather than risk ugly confrontations with protesters. The generally-accepted image of the Vietnam vet back then was one of a psychopathic drug addict. That bothers me to this day. I served for a year in one of the most prolific drug-producing areas on the planet, yet never once saw an American soldier using narcotics. Oh, I recognize that drug abuse became somewhat widespread later on as both the war and society deteriorated. Sadly, that left an indelible stain on the legacy of our fighting men in Southeast Asia. But all of them shouldn't have been painted with the same brush, and I still fiercely resent the commonly-accepted stereotype of the American Vietnam veteran as a drug abuser.

For twenty-five years after I left the Army, not one person outside my immediate circle of family and friends ever thanked me for having served in Vietnam. Then, appropriately enough on Memorial Day, 1990, I was shopping at the Roosevelt Field Mall on Long Island while wearing my "Proud Vietnam Veteran" cap. A young female clerk behind the counter glanced at the inscription on my hat and said rather shyly, "We're proud of you, too."

I was so taken aback that I choked up and left the store without even thanking that lovely girl. When I got home and told my wife Maureen what had happened, all the pent-up emotions came pouring out and I burst into tears. That was a legitimate watershed moment in my life. It also marked the approximate point when America's attitude toward our military began to undergo a dramatic improvement.

Several years ago, one of my clients who had been an avid protester during the Vietnam years approached me. "You know," he said, "I owe you an apology for the way I behaved back then."

I was touched. "You should never apologize for doing what you thought was right," I replied. We remain good friends to this day, which in my view is a wonderful tribute to the concept of human understanding. And my own hostility toward war protesters is long gone now, with one or two notable exceptions.

Today, there's rarely a day when I wear my "Vietnam Veteran" hat in public that someone doesn't stop me to offer a warm "Thank you." Maureen always laughs when that happens because I never fail to become a bit emotional. But I don't mind. And it never gets old, I can assure you.

I'm so pleased to see how well our Afghanistan and Iraq veterans are now treated. Yes, I'll confess to occasionally experiencing a twinge of jealousy. But gratitude offered late is much better than none at all. Whenever I encounter active-duty members of the military, I always make it a point to thank them for their service. Sometimes I'll buy them coffee or cigarettes, or even pick up their lunch tabs. That's my way of showing appreciation for their sacrifices, which I understand only too well. The look of surprise and gratitude on their faces is the best reward I could ever hope to receive. God willing, we can all do something to ensure that our troops never again experience the scorn or outright hatred the Vietnam veterans endured for so many years.

As the expression goes, "Freedom isn't free." In fact, it can be very costly indeed. We Americans today enjoy a way of life and countless privileges that were paid for with the lives of our soldiers, sailors, marines, and airmen. So when you encounter a veteran, I urge you to offer a sincere word of thanks for his or her service. Or, as we Vietnam vets prefer to do, simply say, "Welcome home!"

Today, having reached my 70th birthday, I sometimes reflect on my days as a young soldier resigned to the distinct possibility of not reaching age twenty-two. Then I come to the realization that I've been given a welcome blessing of many more years in which to make a place for myself in the world, to marry my soulmate and to raise a family. I'm very grateful for that. Some of my comrades never had such an opportunity.

The Frost Weeds is meant to show the reader what the early period of the Vietnam War was like, when small groups of American servicemen and their South Vietnamese counterparts waged a relatively unknown and unappreciated conflict against Communist aggression. It is essentially a work of non-fiction, but since I wrote it from a perspective more than forty years after the fact, some of the details are only as accurate as memory serves. I took no notes nor kept a diary during my year in Vietnam. That in itself I now find astounding. I've always been a writer, and to think that I spent a year in a combat zone and kept no records of it is difficult for me to fathom. I've created names for those I could not recall. I've also included several incidents that happened to others. My intent is not to mislead, but rather to give the reader a broader view of the war as it was unfolding at that time. I hope you will enjoy this book as much as I did writing it, and will forgive me for whatever I might have gotten wrong.

Note: The title for this book comes from one of the call signs our radio team used in Vietnam. For the sake of uniformity and clarity, I've used it throughout the story, although in reality we changed call signs regularly, usually on a monthly basis.

———

THE BEGINNING

W HEN I WAS GROWING UP, Dad often lectured me about the importance of going to college. He never had any schooling beyond eleventh grade, and he felt that getting a good education would have spared him from many problems later in life. I never paid much attention to him, though. You know how teenagers are. At age eighteen I thought I knew everything, or at least more than my parents did. But as I was painfully to learn later, Dad was indeed right.

Actually, I ended up taking his advice – sort of. After high school, I enrolled at NYU, partly because I had won a Regents scholarship that would offset a good deal of the tuition expenses. Now don't get me wrong. I was never much of a student. In high school I did well in subjects that interested me, but barely passed the others. Homework was something to be avoided at all costs. I survived only due to my love for reading and an ability to write fairly well.

Things were different at NYU, though. I was neither prepared for nor committed to higher education. And since I wasn't actually about to crack a book, disaster loomed. The only subject I passed was Reserve Officers Training Corps (ROTC), a course in which I excelled. So after one semester of cutting classes and ignoring assignments (but earning an invitation to the "Pershing Rifles," the ROTC honor society), I was ignominiously booted out.

My parents were crushed. There had never been a college graduate in our family, and I had been their best hope. Now that was gone. Three months out of high school I was no longer attending college and going nowhere. I had no idea what I was going to do with the rest of my life.

A series of odd jobs followed, including a six month term as a laborer for my uncle's construction company. I really wasn't much good at that, a fact of which my uncle constantly reminded me. In the spring of 1963 a local bank hired me and I began taking financial courses at night. But a service obligation hung over my head like the "Sword of Damocles." Draft age at the time was about twenty-three. I didn't want to wait three years to be called, so I decided to volunteer my draft. I've always been kind of impatient that way.

In reality, this was a fairly good idea. Enlisting in the Army meant a three year obligation. But by volunteering to be drafted I would only have to serve two. I would be out a full year before I could otherwise expect to be called. Smart, huh? I thought so.

One afternoon during my lunch break, I drove to the local Selective Service office to submit my request. The middle-aged woman behind the desk eyed me with motherly concern. She asked several times if I had discussed this with my parents. I assured her that I had. She just shook her head sadly. That did wonders for my confidence.

The "Greetings" letter my friends and I had often kidded about appeared in the mailbox at the end of August. I was a bit perplexed to find that it actually read "Greeting." Strange how something as insignificant as a missing "s" sticks in your mind when it involves a momentous event in your life. I read the letter and my pulse quickened. Doubt gnawed at the back of my brain. Had I made the right decision? In any case, the die was cast.

I arrived at the United States Army Induction Center on Whitehall Street in lower Manhattan on September 30th. I had taken the Long Island Railroad to Penn Station, and then hopped on the subway for the brief trip downtown. It was a cool, breezy morning… "hurricane weather" we called it back home.

I spent most of the day in a processing area with a large group of draftees. We got poked, prodded, questioned, and marched about in our shorts, shivering from both nervousness and the chilly temperature. At one point a medic drew a blood sample from my arm, then handed me the glass tube. I remember feeling a bit queasy carrying that hot vial. Doctors, psychiatrists, and sergeants tested, re-tested, and examined us at length. I had to laugh when one of them asked me if I liked girls. The way things worked out, maybe I should have said no. I was also surprised to learn that I was partially color-blind. But the doctor said it was a condition that was fairly common in young males. Something genetic. I guess that made me feel a little better.

Finally, late in the afternoon, the military conveyor belt deposited us all in a small auditorium. A trim sergeant in full dress green uniform stepped to a podium at the front of the room. There were three rows of multi-colored ribbons above his left jacket pocket. He silently scanned the group and then sneered. "All right, listen up!" he bellowed. "You scumbags have all somehow passed your physicals. An officer will be here in a couple of minutes to swear you in. Then you'll be leaving for Fort Dix."

I glanced around. So it was finally going to happen. I had been nursing a sort of half-hope that some abnormality would turn up, and they would send me home with an honorable excuse for not serving. Now that possibility seemed to have disappeared.

The sergeant's eyes flicked over our motley group. "Has anybody here ever been arrested?" A couple of hands shot up.

The non-com scowled.

"Is anyone here wanted by the police?" Another hand rose, somewhat tentatively. The sergeant's face darkened.

"Those of you who raised your hands, grab your gear and get the hell out of here! The Army doesn't want your kind."

Broad grins spread across the faces of the three young men. They scrambled to their feet and quickly left the room. I remember wondering if anyone was going to check their claims.

Sergeant "Scowl" watched them leave, and then turned back to us. "The rest of you men form a double line up here facing the rear of the room. When Lieutenant Blanchard comes in, I'll call you to attention. That means you bring your heels together, hands at your sides, stand straight with your eyes forward. No goddamn talking!"

We formed a scraggly line, looking for all the world like a gang of convicts. The sergeant shook his head in disgust, and then left the room. We stood silently for several minutes. No one felt much like talking. Our overseer soon returned carrying a brown clipboard. "Okay, you shitbirds… the lieutenant's on his way." He then busied himself with whatever was on the clipboard and ignored us.

Suddenly the door swung open. Sergeant "Scowl" roared "TEN-HUT!" We all snapped into what we thought was the position of attention. An officer strode quickly to the front of the room where the sergeant met him with a sharp salute. He was also clad in dress greens. I noticed that there was a black stripe running down each leg of his trousers. In my tired mind, he seemed to be wearing a green tuxedo. I had to stifle a chuckle.

Lieutenant Blanchard had silver bars on his shoulders and gold braid on his cap. The crossed rifles of the infantry adorned his lapels. "Sergeant, are the candidates ready for induction?"

"Yessir!"

Lieutenant Blanchard turned to face the uneasy draftees. "Men, I'm going to read you the induction pledge. Repeat after me. When we're finished, you'll be privates in the United States Army." He withdrew a small card from his pocket and glanced down at it. "I... use your name... promise to uphold and defend the Constitution of the United States of America..."

Following the brief ceremony we received sandwiches, coffee and subway tokens. There were thirteen of us consigned to Fort Dix. The names represented a virtual cross-section of New York ethnicity: Dziedzic, Brown, Muscianisi, Ortiz, Quinn, Ohlmiller, Nielsen. Sergeant "Scowl" handed me a packet containing the records of the thirteen new privates. For some reason, I had been designated the group leader. It would be my responsibility to make sure all thirteen arrived safely at Fort Dix. I still can't imagine why they chose me for the job. I was probably the youngest in the group, and I wasn't much interested in taking on that responsibility. But my preferences didn't seem to matter to anyone.

The Army wasted no time with its new recruits. A quick train ride delivered us to the Port Authority Bus Terminal, where a charter waited to take us on the ninety-minute trip into New Jersey. I made a quick head-count before we boarded the bus. Thankfully they were all there. I have no idea what I would have done otherwise. The sun was already setting behind a bank of purple clouds as we pulled out. Some passengers read magazines or paperbacks. It was quiet on the darkened bus. I was tired and quickly dozed off, but it was a fitful sleep at best.

The bus droned steadily south. I recall being awakened by the sound of shifting gears when we turned off the Jersey Turnpike. Night had fallen by the time we passed through the Pine Barrens and reached the outskirts of Fort Dix. The bus pulled up to a brightly lighted terminal in the reception center. Another sergeant climbed aboard to take charge of the recruits. I handed the records to him. He lined us up inside the terminal and called roll. Then he marched us off into the darkness. Some carried small overnight bags as they plodded along in our ragged formation. There appeared to be no common thread connecting us other than that this was our first exposure to the military.

We reached a low rectangular building with a set of double doors at either end. The sergeant, who had said virtually nothing as we marched along, halted our group and went inside. It was now near ten p.m., and there was a bit of a chill in the air. It seemed strange standing outside in the stillness of the night. I hadn't yet gotten my mind around the obvious. We were now operating under the Army's methods and no longer our civilian standards. After a few minutes, the sergeant returned and ordered us to file in four at a time. This was the equipment issue room. As we passed steadily through the building, each man received GI underwear, fatigues, boots, belts, hats, dress uniforms, shaving equipment, socks, shoes and a full assortment of other military gear. By the time I exited through the doors at the far end of the building, I had a duffel bag bulging with hastily stowed Army clothing. Some of it would even fit.

When the last recruit emerged through the doors, the sergeant marched us off into the night again. We crunched along a gravel pathway with our awkward bundles balanced precariously on our shoulders, blindly following our leader. He led us into a nearby reception barracks after first flicking on a light switch just inside the door. A line of bare light bulbs hanging from the ceiling flared harshly to life.

The building was a wooden relic from World War II. There were rows of twin metal bunks flanking either side of a central aisle. Each bunk held a rolled-up mattress and a coverless pillow. There were no sheets or blankets. The sergeant told us to get some sleep and someone would come along in the morning to take charge of us.

I dropped my duffel bag next to a vacant bunk, and unrolled the blue pinstriped mattress on the top rack. Then I untied my shoes and kicked them off. God, I was tired! It was already one in the morning, and it had been a long, trying day. As soon as everyone found a bunk, the sergeant shut the lights and left. My first day in the Army was over. Only 729 more to go! I was already homesick and suffering severe second thoughts about the choices I'd made. I drifted off into a restless sleep, still clad in my street clothes.

We stayed at the reception center for three days, during which we received extensive health and dental examinations. Most of us also spent some time doing KP at the huge mess hall. I was surprised to find that there were machines to peel the mountains of potatoes needed to feed the hundreds of new soldiers from all across the country. I was grateful for that.

There were batteries of tests to determine what military specialty each of us was qualified to fill. We shared the usual jokes about lawyers becoming truck drivers and teachers assigned to the mess hall. No one really believed those stories, but they created a seed of doubt. I thought I did pretty well on the Morse code test, but assumed nothing. That seed had sprouted and was growing roots.

I finally received my new assignment to Company N in the 3rd Training Regiment, along with the rest of my original group. A wheezing old bus carried us to our new home at the farthest reaches of Fort Dix. We stepped down onto the dusty company street in mid-afternoon and looked around.

Four badly weathered wooden barracks stood in a row to the left. At the near end of the line was a decrepit mess hall. Clouds of steam billowed from its chimney, and the clanking of metal trays echoed through the area. Directly across the road sat the company commander's domain, the squat, rectangular orderly room. Thick stands of pine trees stretched for what seemed like miles beyond the barracks. Apparently we were in the most desolate and antiquated area on the post. That in itself was a depressing thought. I felt a strong wave of anxiety sweep through me.

A sergeant emerged from the orderly room and took the roll. He sorted us alphabetically, and chased us into one building or another based upon our last names. Staggering under the weight of my bag, I ran up the rough plank steps into the third barracks.

The interior of the building was much like those in the reception center. Everything was old. I had expected that. On an impulse, I walked into the latrine. A huge cast iron washtub beside the door was half-filled with filthy water. Three ancient toilets lined the wall, one with a crudely lettered DO NOT USE sign on it. There were no partitions to provide some privacy. Grimy mirrors hung above four sinks on the opposite wall. Behind that, a rusty shower head produced a thin trickle of water when I twisted the faucet. I shook my head and wondered what the hell I had gotten into.

Our platoon non-com soon arrived with another group of recruits. Staff Sergeant Leonard Thornton was a trim black man who appeared to be in his late forties. Sergeant Thornton began assigning bunks. Like everything else in the Army, it was done alphabetically.

Most of the platoon was composed of a National Guard unit from Massachusetts fulfilling its six month active duty commitment. After advanced training they would go home to another five years of weekend drilling. I could have done that too, but had decided against it, much to my regret at the moment.

Eight weeks of basic training followed. My one semester of ROTC in college had begun to prepare me for this, and I soon realized that I was a pretty good soldier. I hated the constant harassment from the drill sergeants, but excelled at marching, rifle drill and marksmanship. We ran daily through the sandy Pine Barrens carrying our rifles, packs and steel helmets. Our bodies quickly became lean and hard. On the rare occasions when we had some free time, my platoon mates and I liked to go to one of the post theaters to see the latest movies. The drill sergeants seemed to ease off a bit as we neared the end of training.

Around the seventh week, we received our advanced assignments. Sergeant Thornton came into the barracks one afternoon following chow. He had a platoon roster and went down the list, announcing the Military Occupational Specialty (MOS) for each man. When he got to me he said, "Oh-liveri, you're an oh-five-one."

I scratched my head. "What's an oh-five-one, Sergeant Thornton?" The way he'd said it didn't sound too promising.

Thornton glanced up from his roster. "Intermediate speed radio operator." Noting my puzzled look, he added, "Morse code."

A broad smile creased my face. I KNEW I had done well on the code test at the reception center. Hot damn! This was a lot better than going to advanced infantry training (AIT) like most of the rest of our platoon. Instead I would be moving just across the post to attend the Intermediate Speed Radio Operators Course (ISROC) at Company B in the 5th Training Regiment. Good deal, I thought. I'll be able to go home just about every weekend.

Thornton quickly brought me back to reality. "Don't y'all be gettin' too happy now," he warned. "You ain't 'zactly gonna be linin' up for no poontang over there. Half them trainees don't make it through that course. Then the dumb shits wind up in AIT anyway. And if you do grad-jee-ate, you'll prob-ly get sent to Vee-et-Nam."

That was classic Thornton: subtlety and encouragement all rolled into one. I don't think I'd ever heard him say so many words at one time. But I was only half-listening. It wasn't until much later that I realized how right he was.

We graduated from basic on a cold, bright Friday morning in December. The platoon sergeants marched us in formation to the regimental theater, where the battalion commander, a major, addressed the company. I don't recall his exact words, but it was something to the effect that we had proved ourselves as soldiers, and now we must go on to do our duty as best we could. We thought we were really hot stuff.

After the ceremony, we made our last visit to the Company N mess hall for lunch. Following that, the recruits began to move out to their new assignments.

I was among the last troops still remaining in the company area. We stacked our gear outside the barracks and awaited the scheduled ride to our new assignments. Eventually a ¾ ton truck, its gears grinding, pulled up outside the orderly room. We threw our bags into the back of the uncovered vehicle and then climbed over the tailgate. I recognized several soldiers from the other platoons who were also heading for ISROC. When we were all on board, the truck driver rolled off for the ten-minute drive to B Company, located near the post hospital. Upon arrival, we unloaded our gear and immediately reported to the First Sergeant.

B Company was entirely contained within a modern 3-story brick building. This was a far cry from the somewhat primitive conditions we had endured in basic training. 1st Lieutenant Peter Kontanis, a hard-nosed infantry officer known for his strict disciplinary tactics, commanded the company. A new group of trainees arrived every other week to begin the three-month course. I was to be part of Class 26, the final group of the year 1963. Kontanis was responsible for pushing us along to graduation and weeding out marginal or inept trainees. We soon learned that he did his job well.

After checking our orders, the white-haired First Sergeant escorted us to a platoon bay on the second floor. There were bunks for fifty men lining both sides of the room. Behind each was a double gray metal locker. Many of the bunks were still vacant, since the bulk of the class had yet to arrive.

"Get yourselves squared away," growled the First Sergeant. "Then report to the orderly room if you want a weekend pass."

No further urging was necessary. We quickly chose bunks and stowed our gear in the lockers. The First Sergeant had left us a roll of masking tape and a felt-tipped pen. We used that to make name tags, and plastered them to the foot of each bed. I stripped off my fatigues and changed into a Class A dress uniform. Within an hour I was aboard a bus headed up the Jersey Turnpike to New York. Morse code went on the back burner for a couple of days.

ISROC

THE INTERMEDIATE SPEED RADIO OPERATORS Course (ISROC) was taught at a training facility located about half a mile across an open parade ground from the B Company barracks. Our class marched in order to the radio school each morning. We returned for lunch, and then marched back again for the afternoon session.

Fort Dix is a cold, wind-swept bitch of a place in the winter, subject to extremes of weather. We often plodded to our daily sessions through knee-deep snow and arctic temperatures. In January and February of 1964, it was not a pleasant trip. You could freeze your ass off several times a day marching between the barracks and radio school.

The Army's methods for teaching Morse code were very rudimentary. The school consisted of several large training rooms, each containing long wooden tables subdivided into small cubicles. The trainee sat at his station wearing a set of headphones. On tape, an instructor repeated groups of letters, and then tapped out the Morse equivalents. It was truly learning by repetition.

"I... DIH-DIT
I... DIH-DIT
I... DIH-DIT
V... DIH-DIH-DIH-DAH
V... DIH-DIH-DIH-DAH
V... DIH-DIH-DIH-DAH."

After listening to a set of six letters several dozen times, we were tested on our retention. If the trainee could accurately record the slowly transmitted signals, he moved on to another set of letters, and finally, to numbers. A talented candidate might absorb the entire code within a week. But it could be a maddening process. By the end of the day, you wanted to rip out the goddamn tables and throw them through the window.

Once we learned the code, we began to work on our speed. That was the hardest part. We started at a very slow five words per minute. This gradually escalated to seven and then ten. As our skills grew we progressed to twelve words per minute, a key level. If you made it that far, you had a good chance of completing the course. Sixteen words per minute was the maximum. We could not graduate until we were able to transmit and copy at that speed. For some reason, I found it easier to transmit than to receive.

The failure rate was surprisingly high. Most trainees were eventually able to master the code, but many simply couldn't develop enough speed to graduate. And there was a time limit for each level. If you failed to pass a speed test within the allotted time period, the school dropped you, and you got assigned to another MOS, usually infantry. Some candidates just didn't want to be radio operators and failed intentionally. Others dragged out their training as long as possible in order to delay reassignment to less desirable duty. Whatever the reasons, more than fifty per cent of some classes flunked out. As a result, the cadre often pushed less experienced trainees ahead to fill out the ranks of understrength graduating classes.

Lieutenant Kontanis knew all the tricks, and tolerated none of them. The B Company commander was a major contributor to the washout rate. He seemed to take an almost sadistic pleasure in harassing the trainees. I suppose this was the Army's way of ridding itself of mediocre candidates who weren't strong enough to do the job intended for them. Kontanis had a well-deserved reputation for "thinning the herd", and the prick wasted no time living up to it.

Several trainees were detached from class each day to perform company duties such as KP and latrine detail. When our turn came up, Doug Potter and I drew the second floor latrine with another soldier. The three of us worked diligently all that morning scouring sinks, toilets and showers. When we were done, the fixtures absolutely sparkled. The other trainee found some clean rags in a closet, and we began scrubbing down the tile floor.

The First Sergeant entered the latrine as we worked. When he spotted the small pile of fresh rags, his eyes bulged out of his head as if he were some half-assed cartoon character. He grabbed the other trainee by the collar and yanked him to his feet. "Are you out of your goddamn mind?" he bellowed. "Why did you tear up these sheets?"

The soldier seemed confused. "We didn't tear up any sheets, First Sergeant. We found these by the slop sink."

The First Sergeant was beside himself. "Don't give me that crap! This is government property you fuck-ups destroyed." He glared at us. "All of you come with me."

The senior non-com escorted three unnerved soldiers to the orderly room. We waited outside while he went in. I looked at Doug and shrugged. He was a couple of inches shorter than me and stocky. Doug had a tendency to be a bit brash, usually fun-loving and a little loud. I had first met him when I originally got to radio school. He and another soldier had been playfully wrestling on the platoon bay floor. We hadn't had much contact since then, however. Now that we both seemed to be in a little trouble, I didn't know whether to laugh or shit my pants. When the First Sergeant finally emerged, he pointed at me. "You... inside!"

Kontanis was seated at his desk examining a loose-leaf manual. He didn't look up as I marched forward and saluted. "Private Oliveri reports to the Company Commander, Sir."

The lieutenant ignored me and began reading aloud from the manual. It was the procedure for an Article 15, or company punishment. I couldn't believe it. We had done nothing wrong, yet we were about to receive official reprimands that would be recorded in our personnel files. The end result was usually loss of privileges, including the much valued weekend pass. None of us wanted that. We had few enough privileges as it was.

I risked speaking up. "Sir, if I may interrupt…"

Kontanis stabbed his forefinger viciously into the manual. "No, you may not!" He resumed quoting the procedures. When he had finished, he raised his head for the first time. "Private Oliveri, I'm charging you with the deliberate destruction of government property. Do you have anything to say?"

This was bullshit. I felt trapped. Outraged and shaken, I struggled to maintain my composure. "But, Sir… we didn't destroy any property. Those rags were in the supply closet." I was painfully aware that it sounded like whining.

Never having been this close to Kontanis before, I hadn't realized how dark and bushy his eyebrows were. I half-expected him to pull out a cigar and do a Groucho Marx imitation. Despite being so upset, I struggled desperately to keep a straight face. It's a characteristic of mine that I often react to stress by laughing. It's not necessarily a good attribute because it can make you appear guilty even when you're not.

Kontanis glared at me from beneath those eyebrows. "Do you understand that you have the right to refuse an Article 15 and accept a General Court Martial?"

"Yes, Sir. I do.

"Do you wish to refuse the Article 15?"

I swallowed. "No, Sir. But I would like to say again that we did not destroy any sheets."

Kontanis leaned back and sighed. "Okay, private. You give me the name of the soldier who tore up those sheets within the next twenty-four hours, and I'll forget about this."

I took a deep breath. I didn't like being intimidated this way. "I can't, Sir," I said with finality. "I don't know who did it. Those rags were already torn up when we found them."

Kontanis' eyes smoldered. "Get out of here." His voice was an ominous whisper.

I saluted and executed a sharp about-face. Doug and the other trainee were outside the orderly room. I wanted to talk to them, but the First Sergeant ordered me back to the latrine. Later we compared notes and found that we had all told the same story. That was good, but we figured we were screwed anyway. I couldn't believe all the fuss over a handful of rags.

I glanced at Doug. "What do you think?"

"I guess we wait." The stocky blond didn't seem overly concerned. That annoyed me.

We sweated out a few days, but for some reason, Kontanis never brought any charges against us. Maybe he was satisfied thinking he had thrown a good scare into us, or else his case was just too weak to proceed. I didn't care which as long as I still had my weekend pass. And possibly as a result of our ordeal together, Potter and I became good buddies.

After the incident, we resumed our studies at ISROC with a vengeance. During the fourth week, I had completed twelve words per minute and was working toward sixteen. Doug had passed the test for ten words, barely, but was having difficulty getting to twelve. When we talked about this, I learned something I hadn't realized before.

"Doug, I think I'm gonna take the test for sixteen tomorrow."

My friend turned away from me. "You should, Jimbo. You're

really good at this stuff." Something in his voice caught my attention.

"What's the matter? You don't sound like you're happy about it."

Doug sat on his bunk and rubbed his eyes. "Don't you understand what's gonna happen here? If you pass sixteen, they're not gonna let you hang around for another two months. Some of those classes ahead of us are down to less than half strength. They'll bump you up and graduate you early." He paused and frowned. "I was kind of hoping we'd finish together."

So that was it. I thought for a moment. "Well, there's no guarantee that I'll pass."

"Hey, I told you. You're good at this shit."

"Come on. A lot of guys never make it to sixteen. You know that. What happens if it takes me a couple more weeks?"

"Nah, not you."

I chuckled. "All of a sudden I feel a brain cramp coming on."

Doug's eyes sparkled. "If they catch on, your ass is grass."

"Well then, you better shake your rear end and pass twelve so I don't have to stall too long." I slapped him on the back.

Two days later, Doug passed the test for twelve. We decided to go for sixteen together the following week.

On the morning of the test, a huge blizzard struck Fort Dix. When we marched in formation to ISROC there was a foot of drifting snow on the ground and the wind was howling. It was a virtual whiteout. I was hunched so deep inside the hood of my field jacket that all I could see was the swirling snow directly in front of my nose. If we hadn't made this trip so many times previously, I'm not sure we could have found the school. I had never been so cold in my life. When we finally got there, the austere code building seemed as warm and cozy as someone's den. A feeling of contentment and well being crept over me as the warmth began to penetrate my body. I was relaxed, supremely confident and ready to do battle with sixteen words per minute.

Doug and I took adjoining seats at the test table. An instructor handed us score sheets and pencils. We adjusted our headsets and waited. It was a relief when the beeping signals finally began.

I wasn't having much trouble with the test. Occasionally I glanced across at Doug. He seemed to be struggling. Sometimes he closed his eyes in concentration, or at least that's what I thought it was. I hoped it wasn't resignation. I finished up my own sheet and handed it to the sergeant. Then I went out of the room and waited.

One good thing about taking this test was that you got the results quickly. About ten minutes later, the instructor emerged from the exam room with my score sheet in his hand. He said simply, "Private Oliveri...Pass," and then returned to the testing. I smiled.

Doug came out shortly afterward. He didn't look too happy. He took a seat beside me and said nothing. It was so quiet I could hear the ticking of the clock on the opposite wall. I sat there watching the second hand creep around the dial. It was maddening how it seemed to take forever to click off a single minute. A ruptured snail moved faster. Finally our instructor opened the door. Doug and I both leaned forward as he shuffled the papers in his hands.

"Uh, let's see. Private Potter... I've got yours here someplace." He fumbled through the forms. I wanted to strangle him. "Ah, here it is. Potter... Pass."

Doug turned to me with a broad grin. "Well, ain't that a bitch?" We slapped hands in jubilation. Whatever happened to us now, at least we would face it together.

Our orders came quickly. We were instructed to transfer into the Class 22 bay. It was not a long journey by any means. Doug and I simply had to move our gear down one floor. With our new class at less than half strength, there was no need for anyone to quarter in the main bay. We were assigned a small room to share. We were no longer required to fall out in the bitter cold for the twice-daily formations. Kontanis stopped harassing us. The First Sergeant virtually ignored us. Doug and I attended our training sessions and enjoyed a considerable amount of free time, much of it spent drinking coffee at the PX. We were feeling pretty good about ourselves. This was the equivalent of what passed for heaven at Fort Dix. Too bad it didn't last very long.

There was one negative side to all this. By being bumped ahead into Class 22, Doug and I missed the technical training for other equipment we could expect to use as radio operators. I had no way of knowing it at the time, of course, but that would eventually cause me a good deal of grief.

At our training sessions, we took turns sending and receiving practice messages on an ANGRC/9 ("Angry/9") radio. We had to copy or transmit encrypted three-letter groups, and then decode them using shackle sheets. One of the messages we used was purportedly from an American unit operating along the Mekong River. It was a situation report about contact with a group of enemy soldiers. After I finished transcribing it, I re-read the text. It seemed so far-fetched. Where the hell was the Mekong, anyway? Thailand? Burma? It was difficult to take these games seriously.

One afternoon several weeks later, Doug stormed into our room. A dark scowl contorted his face. I looked up from the dress shoe I had been spit-shining with a moist cotton ball. "What the hell's wrong with you?"

"Plenty. I heard you could go down to headquarters and check on your next assignment. I just came from there. They said I'm going to Southeast Asia."

I shrugged. "Southeast Asia? Hey, that's not so bad. Must be Thailand. We've got a couple of big bases there."

Doug snarled. "Like hell. It's Vietnam!"

I whistled softly. "Jesus. There's a shooting war going on over there."

Doug nodded. "Yeah, and that's not all. They said most of our class is headed there too." He pointed his finger at me dramatically. "You'd better get your ass down there now and find out about yourself."

He certainly had my attention. I dropped the shoe polish and cleaning equipment. Snatching my cap from the bunk, I grabbed my field jacket and was quickly out the door. I dashed down the stairwell, taking the steps two at a time. Within half an hour I was back.

Doug eyed me as I came into the room. "Well?"

I leaned against my locker and pulled off my hat. "Looks like we're going together, buddy."

Doug shook his head and flashed a wry smile. "I figured."

I glanced out the window. The snow cover seemed a lot less clean than it had several weeks before. A sudden thought made me chuckle. "Hey, Doug. Do you remember when they called a formation to hear that Special Forces Captain? He was looking for volunteers to join the Green Berets. We all said, 'Fuck him... we don't wanna go to Vietnam!'" The irony of the moment drew another chuckle from me. "So where do we wind up?"

Doug slapped me on the back. "Vietnam, my man!"

———

GOING TO WAR

OR THE REMAINDER OF OUR time at ISROC, Doug and I stayed in our two-man room that had been previously occupied by upper classmen who had since moved on. Until we graduated, we received semi-preferential treatment, or at least what passed for it at Company "B." We took full advantage of that.

After completing the course in March of 1964, Doug and I received almost identical orders for transfer to Vietnam. Mine read:

> **DEPARTMENT OF THE ARMY SPECIAL ORDERS NO. 77 DATED 18 MAR 1964**
>
> OLIVERI, James A., US51518350 Pvt (E-2) 051.10 TRN USATC Inf (1387)
>
> Ft. Dix, N.J. Aloc. Jun 64 D-41. Aval date 4 May 1964 to arr OS dest NLT 8 May
>
> 1964. Scty clnc secret. BPED 30 Sep 1963. ETS 29 Sep 1965. EDCSA 4 May 1964.
>
> By order of the Secretary of the Army:
> Earle G. Wheeler
> General, United States Army
> Chief of Staff

Now came regular visits to headquarters for processing. We also reported to the clinic for shots – lots of them. All personnel going to Southeast Asia were inoculated against a horrendous litany of tropical diseases including cholera, plague, typhus and God knows what else. My shot card was four pages long. We also rushed to complete any dental work in progress. There were few dentists in Vietnam, so the Army removed my wisdom teeth as a precautionary measure before releasing me.

On April 5th, Potter and I said our goodbyes to the remaining friends we had made at ISROC. Many of them would soon follow us to Vietnam. We vowed to meet again overseas.

As I left our room for the last time I noticed something lying on my bunk and picked it up. It was a green religious card bearing a portrait of St. Jude, the patron saint of lost causes. How appropriate. Apparently Ed Naticha, my soft-spoken, balding buddy with a warm, friendly smile who was in the class behind us, had left it there. On the back he had written, "Jim, best of luck 'til we meet again. Your friend Eddie."

I was touched. As a former altar boy, Eddie understood that I was headed into harm's way and might need a little divine intervention at some point. His gift was, to me, a much welcome blessing. I never saw Eddie again, but I still have that little card sitting prominently on a shelf in my office. For all I know, it may actually have done some good.

I shook hands with Doug at the post bus terminal as he boarded a charter bound for Buffalo and I waited for one headed to New York. We were both booked on board Military Air Transport Service (MATS) flight number P-245 out of Oakland on May 5th that would carry us to Saigon. Doug and I parted, agreeing to join up at Travis Air Force Base. Until then we would each spend a thirty day leave at home.

After my second week of furlough, things began to fall apart. I came down with what I thought was just a bad cold. But I began to run a high fever and felt so weak that I could barely stand. I couldn't take a breath without wheezing. By the end of my third week I was so sick that Dad drove me to St. Albans Naval Hospital in Queens for an exam.

The cold dampness of Fort Dix had apparently taken its toll. I was admitted to the hospital with acute bronchitis. For six days I got out of bed only for reveille or to go to the bathroom. As my departure date approached I was starting to feel better, but I figured there was no way I would get out in time to make the original flight. I wrote to Doug and told him not to expect me in Oakland. I promised to catch up with him later.

On the morning of May 5th, after almost two weeks at the hospital, the Navy doctor handling my case told me he was releasing me that afternoon, and I could go back on leave. I was incredulous. "But, Sir," I complained. "I'm scheduled to leave for Vietnam tomorrow. There's no way I can get ready by then."

He was less than sympathetic. "Oh, you'll manage," he said as he began to walk off down the corridor. He paused to glance back. "Good luck, by the way."

Leave it to a Navy doctor to screw over the Army. That was one of my kinder thoughts. I was still seething about this unexpected development when Dad picked me up later that afternoon. We said little during the trip home. I scrambled to book a last-minute flight to San Francisco and then packed my bags. I didn't sleep much that night.

A small caravan escorted me to the airport the next morning with my buddy Richie driving one car. It was a gray, overcast day. My plane was scheduled to depart at noon. When the flight was announced for boarding, my mother and grandmother began to cry. It was a bit of an emotional scene as we waved goodbye and I turned to pass through the gate. I climbed aboard the aircraft and chose a seat on the side facing the terminal. The plane began to back out, preparing to roll onto the runway. I squinted through the clouded porthole. As we pulled away, I could see my family still standing there, waving forlornly at the departing aircraft.

I don't remember much about the flight to San Francisco, except for a majestic view of the snow-covered Rockies as we crossed high over that rugged mountain range. By the time we began our descent over California my emotions were once again under control. The parting was history. My sense of adventure was slowly returning.

After disembarking from the plane, I stopped at a Western Union booth in the terminal. An attractive young woman with short blonde hair stood behind the counter and smiled at me. She appeared to be in her late twenties. I reached for a yellow message blank and quickly composed a telegram for my family:

> Arrived safely San Francisco Stop
> Leaving for Saigon Stop
> Will write soon Stop

Exactly ten words, the Western Union limit. Written like a true professional radio operator, I thought smugly. I handed the paper to the waiting attendant. She read it through and glanced up at me. "Good luck over there." She smiled again. I thanked her and walked out into the terminal.

Travis Air Force Base was a forty-minute bus ride from San Francisco. I marveled at the spectacular view of the Golden Gate Bridge with the late afternoon sun reflecting from its network of reddish-orange girders. The bus ground steadily across the bridge and continued on to Travis. Once inside the airbase I reported to the reception desk and handed over my orders. An airman took my baggage. The flight was scheduled to depart in just over two hours.

The itinerary called for twenty hours flying time to Vietnam, with refueling stops in Alaska, Japan and the Philippines. That meant at least a full day before arrival in Saigon. The collar on my khaki uniform shirt was already beginning to feel gritty, and I still had to fly halfway around the world. Charming.

Walking past a coffee shop, I suddenly realized how ravenously hungry I was. I went inside and bought a hot dog and a cup of coffee. After wolfing down both, I began to search for Doug. I wondered if he had even arrived yet. A smile crossed my face as I thought about how he would react when he saw me.

After scouting around for just a few minutes, I spotted Doug sitting on a green wooden bench reading a newspaper. I walked up beside him. "Hey, Loser. How are you?"

Doug dropped the paper in surprise and leaped to his feet. "Jimbo! What the hell are you doing here?"

"Leave it to the Navy to give me the shaft," I bitched. "They kicked me out of the hospital yesterday just in time to make this trip."

"Are you OK?"

"Yeah, I guess so. A little weak, but I'll make it."

To tell the truth, I felt much better after seeing Doug. Going off to a war zone seemed a bit less foreboding now that I had a friend along for the ride.

Doug clapped me on the back. "Well, you asshole, I'm glad to see you. I thought I was gonna have to make this trip alone."

We exchanged some sordid lies about what we had done on leave, knowing full well that neither of us believed the other. Finally we just dropped the small talk. When our flight was posted for departure, we reported to the appropriate gate. Our plane was clearly visible through the open glass doors. I was mildly surprised to find a sleek silver and blue Pan American 707 waiting on the tarmac. I had assumed it would be a military jet. Doug and I exchanged glances. This was going to be much better than we had expected.

We chose seats on the right side of the aircraft, just to the rear of the backswept wings. I settled in next to the window while Doug sat beside me in the center seat. A short, balding staff sergeant who appeared to be in his early forties took the aisle spot. He ignored us.

The plane took off promptly at 2200 hours, ascending at a steep angle before leveling off at cruising altitude. The flight north to Anchorage would be mainly over the ocean. It was a black, moonless night. We quickly realized there would be little to see. Once the novelty began to wear off, fatigue took over. I soon drifted off into a fitful sleep.

It was still dark when we touched down on Alaskan soil. With an hour layover for refueling, we left the plane to stretch and walk around. We looked for signs of the massive Good Friday earthquake that had struck the area recently, but were disappointed to find only a single small pile of rubble at the far end of a remote corridor. This had probably once been a concrete block partition. A few soldiers snapped some pictures and then moved on. We were all clad in summer dress uniforms, and the Alaskan night was briskly cool.

The sun was just peeking above the horizon as we re-boarded the plane. The next leg of the journey would be the longest, thousands of miles across the open Pacific Ocean to Tokyo.

Shortly after takeoff, the crew of three stewardesses began to serve breakfast. We had hardly noticed them during the night. They were all young and attractive, but one, a raven-haired Eurasian girl, was particularly stunning. Doug and I sat fixated, unable to keep our eyes off her whenever she passed along the aisle.

Were it not for the pretty stewardesses, the trip would have seemed interminable. The crew served us a meal every few hours. Breakfast, lunch, dinner—it didn't matter; they were inter-changeable. There was little else to do so most of us napped between meals. The vast azure Pacific passing below mesmerized me. It seemed endless. Pale wispy clouds occasionally closed around us, blocking our view of the water. Later I spotted the V-shaped wake of a large ship below. It was the only sign of life I saw during the entire flight.

We were all growing restless by the time we reached Japanese air space. To make matters worse, after we landed in Tokyo we had to stay aboard during refueling. The extent of our exposure to Japan was a brief glimpse of beautiful Mount Fujiyama through a porthole. We were soon on our way to the Philippines.

The relatively short flight to Manila was also the least endurable. We were all tired, cramped, cranky and bored. With another stop still ahead, the excitement of finally reaching our destination had not yet begun to set in. But the last layover quickly changed our mood.

The airport in Manila was surrounded by a horseshoe-shaped bowl of lush, green mountains. In combination with the brilliant blue skies and aqua-tinted ocean, the effect was startling. It was 83 degrees when we stepped off the plane. I had never seen a more beautiful panorama. It was almost as if we had been dropped into Paradise. I silently cursed myself for leaving my camera on board.

Everyone seemed strangely subdued when the powerful jet at last lifted off once again. The entire atmosphere of the flight began to change. Tension crackled through the hushed aircraft. The crew served a hasty meal and then retreated. They seemed to be avoiding contact with the passengers. I guess they knew from experience that some of us would not be making the return flight the following spring.

As we approached the Indo-Chinese mainland, the plane slowed perceptibly. The pilot's voice came up on the intercom, announcing that the temperature at Tan Son Nhut Airport was 92 degrees. The aircraft was beginning its descent toward Saigon. It was early afternoon on May 6th, the same date we had left Travis. Somewhere over the Pacific we had crossed the international dateline and gained twenty-four hours.

The 707 continued its sharp descent during the final phase of the approach. There was a rumbling vibration beneath our feet as the landing gear extended and locked into place. Moments later the plane touched down on the runway with a squeal of tires. We seemed to be traveling at a high rate of speed. I later learned that this was done to minimize our chances of being hit by enemy sniper fire. I'm glad I didn't know that at the time.

The plane turned off onto a siding and rolled to a stop inside a sandbagged revetment. The piercing whine of the turbines quickly diminished and then ceased. The crew popped the hatch. Hot, moist air poured into the air-conditioned cabin, fogging the eyeglasses of those who wore them. The concrete runway beyond shimmered in the blazing heat. A khaki-clad lieutenant stepped into the craft. There were dark sweat stains under his armpits. He blinked rapidly, trying to adjust his vision to the relatively dim interior of the plane. "Welcome to Saigon!" he called out cheerfully. "Please follow me."

SAIGON

M Y PULSE QUICKENED AS WE filed off the plane into the searing Saigon sunshine. We're finally here, I thought, gazing about at the curious scene before us. We followed the lieutenant to a squat concrete-block reception building nearby. Having left a spring-like California just the previous day, we were quite unprepared for the intense heat. It was somewhat like stepping fully clothed into a sauna. Perspiration boiled up from our pores and quickly soaked through our already limp uniforms.

Fortunately the building was air-conditioned. The contrast with the outside heat was striking. My khaki shirt suddenly felt clammy. The cool air threw a chill into my body as it washed over my damp clothing. I probably would have appreciated it more had I known that it would be almost a year before we were to experience such luxury again.

One large room served as an auditorium, with the far wall covered by a projection screen. A wooden podium stood before it. Rows of theater seats faced the screen. After we were all seated, several NCOs circulated among us and collected our orders.

We rose to our feet as a major named Hostedt entered the room and strode to the podium. "Good afternoon, gentlemen," he began. "Welcome to the Military Assistance Advisory Group, Vietnam – otherwise known as MAAG." He pronounced it "mag." "You should be aware that MAAG will be superseded within thirty days by the Military Assistance

Command, Vietnam, or MACV (Mack-vee). You men are among the last to be assigned here under MAAG.

"Let me give you a brief overview of the military situation here in the Republic of Vietnam." He turned to the screen and unrolled a map suspended above it. From behind the podium he produced a wooden pointer with a black metal tip. The major tapped the long, curving outline of the Vietnam coast depicted on the map and continued.

"Vietnam is divided into four military regions. Farthest north is I Corps (he pronounced it 'Eye' Corps), stretching south from the DMZ to Quang Ngai Province. This region contains Da Nang, the country's second largest city, and Hue, the ancient imperial capital of Vietnam.

"II Corps runs from Kontum Province to Binh Thuan Province. This area is known as the Central Highlands, and includes the resort cities of Nha Trang and Da Lat.

"The dividing line for III Corps runs along Tay Ninh, Binh Long, and Phuoc Long Provinces. This is the region containing the capital city of Saigon, where you're located right now."

Major Hostedt punctuated his presentation with firm thrusts of the pointer. "And finally, IV Corps lies below Saigon in the flat delta area formed by the Mekong River. The Plain of Reeds and the U Minh Forest can be found here."

The major turned back to his audience. "Most of you will be assigned to slots in II and III Corps. Some will go to I Corps or south to the Delta. Are there any questions so far?" No hands went up. Hostedt motioned to a bored-looking sergeant standing at the rear of the room. My guess was that he had heard this presentation a hundred times. "Okay, sergeant... pass out the schedules."

Hostedt continued as the non-com moved up and down the aisles. "When we break here shortly, you'll all be photographed for military records and ID cards. After that, buses will be available to transport you to your temporary quarters. Officers will be housed at the Caravelle Hotel, enlisted men at the Capital."

Doug and I glanced at one another. A hotel? What the hell kind of hardship tour was this? We both grinned.

Major Hostedt briefed us for another half hour on some of the more mundane things we needed to know, such as converting U.S. dollars to Vietnamese piasters, the typical rates for various services, the locations of facilities, understanding Vietnamese customs, and more. Then he began to wrap up the session. "Be sure to check your schedules. For the next three days you'll be attending indoctrination meetings in this compound. We'll begin tomorrow morning at 0900. As soon as you've been photographed, you're dismissed for today."

Doug and I shuffled out of the briefing room with the rest of the group. After posing impatiently for one quick photo, we exited the building and joined the crowd milling about outside. Within minutes, several gray military buses pulled up. Officers boarded the first in line bound for the Caravelle Hotel. Enlisted men occupied the remaining two vehicles. When everyone was aboard, the small convoy rolled off.

All the windows on our bus were open, but covered by heavy wire mesh. Doug fingered the tough metal strands. "I guess this is to keep the gooks from throwing grenades in here." I glanced at him with raised eyebrows. That hadn't occurred to me.

We passed through the barbed wire gates at the airport entrance. Two South Vietnamese military policemen (Quan Canh) wearing white-striped helmets and armed with M-1 carbines stood guard behind a sandbagged position. To some Americans they were derisively known as "White Mice" due to their painted helmets and slight stature. We eyed them as the buses chugged forward onto one of Saigon's main arteries.

The scene unfolding before us was incredible. Vietnamese women wearing loose pajama-like outfits and cone-shaped hats lined the streets. Some of them staggered along under wooden "chogey sticks" that held massive bundles suspended from either end. The road was flooded with people on small motorbikes, who jockeyed for position with hurtling French taxis. Hundreds of others rode bicycles, seemingly pedaling for dear life as they were swept down the highway by this foaming current of runaway humanity. The entire conglomeration barreled along at breakneck speed without any apparent traffic control. It was unlike anything I had ever seen before.

The city of Saigon itself was surprisingly modern. Its streets were lined with sturdy stone and stucco buildings, most of them painted light colors to reflect the heat. Central islands planted with palm trees divided the opposing streams of traffic. Civilian policemen stood atop concrete pedestals at the main intersections. They struggled in vain to impart some sense of order to the chaos flowing by. But the undisciplined human torrent mostly ignored their gestures and shrill whistles.

Our bus ground alongside the Dong Nai River, which ran through the center of the city. The twin spires of a massive cathedral rose in the distance. We gawked at an immense U.S. Navy LST lying at anchor in the river, its battleship-gray silhouette adding a stark, miniature skyline to the shore.

We continued down tree-lined Tu Do Street. Formerly called the Rue Catinat during the French era, Tu Do was the main artery of "The Paris of the Orient", as Saigon was known. Shops displayed the latest fashions from France. Here and there, white-suited Frenchmen still sipped rich coffee at sidewalk cafes. We gaped at a long line of youngsters in front of a movie theater whose marquee advertised the recent American film "Merrill's Marauders." All the wording except the title was in Vietnamese. Doug and I later went to see the movie, but left quickly after finding that none of the dialogue was in English.

The bus finally passed into Cholon, Saigon's twin city. Most of Cholon's residents were ethnic Chinese and foreign businessmen. The Capital Hotel was located there, at a point where the road split into two thoroughfares.

Our vehicle pulled up in front of the six-story structure and wheezed to a halt. The sidewalk around the hotel was lined with barbed wire. The front entrance was sandbagged and guarded by armed police. Balconies fronted with wrought iron railings encircled each floor of the building. For additional protection, more barbed wire stretched from the railings of the first three floors to the bottoms of the balconies directly above. A huge Coca-Cola sign rested atop the roof.

We filed inside to the desk, showed our orders, and were assigned a room together. Doug and I were the lowest ranking enlisted men in the group, so naturally our room was on the fifth floor. There were no elevators. We rolled our eyes. Rank obviously had its privileges. Junior personnel had more stairs to climb.

It was already late afternoon, and we were spent, so Doug and I wasted no time in getting to our room. We dropped our gear and looked around. Two single beds projected from the far wall. They had no bedsprings; the thin mattresses were laid directly over plywood frames. There were no windows, but full-length wooden shutters opened onto the balcony. Even with the light on, it was quite dim inside the room. Vietnamese electrical power was inconsistent, subject to wide swings of voltage. Brownouts were the rule rather than the exception.

I opened the shutters and stepped out onto the balcony. The panoramic view of the city held me spellbound until Doug came out to join me. "Quite a sight, isn't it?" he said.

"Yeah," I replied. It sure is."

We decided to have dinner in the main dining room on the ground floor instead of going out. Exhausted, we quickly returned to our room and took turns showering. Doug was first into the bathroom, where he found the water tank for the toilet mounted on the wall with a pull-chain hanging from it. There was an ancient cast iron bathtub with a shower head the size of a saucer projecting above it. Doug called out, "Hey Jim! This plumbing's older than me!"

I chuckled. Stretching out on my bed, I watched a small gray lizard walk upside-down across the ceiling. Our first day in Vietnam had been fascinating, but it was done. After a quick shower, I soon fell into a deep, dreamless sleep.

We had a modest breakfast in the cafeteria the next morning before catching the bus downtown. Most of our day was taken up with one orientation meeting after another. During the afternoon, we received orders to replace two radio operators in the city of Quang Tri. "Where the hell is Quang Tri?" muttered Doug.

I studied a map on the wall. "Here it is – all the way up north in I Corps. Right near the DMZ. Can't go much further and still be in South Vietnam."

"Great. Sounds like they're really sending us to the damn boonies." Doug was being his usually optimistic self.

Before breaking for the day, we drew field equipment, including steel helmets and jungle boots, from the supply room. After stowing our gear, the next stop was the weapons room.

A young corporal stood behind a half-door separating the room from the hallway. His elbows rested on a wooden shelf atop the door. He was chewing gum as he casually eyed us. We handed him copies of our orders. "Radio operators, huh?" he said, and disappeared into the back of the room. When he returned, he dropped two .45 automatics on the shelf, complete with holsters and pistol belts.

I stared at the handguns. "Wait a minute... I've never even fired a .45 before. How about a rifle instead?"

The corporal snapped his gum and rolled his eyes. "I wouldn't worry about it, pal. You guys probably ain't comin' back anyway."

I hefted the pistol and fixed him with an icy glare. "Hey, man... why don't you just take this thing and stick it up your fat ass?"

The clerk threw up his hands in mock horror. "Whoooah! That's no way to talk to a corporal."

I started to step forward, but Doug moved between us. He snatched the remaining weapon from the shelf and stashed it in his duffel bag. "Better listen to him, Jimbo." His voice dripped with sarcasm. "What we obviously have here is an experienced combat veteran. The VC raid this supply room all the time, you know."

The corporal's smile vanished. He slammed a clipboard down on the shelf. "Just sign the goddamn papers and take off, wise ass."

On the bus ride back to the hotel I was still fuming, maybe because I feared that the corporal's prediction might actually come true. He had, after all, merely voiced something that had already been in the back of my mind. But Doug would have none of it. "Forget that jerk," he growled. "He's just a rear-echelon asshole." We never discussed the incident again, but it remained rooted in my subconscious.

Doug and I completed our orientation the next afternoon. We were scheduled to fly up to Da Nang the following morning on a C-123 cargo plane. From there we were to make connections with an "Otter", a twelve-seat commuter aircraft stopping first at Hue and then continuing on to Quang Tri. To celebrate our last night in Saigon, we planned to go downtown to the enlisted men's club.

Shortly after dark we flagged down two cyclo drivers outside the hotel. The three-wheeled pedicab was a popular means of transportation in Saigon. It had a buckboard-type seat mounted up front astride two large bicycle wheels. A canvas top shielded the passenger from the weather. The driver sat behind on what looked like the back half of a bicycle. Most of the cyclo drivers we saw appeared to be comparatively older men. They had heavily-muscled calves from years of steady pedaling. And they loved to overcharge Americans.

Doug tried to explain to the drivers where we wanted to go, using a combination of English and pidgin Vietnamese. One of them listened carefully and nodded. "Ah… two hunra' pee," he exclaimed. I understood that. He wanted two hundred piasters, or about two dollars, for the trip.

Doug grimaced and made a great show of his displeasure. "Sau! Sau!" he cried in outrage, using the Vietnamese word for "bad." He pointed his index finger at the side of his head and slowly rotated it. "Dinky-dau!" (Crazy), he roared. "We pay one hundred pee."

The drivers flashed broad grins. I had to laugh. I guess that was more money than they had hoped to get in the first place. We probably could have sealed the deal for fifty piasters. "OK!" said the first driver. "We go." Somehow I felt we'd been taken, but… ah, what the hell?

When we arrived at the club ten minutes later, Doug paid the two drivers. "Probably a couple of friggin' VC," he snorted as they pedaled off. I shrugged. We turned and went inside.

The interior was a cheap imitation of an American night-club, with small round tables arrayed in front of a low stage. Servicemen wearing civilian clothing already occupied many of the seats. A brilliant spotlight shown down on a Vietnamese vocal group performing the Beatles' current hit song, "I Want to Hold Your Hand." A long, curved bar was located on the left side of the main room, partially obscured by a bamboo screen. Several Americans sat on stools carefully nursing their drinks. Directly opposite the bar, shielded by a bamboo screen, was a small gambling area containing a dozen shiny slot machines.

Arrival in Saigon, May 1964.

A smiling hostess met us at the door. She was clad in an orange ao-dai, the loose-fitting native dress worn by many Vietnamese women. She escorted us to a table in the middle of the room, took our drink orders, and quickly retreated. We sat back to watch the show.

The group was actually quite good, and performed several recent American rock hits. Doug jabbed me with an elbow. "Almost like back home, isn't it?"

After a couple of drinks, we were beginning to feel a bit tipsy, so we decided to return to the hotel, remembering the midnight curfew. But before we left Doug veered into the gambling nook and began pumping nickels into a "one-armed bandit." I watched in fascination, never having seen slot machines before. Within a few pulls he hit a small jackpot. "Lucky bastard," I muttered.

We then made our way outside, where a blue and silver taxi was cruising the street. Doug hailed it. It would be safer and quicker for two boozed-up soldiers than riding in an open cyclo at that hour. Besides, I didn't feel like dealing with those two VC again. The driver dropped us in front of the hotel, and we boisterously stumbled up the stairs to our room. Within minutes we both fell into a deep, alcohol-induced sleep.

I awoke the next morning with a pounding headache. Someone had lined my throat with sandpaper during the night. There was just enough time to shower, dress and grab a quick cup of coffee before the bus arrived to take us to Tan Son Nhut. We raced downstairs, spilling assorted gear along the way.

Our three days of semi-luxury ended abruptly when we boarded the C-123. It was a typical military transport, completely devoid of physical comforts. There were no seats, for one thing. Rows of cargo netting hung from the fuselage. We settled into it as best we could, sharing space with a dozen other soldiers and their baggage. Comfortable is not the word I would use to describe the netting. I turned to Doug. "By the time we get to Da Nang," I groused, "our asses are gonna have stripes."

The cargo doors whined shut. Both engines coughed, sputtered, and roared to life in turn. The noise was deafening. We taxied out onto the runway and took off. It was a long, loud ride to Da Nang.

Upon arrival at the Republic of Vietnam's second largest city, we discovered that the Otter that would carry us further north wasn't due to arrive until the following morning. Instead, a truck waited to transport us to the advisors' hotel. We tossed our gear into the back of the vehicle and climbed aboard.

The hotel was a beautiful white stucco building, four stories high. Like so many of the structures in Vietnam's cities, it had open-air balconies surrounding each of its levels. A broad path of red patio blocks lined on either side by brilliantly blooming flower beds led to the front entrance. There was a small but well-equipped radio shack on the roof. Twin antenna poles towered above it. Doug and I stood for a moment, captivated by the view. "Man," I murmured wistfully. "I wouldn't mind staying here."

"Yeah, right," sneered Doug. "That might happen."

We were assigned quarters in the transient area and ate dinner in the main dining room. Later we watched, appropriately enough, a World War II movie entitled "The Red Ball Express" in the day room. When we finally turned in for the night, we found the beds enclosed with mosquito netting and a small electric fan beside each. We slept in relative comfort.

The truck returned the next morning to take us back to the airstrip, and we were truly sorry to leave. A born cynic, Doug muttered, "Ain't no way Quang Tri can be as nice as this." The guy was becoming a veritable Nostradamus.

The Otter sat waiting for us at the strip. It was scheduled to hopscotch to Quang Tri, first stopping sixty miles up Highway 1 at Hue to drop off some other passengers. If all went well, we would be at our new station in about two hours.

The courier plane took off into a sparkling blue sky. The pilot leveled off at 1500 feet and followed the highway north to Hue. We peered curiously through the round portholes, watching the terrain pass below. When we arrived over Hue, the pilot cut the engine and coasted in a wide arc over the city.

We could see the ocean just to the east. The Perfume River passed through Hue as it flowed down to the South China Sea. We caught a quick glimpse of two bridges spanning the river before the Otter floated down to a gentle landing. The plane rumbled along the runway, gradually decelerating until it came to a complete stop. The other passengers unbuckled their seat belts and prepared to exit. Doug and I remained in our seats, waiting for the craft to take off again on the final leg of the journey.

After the doors swung open, everyone else disembarked. Then a soldier dressed in green fatigues and a floppy jungle hat appeared in the doorway. He squinted inside the plane. "Any radio operators on board?" he asked. It was Tony Thompson. He had been in the class ahead of us at ISROC, and we knew him casually.

"Yeah," I called out. "Hey, Tony... how are you?"

Thompson's eyes widened in surprise. "Well, whattaya know? Come on down, you guys."

"We're supposed to go on to Quang Tri," said Doug.

"Nah," replied Tony. "Everyone gets out here. This is the headquarters for northern I Corps."

We shuffled down the aisle, tossed out our baggage, and jumped down onto the runway. We had arrived at Tay Loc airfield inside the Hue citadel.

———

I CORPS

T HOMPSON LED US INTO A low stucco building adjacent to the landing strip. One small room at the near end housed the communications center for Advisory Team #3 headquartered in Hue. Inside mounted on a wooden bench was an "Angry/9" radio exactly like the ones we had practiced with at ISROC. The room was strewn with the paraphernalia of a commo hub.

A tall, blond sergeant who appeared to be in his mid-thirties was monitoring the radio. He peered at us over the top of his glasses as we walked through the door. Thompson said, "This is Sergeant Kane. We call him 'CHOP', short for Chief Operator."

Kane stood up and grinned. "What have we got here? Radio operators, I hope."

I stuck out my hand. "Jim Oliveri. This is Doug Potter."

Kane gave us both an enthusiastic handshake. "Man, do we need you guys. We've been working double shifts since the two operators you're replacing went home last week."

I noticed Thompson rolling his eyes and wondered why he had done that. He said, "Want me to drive them up to the hotel, Chop?"

"Yeah. Make them comfortable. We don't want them to get away." Kane chuckled and turned back to the radio that was hissing and popping softly behind him.

Thompson led us through the door to a jeep parked just outside the building. Kane called after us, "Say, do you think one of you guys could take a shift tonight?"

I looked at Thompson. He shrugged. "Sure. I'll take a shot at it." I hadn't expected to start so soon, but I was willing to give it a try.

"Great," replied Kane. "Lansing is on tonight. He can show you the ropes and break you in. We've been working twelve-hour shifts, but we can shorten that as soon as you guys get into the rotation. OK, I'll see you later."

We tossed our bags into the back of the jeep and climbed in on top of them. Thompson lurched off down the dirt road, trailing a cloud of orange dust. He gave us a quick briefing as we rode. "He's a goddamn character. He doesn't usually take a shift, but we've been so shorthanded he's had to. You'll get used to him. Our boss is Captain Schader, the commo officer. We call him 'Captain Shithead.' Doesn't do a damn thing for us. Just rides around the city all day taking pictures."

We turned left onto a slightly wider dirt road. "That was Tay Loc Airfield we just left," continued Tony. "We're inside the Hue Citadel."

Hue (Way) was formerly the imperial capital of Vietnam. The ancient Vietnamese constructed the Citadel as a residence for the Annamese emperors. It enclosed the revered Palace of Peace, one of the most important shrines in Indo-China. The Citadel was roughly two miles square. Its brick walls were sixteen feet high, ranging in thickness from sixty to two hundred feet. The entire structure was surrounded by a wide water-filled moat, its surface speckled with green aquatic plants. Built along the banks of the Perfume River, the Citadel had a distinctly medieval appearance. Stone watch-towers dotted its walls. The yellow and red striped South Vietnamese flag flew from its highest point, a huge flagpole located near the Palace of Peace at the south wall.

The 1st Division of the Army of the Republic of Vietnam (ARVN) had its headquarters compound inside the northeast corner of the Citadel. The American advisory team also maintained a modest command post there. U.S. personnel commuted daily between the Citadel and the advisors' hotel just across the river. Hue was one of the most secure and peaceful sites in all of Vietnam. For both Vietnamese and Americans alike, it was a preferred duty station.

Our jeep bounced along and passed through one of the huge stone gateways leading out of the Citadel. With a clash of gears, Thompson turned left again onto Tran Hung Dao Street, running alongside the river. I spotted the two bridges we had glimpsed from the air. The one upriver to our rear was a simple railroad bridge. Ahead and to our right lay a more heavily-trafficked steel girder structure.

The French had built the Nguyen Hoang Bridge across the Perfume River about thirty years earlier. It was a graceful truss-type span consisting of a series of arched segments set atop concrete pilings. There was room for only a single lane of traffic in either direction. Pedestrian walkways lay outside the vertical supports on both sides, enclosed by wrought iron railings. The entire structure towered about twenty-five feet above the gently flowing river. It was one of the favorite vantage points of the Americans, who frequently used it to take photographs of this bustling Asian metropolis. The Nguyen Hoang Bridge was one of the focal points of Hue, essentially serving as the main link between the north and south sections of the city.

We drove past a colorful pagoda located in a small public park. Thompson turned right onto Duy Tan Street and continued south to the bridge. Other than military vehicles, there were few automobiles in Hue. Most of the populace traveled either on foot, by bicycle or on cyclos. Tony braked frequently to keep pace with the slower moving traffic. We inched across the spans until we reached the south shore.

The advisors' hotel was situated on a corner just beyond the ramp to the bridge. There was a small concrete traffic platform in the middle of the intersection manned by a Vietnamese police officer. Thompson signaled for a left turn, and the policeman motioned us on. Tony pulled into the lot behind the building and slipped into a vacant parking space.

The cream-colored hotel seemed much less luxurious than its counterpart in Da Nang. Doug had certainly been right about that. The exterior was stucco, naturally, and the obligatory balconies surrounded its three stories. The front entrance was sealed and sandbagged for security, since it was merely a few feet from the street. The parking area was ringed with coils of barbed wire. A long two-floored structure adjacent to the left rear of the hotel served as a separate billet for officers, and also housed the dispensary. There was a large screened room upstairs that was used for meetings and movies. About one hundred men of Advisory Team #3 were based in this compound.

A Vietnamese maid was rinsing a mop in a metal bucket outside the entrance as we approached. She flashed us a shy smile. I nodded politely in return.

Inside the hotel was a small lobby containing a mailroom and a barbershop. There was a large dining room to the left. Thompson peeked into the tiny mailroom. A middle-aged sergeant was sorting envelopes into a wooden rack. Tony called out, "Hey, Sergeant Haight... Got a couple of new customers for you."

Haight didn't bother to look up, and continued working. "Leave me a copy of their orders and put them in your room. You got empty bunks up there."

Thompson glanced at us and shrugged. "Come on. I'll show you your new home."

We hauled our gear up to the second floor. I was thinking about how nice it would be to find a permanent home for this stuff so we could quit carrying it all over God's creation. Anyway, our assigned room was a large one containing five mosquito-netted beds. Two were currently vacant. There was a bathroom located at the far end of the room. Doug and I selected bunks, and then went about sorting our clothing and equipment.

Thompson explained the dining procedures while we worked. At meal time, we were expected to check in with a clerk who sat inside a small cubicle at the front of the mess hall. He would record our names, and then hand out round metal chits stamped HUE MESS. The waitresses would collect these when they served the food. At the end of the month when we were paid, we could settle the bill for each meal we consumed. Of course, we would not have to pay for any meals we missed while we were in the field. Overall it was an equitable arrangement. And best of all, the food was quite good.

Doug and I met Specialist 4th Class Ray Lansing at dinner. He was a career soldier in his late thirties who was scheduled to return home in a couple of weeks. The light-haired, balding Lansing was known for carrying a long-barreled .38 when he was on duty. He was also one of the best radio operators in Vietnam.

Lansing said, "I hear one of you is taking the graveyard shift with me."

"That's me," I replied.

"Good. I'll meet you down here at 1930. The Colonel wants us to make sure we're off the streets before dark."

After dinner I went upstairs to rest. It had sounded like it was going to be a long night. I lay on my bunk for about half an hour, but I was too full of nervous energy to close my eyes. At 1915, I splashed some cold water on my face, strapped on my .45, and went downstairs.

Lansing was waiting in the lobby, holding a thermos of coffee he had just filled in the kitchen. "All set?"

I nodded. We went out through the rear screen door into the parking lot. Lansing slid behind the wheel of the commo jeep while I climbed into the front seat beside him. We lurched out of the compound and headed across the bridge.

There was very little traffic as twilight approached. Except for those of us on duty, no Americans were on the streets at night. Even the locals seldom used the bridge after dusk. The soft lights of the city reflected from the darkening waters of the river as we sped past the Citadel walls. I noticed that the flag atop the huge pole had been lowered for the night. When we reached the airfield, Chop Kane was standing in the doorway of the radio room.

"You guys are early."

Lansing smiled. "Our new romeo oscar (radio operator) is real anxious to get started."

"That's good," said Kane. "Everything's been quiet. No traffic since early this afternoon."

"Okay," replied Lansing. "We'll see you in the morning."

Kane hopped into the jeep and sped off. We turned and went inside. It was a humid evening. The commo room was hot and stuffy, and the air smelled stale. Lansing placed the thermos on the bench, and then pulled two chairs around to the front. "Grab a seat," he said. I sat down and eyed the familiar green metal radio with its various dials. The "Angry/9" crackled and hissed softly.

Lansing turned to me. "The first thing I usually do is send out a net call to make sure everyone's OK." He flicked on the transmit switch, picked up the telegraph key and rested it on his knee. He began tapping out the letter "V" repeatedly. This alerted the other stations that a call was coming. Lansing followed up with an alpha-numeric grouping used to designate a net call, and an interrogative asking for traffic. So far none of this was unfamiliar to me.

Quang Tri was the first to respond. The radio in the advisors' compound there ran on regular electric power, while the operators at the other stations had to run outside and manually crank up their gasoline generators before transmitting. The stations began checking in one by one. Their dits and dahs each had a distinctly different tone. They all replied that Lansing's signal was coming in loud and clear, and that they had no messages to send.

Lansing rogered each transmission by tapping the "out" signal: dih-dah-dih-dah-dit. The other stations responded with two quick dits each. Apparently this was a little game they played when there was no important traffic.

Lansing flipped off the transmit switch and sat back. "Well, let's see... I'll give you a quick rundown of our setup. We've got anywhere from five to ten stations in the 'Frost Weed' net, depending on what's going on. There are permanent stations here and at Quang Tri. We have operators at Ta Bat and A Luoi out in the A Shau Valley. There's also a Special Forces camp in the A Shau, but they have their own net. Once in a while, if ARVN has an operation going, we'll send someone out there for a week or so."

He pointed to a small map of I Corps on the wall. "There's an operator up here at Lang Vei near the Laotian border. There's another Special Forces camp about five miles from Lang Vei at Khe Sanh. Again, they're not part of our net.

"From time to time we'll send operators up to places along the DMZ like Cam Lo, Gio Linh, and Con Thien. But that's usually just for a couple of days." He tapped the map. "You might as well take a look at this so you'll get an idea where everyone is."

Lansing poured himself a cup of coffee while I studied the map. He took a gulp of the steaming brew and then said, "That A Shau Valley gives me the creeps. If you ever get out there you'll see what I mean. It's real isolated. Usually the only way in or out is by air. I was there once for more than two weeks without a plane coming in because of the weather. No resupply. We lived on rice and tea the whole time. Sometimes the fog rolls in and doesn't move for days. I used to worry a lot about getting hit during the rainy season. You're pretty much on your own in that case." He shook his head. "Yep, that place scares the hell out of me."

I was duly impressed. If a veteran operator like Lansing feared The Valley, there had to be a good reason. I made a mental note to learn all I could about the A Shau. I asked a few technical questions, but our conversation petered out after a few minutes. Lansing peered across at me. "OK, let's see what kind of 'fist' you have."

My mentor disconnected the antenna leading into the radio, and then pointed to the telegraph key. I slid across and grasped the flat black knob. Lansing handed me a code sheet. "Here. Transmit these groups at twelve words per minute."

I adjusted the key to my touch and began pounding away in a steady pattern. Lansing nodded approvingly. "Not bad," he said. "Pick up the speed a little."

I complied, tapping out the code in a clear, easy to read manner. Next he slid a notepad across the table. "OK, now you copy while I send." He started cranking out three-letter groups.

I followed without much difficulty. After about thirty seconds, Lansing put down the key and smiled. "That was outstanding. You didn't miss a single letter. As far as I'm concerned, you can go right in the rotation."

I beamed, feeling that I'd passed an important test. Lansing reconnected the antenna and sat back. Except for the soft chirping of the radio, the night was again still. "Listen," said Lansing. "We hardly ever get any traffic at night. Too much interference. Why don't you sack out for a while? You can relieve me at 0200."

I sprawled out on a bamboo couch against the wall, and watched a pair of geckos chase each other across the ceiling. My eyelids began to droop and finally closed. When I opened them again, daylight was streaming through an open window. Lansing was standing in the doorway gazing out across the landing strip. He glanced at me as I sat up. "Ah, hell, Ray," I said. You never called me."

Lansing shrugged. "No problem. I conked out, too. Nothing was happening anyway."

I flashed a sheepish grin and tried to smooth my rumpled uniform. "Say, where do you pee around here?"

Lansing chuckled. "You can go around the back of the building. Nobody will say anything."

When I returned from relieving myself, Thompson and Doug pulled up in the commo jeep. "You guys ready for breakfast?" called Doug as he hopped out of the vehicle. "They're cooking up a shitload of bacon and eggs."

Lansing came over to join us. Thompson motioned to Doug and said, "We're gonna work together today. Chop said if everything is okay, they can both go in the rotation starting tomorrow."

Specialist Lansing smiled. "That's good news."

We left Doug and Tony to take over, and sped back to the hotel, where a hearty breakfast awaited us.

HUE CITY

I WAS ON DUTY AT THE radio shack in the Citadel when Tony Thompson went out to Ta Bat. I wished him luck as he boarded a Caribou resupply plane headed west to the A Shau Valley. For the next several hours I attended to the routine operation of the radio net.

Some time around noon, I heard a flight of helicopters approaching the landing strip. The steady drumbeat of their rotors was clearly audible even though they were still some distance off. It had been a hot, uneventful morning thus far, so I stepped outside the radio shack to watch them come in.

Three big ARVN (Army of the Republic of Vietnam) H-34 choppers soon arrived and began to settle slowly onto the near edge of the runway, scattering dust and debris in a blinding cloud. As soon as they touched down, several squads of South Vietnamese infantry descended from the craft. The crew of the helicopter nearest me went to work unloading a stack of cumbersome green rubber bags. I realized with a start that these were the bodies of South Vietnamese soldiers killed in battle. The VC had sprung a lethal ambush on a patrol somewhere to the west, killing more than a dozen friendlies. It had been a humiliating setback for the ARVN, who could claim no enemy casualties in return.

I watched in macabre fascination while the H-34 crewmen tossed the bags down onto the runway as if they were so much firewood. The war suddenly hit close to home. Until now Vietnam had seemed more like a resort area than a battle zone. But that misconception was brutally driven from my mind this day. Here were men who had actually died. This morning they had been live human beings, laughing, talking and planning for a future they hoped would be free of war. Now they lay silent and cold in those latex cocoons, their dreams forever terminated. For the first time I felt fear. It was an unsettling experience. I couldn't help but think about what that weapons corporal back in Saigon had said. Maybe the bastard knew something I didn't. I stepped back inside the radio room. Glancing down at my hands, I was surprised to find them trembling.

Advisory Team #3 hotel in Hue.

Fortunately, there was quite a bit of traffic on the net that day to take my mind off the incident. But later that afternoon another interesting event occurred. General Thi, the ARVN commander of I Corps, arrived at the Citadel by helicopter, probably to be briefed on the ambush.

Nguyen Chanh Thi was a powerful general, extremely popular with his soldiers and among the Buddhist populace of the northern provinces. He was a strong-willed patriot who would later be banished to the United States following a bitter feud with Premier Nguyen Cao Ky. Known as "the warlord of the north", Thi was undoubtedly the single most influential man in the Vietnamese military. The American advisors considered him a "real fighting general" and a capable tactician. In his younger days, Thi was a courageous paratrooper who had been captured and imprisoned by both the Japanese and the Viet Cong. When he stepped off the helicopter at Tay Loc, General Thi was dressed in tailored camouflage fatigues, and wore a maroon beret. He had a thick, droopy moustache.

An olive-colored staff car sped past the commo room and approached the group that was now disembarking from the helicopter. When I saw the flag bearing three gold stars fluttering from the hood of the vehicle, I knew immediately who our visitor was.

Thi clambered into the rear seat of the car with an aide, and the vehicle quickly turned back in my direction. As it neared the radio shack, I stepped forward, snapped to attention, and saluted. The car slowed and halted momentarily just outside the radio room. General Thi leaned forward and smiled at me through a side window. Thi liked Americans, and seemed to appreciate being recognized and acknowledged by this young U.S. soldier. He returned my salute. The car then accelerated again and disappeared up the road, leaving behind a cloud of swirling red dust. Several truckloads of ARVN troops followed in pursuit, forming a mini-caravan that made its way rapidly to Division headquarters. The excitement was over for the moment, and so was my shift. Doug had arrived to take over.

Traffic at Tay Loc airfield remained fairly heavy. Helicopters chugged in and out sporadically. An American L-19 "Bird Dog" observation plane was based there, and made daily flights to the west. The "Otter" commuted on a regular courier run between Da Nang, Hue and Quang Tri. And the medium-sized "Caribou" made frequent resupply trips to The Valley and beyond.

One morning shortly after General Thi's visit, I was on duty when I heard the single-engine L-19 pass overhead as it circled the Citadel. Incoming craft usually touched down at the far end of the runway and then taxied to the holding area near the radio shack. With nothing happening on the net, I strolled outside to watch the "Bird Dog" come in.

It was a typical Hue morning. The sky was a brilliant blue with the temperature hovering around 90 degrees. The light aircraft bobbed slightly as it approached, waggling its wings as gentle air currents drifted up from the hot ground. Visibility seemed ideal. The plane appeared a bit high as it arrived over Tay Loc. At the midpoint of the runway, the pilot must have realized that there wasn't enough room left to land safely. He gunned the engine in a desperate attempt to abort the approach and circle around again. The motor stalled out and the plane dropped like a stone. It passed over my head and impacted nose-first into the shallow moat beyond, where it flipped over onto its back.

For a moment I couldn't believe what I had just seen. Then I dashed out onto a dry earth dike extending into the moat. By the time I reached the downed aircraft, several ARVN soldiers had successfully freed the pilot – I can't recall his name – from the cockpit. He seemed unhurt but appeared to be in shock. His flight suit was soaked and smeared with mud. A Vietnamese soldier and I helped support him as we made our way ponderously back toward the commo shack. Once inside, we sat the still disoriented pilot on the bamboo couch and I raced for the landline. The duty officer at headquarters answered and I told him what had happened. "Roger," he replied. "We're on the way."

At this point I heard Thompson calling net control on voice. He must have been trying for some time because he sounded annoyed. I snatched up the mike and responded, "This is Frost Weed Alpha. Please stand by. We have an emergency situation here. Out."

A jeep and a ¾ ton truck screeched to a halt outside within minutes. A lieutenant and a master sergeant scurried into the commo shack and quickly examined the pilot. When he seemed to have regained his composure they hustled him into the truck and drove off. I called Thompson back, apologized and took his message, but he still sounded irritated.

The L-19 was eventually salvaged, but I never saw that particular pilot again. I don't know if his tour of duty was concluded or if they just sent him home as a result of the accident. In any case, he was not the last to suddenly vanish from Advisory Team #3.

Several days later I picked up a coded message from Thompson. After rogering receipt, I deciphered the transmission. It was a priority message, and when I read it, I understood why. A patrol out of Ta Bat had sighted Chinese trucks moving down the "Ho Chi Minh Trail" in Laos, just to the west of The Valley. This was an important development. I rang up headquarters on the landline and told them about the message. They immediately sent a driver over for it, rather than electing to wait for the regular courier run later in the day. Things were picking up in the A Shau.

It was around this time that Chop announced his plans for Doug and me. "We'll be setting up permanent stations soon at Cam Lo, Gio Linh and Con Thien," he said with a grin. "You guys will be going up there to man the radios."

This was not good news. Those three locations were near or north of Highway 9 in Quang Tri Province, virtually within hailing distance of the DMZ. According to Kane, each of us, along with an American advisor, would be assigned to a Vietnamese unit operating in one of those areas. We would live and work more or less permanently out of an armored personnel carrier (APC). Chop didn't seem much concerned with what risks we might experience while performing this duty. I understood then why Thompson had been less than complimentary about him when we first arrived. And of course we never heard any words of encouragement from our esteemed commo officer, Captain Schader, either. In fact, we never heard anything at all from him. We were not only novices, but entirely on our own as well.

Doug and I were not happy. To us it sounded like we would be in for some rugged and dangerous duty. If we had to function that way for the rest of our tour it would make for a very long year indeed. Fortunately, none of it ever came to pass. I'm not sure if I Corps command discarded the plan or if Kane was merely trying to exert some domination over us by alarming two green privates. Maybe both. In any case, Doug and I spent a couple of uncomfortable weeks worrying about our immediate future.

The situation with Captain Schader was especially perplexing. As our boss, it would seem reasonable that he'd check on us periodically to be sure that we were doing our jobs properly. But he never once made an appearance at the Tay Loc radio shack. As far as inquiring about our personal welfare or asking if we needed anything, that didn't happen either. What he actually did all day was a mystery to us. During our first month in Hue, absentee management was the modus operandi at MAAG Radio.

Lansing went home that same week. I was sorry to see him go, but I was happy for him too. I had grown fond of the soft-spoken, impassive Spec-4. Toward the end of the week, Doug and I were both off duty until the afternoon. Someone mentioned that a group of advisors was going down to the ocean for a swimming trip, so we decided to join them. It was a good day for the beach: hot and humid, with bright, searing sunshine.

Seven of us made the trip. The Vietnamese driver dropped us off at the shore, and promised to be back in the afternoon. Hue was considered so secure that no Americans carried weapons while off duty. Doug and I walked barefoot to the water's edge. We were impressed. The coarse sand had a pale yellow tint. The blazing sun sent brilliant blue and white sparkles radiating from the gently rolling South China Sea. Several dozen locals clad in shorts milled about the beach or chanced an occasional dip in the warm surf.

We stripped down to bathing trunks and eased onto the burning sand. Someone noticed two Vietnamese men standing beside a water-logged canoe in a small tidal pool. Two of our companions wandered over and soon arranged to rent the leaky vessel.

The seven of us piled into the canoe as if we were on a Sunday outing back home. Doug snickered and said, "I hope this thing isn't named the Titanic." We began paddling madly with our hands, and laughed and whooped with glee as our craft started to make headway. Somehow, we managed to swing what passed for the bow of the over-loaded canoe into the oncoming swells.

About fifty feet from shore, a small breaker swamped the boat, and it sank like a rock. I swallowed a mouthful of salt water, and came up spluttering. Doug and the others were flailing about nearby. We struck out for the beach.

As we stepped dripping and laughing from the surf, the two Vietnamese men came running. They were furious at the loss of their boat, and hopped up and down in the sand while chattering madly at us. I couldn't even begin to guess what they were calling us. I didn't know whether to laugh or to worry that we could be in trouble. A crowd of bathers began to gather. Most of them seemed amused by the bizarre spectacle we had created.

One of the other Americans, an Air Force sergeant, broke from the group and strode over to where his clothing lay on the sand. He pulled his wallet from the pocket and withdrew a handful of piaster notes. Then he handed the money to the indignant Vietnamese men. They immediately ceased their angry gyrations and stalked off, still muttering to themselves. They glared back once or twice, but we pretended not to notice.

By the time our ride arrived, my skin was already turning bright crimson. I had underestimated the strength of the tropical sun and had stayed far too long without a shirt. When we got back to the hotel, my shoulders had already begun to blister. The pain was unbearable during the night. I had to lie on my stomach in order to get any sleep at all. The next morning, Doug was very sympathetic. "What a yo-yo," he said. "If you had olive skin like a real Italian, you wouldn't have this problem." I wanted to shoot him the bird, but raising my arm caused just too much pain.

I had to work my shift that day without a shirt. Later that afternoon, Sergeant Harris, the detachment medic, treated me in the dispensary and diagnosed second degree burns. He gave me a foul-smelling ointment to apply to the blisters. For the rest of my tour, I stayed out of the sun whenever possible. As I write this many years later, the scars on my shoulders are still faintly visible.

Doug and I continued to alternate shifts. One afternoon as I sat at the radio, the landline jangled. I picked up the receiver. "MAAG (Military Assistance Advisory Group) Radio, Private Oliveri speaking, Sir."

"Oliveri, this is Lieutenant Lacey at headquarters. Hue is under a state of emergency, and vehicular traffic is prohibited until further notice. I suggest you remain indoors and stay alert. We'll let you know if the situation changes."

What the hell was this all about? I walked to the door and peered outside. Several ARVN soldiers were moving about near the fuel storage area across the runway. The air above the landing strip shimmered in the heat. Everything seemed normal. I returned inside and sat down beside the radio. The "Angry/9" hissed and popped softly in the background.

I was perplexed. I had no idea what was going on, and, indeed, nothing unusual seemed to be happening. My hand slid down to my pistol belt, and I removed the .45 from its holster. I chambered a round with a metallic click, and then laid the weapon on the table beside the radio. I leaned back against the wall, facing the door.

There was no traffic on the net. Maybe it was my imagination, but the ARVN guards seemed to be hanging closer to the commo shack than they usually did. I was tense. Beads of perspiration began to form on my forehead, and it wasn't from the heat.

Moments later, a routine message came in from one of the outposts. I rogered the transmission and began to copy. While I was printing the coded groups, a Vietnamese soldier appeared in the doorway. He made no attempt to enter the room, and merely stood quietly in the entrance. He smiled benignly at me.

I tried to act unconcerned and continued copying the message. But I slid my left hand slowly along the counter until I gripped the pistol. When the soldier saw this, his smile faded into a frown and he shook his head. Then he disappeared from the doorway.

I finished transcribing the message, and then walked to the door, weapon in hand. There was no one in sight. The soldier was probably just trying to be friendly. Or maybe he was scared, too, and was just seeking some form of reassurance. I guess my threatening gesture was not what he had expected. In any case, he was gone. I wiped my brow with the back of my forearm, still wondering what the hell was going on.

About an hour later, Lacey called back to tell me that the alert had been lifted. My relief would be along at the regular time.

Doug had the whole story when he arrived. Apparently the local Buddhists had planned a rally to protest General Nguyen Khanh's government. The Vietnamese authorities had advised the Americans to stay off the streets until it was over. The protest never materialized for some reason, and the alert had been cancelled.

The incident with the ARVN soldier still bothered me, and I told Doug about it. "Listen," he said. "You did the right thing. How the hell could you know what he was up to?" I guess he was right. The whole situation was really confusing.

Doug and I continued to alternate shifts through the end of May. Chop Kane sat in now and then so we could switch off. We soon realized that Kane could be a major pain in the ass. He was an exasperating prima donna more interested in wangling a promotion than in running an efficient radio net. We rarely saw Captain Schader, who was supposed to be our communications officer. In essence, control of the MAAG Radio net was in the hands of two very novice privates.

Near the end of the month Potter and I were promoted to PFC. No doubt it was an administrative decision made in Saigon without input from Kane or Schader. At any rate, Doug was soon sent out to A Luoi to relieve Ken Keller, the operator there.

I was on duty when Keller returned from The Valley aboard a Caribou. Ken was a lanky, curly-blond from Ohio with a high forehead and an easy smile. He hopped down from the cargo gate with his duffel bag slung over one shoulder. We had often talked on the radio, but had never met in person. It was a strange experience to finally put a face on the voice. His demeanor reminded me of Lansing. I took an immediate liking to him.

Sgt. Kane reluctantly worked a swing shift that night. After dinner, Keller, Doug and I went up to the enlisted men's club to get better acquainted. The Hue EM Club was located on the third floor of the hotel. Two sides of the room were screened in and opened onto a balcony. A modest bar in the center of the room was trimmed with black vinyl armrests and had a padded front decorated with brass studs. A Vietnamese bartender stood behind the counter. He smiled politely as we entered the room. The Vietnamese were always smiling. It seemed like a charming mannerism until you realized that the grin often wasn't sincere. Many Vietnamese secretly loathed the Americans even as they smiled at them. We quickly learned to ignore their shallow friendliness.

We ordered drinks and then sat at one of the vacant tables across from the bar. Another soldier dressed in civilian clothes stood at the rear of the room pumping nickels into the club's single slot machine. The "one-armed bandit" whirred softly, occasionally emitting a tinkle as it disgorged a few coins into a metal tray at its base.

The three of us talked about Vietnam in general and I Corps in particular. Keller had arrived in-country a month before Doug and me, and had been at A Luoi for the previous three weeks. Ken had just enjoyed his first hot shower in that time. "To tell you the truth," he said, "A Luoi's not that bad. It's newer than Ta Bat, and a lot cleaner. But, man, I gotta tell you, it is boring out there. There's absolutely nothing to do all day. My three weeks seemed like three months."

I sipped my drink, deep in thought. Doug didn't seem to be paying much attention as he listened to the soldier in the rear swearing at the slot machine. But then he asked, "Do you ever run into the 'Green Beanies'?"

"Special Forces? Nah. Their camp is too far down The Valley. But sometimes someone will walk in from Ta Bat. There's a rough trail between the two outposts. Actually they're within artillery range of each other. The ARVN gunners are pretty good, too. They've got The Valley well registered in case of an attack."

This all sounded very hairy to me. "Any other Americans out there?" I asked.

Ken nodded. "There's an officer. But I never saw much of him except when he wanted to send a message. He usually stayed with his counterpart in the ARVN bunker. Tell you what, there were times when I really felt isolated. You can't hardly talk to the Vietnamese, and nobody else ever tells you anything. I always felt like I was gonna be the last to know when something was about to bite me in the ass."

None of this was making me feel any better. "Well," I said, "I guess we'll find out for ourselves."

Keller nodded again. "For sure."

With three operators now available, I wasn't on the schedule for the following day. I decided to use the opportunity to get better acquainted with the city of Hue. Armed with a map Thompson had given me, I set out to cover the region south of the river. Carrying only a camera, I traversed the area on foot. It was a clear sunny day. Some scattered light clouds floated gently across the morning sky. The temperature was in the low 80's, cooler than usual and ideal for walking. And for once it was relatively dry. I could have rented a bicycle from one of the local merchants for a few piasters, but decided against it. I wanted to take my time.

Starting from the Advisors Compound, I strolled to the Joan of Arc Cathedral, one block south on Duy Tan Street, which was actually an extension of Highway 1. I snapped several photos of the Roman Catholic church and school run by Vietnamese priests and then moved on.

Turning east, I walked several blocks to Hue Stadium, scene of the massive Buddhist protests several years before. Doubling back, I stopped briefly at the Treasury building and took several more photos of that imposing structure.

I swung north to Le Loi Street, which ran parallel to the Perfume River, pausing to admire the beautiful Cercle Sportif, an old French country club. Carefully manicured tennis courts surrounded the facility, flanked by lovely grassy banks sloping gently to the river. There was a large rectangular swimming pool on the grounds with a high diving board at one end. Several patrons were splashing happily in the crystal waters. The Cercle Sportif was renowned for serving the best food in Hue.

Continuing east along Le Loi, I soon reached the Capitol Building and the Public Health and Hospital Complex. The attitude of the Vietnamese civilians on the street was amusing. American sight-seers were still a novelty in Hue. They eyed me curiously as I snapped photo after photo. If any happened to cross my line of sight as I aimed the camera, they always turned and smiled into the lens. I was reminded of little children hamming it up for a photographer.

Now heading back toward the hotel two blocks west, I paused one last time to snap Hue University with its adjacent soccer field. My walking tour had taken just over two hours, and the sun was beginning to get hot. I decided to return to the compound for lunch.

When I reached the hotel, Captain Shader was just emerging from the dining room. He came over to me. "We're bringing Thompson in from Ta Bat tomorrow. You're going out in his place."

I tried to appear unconcerned. "Okay, Sir."

"Take plenty of gear. You'll probably be out there a few weeks." He stalked off without another word.

I glared after him. What a jackass, I thought. Our commo officer didn't give a damn about any of us. He was probably headed for the bar in the officers' club. In the meantime I had work to do. Tomorrow I would be in the heart of the A Shau Valley, one of the wildest places in I Corps. I had suspected all along that I would probably wind up there eventually, but it was still unsettling now that it was so imminent. I knew I wasn't going to sleep much that night. And I had no way of knowing it, of course, but I would spend precious little time in Hue during the ensuing eleven months.

So that was my "war" during the month of May, 1964. But things were about to take a dramatic turn.

———

INCIDENT AT
TA BAT

T A BAT WAS A PRIMITIVE outpost located in the remote A Shau
Valley adjacent to the Laotian border. The Vietnamese
36th Ranger Battalion, advised by an American officer,
called Ta Bat home. The A Shau was probably the most wildly
beautiful and severely contoured area in South Vietnam. It
contained some of the most impassable terrain in Southeast
Asia. Elephants were known to roam there, and an occasional
tiger sometimes came down from the hills in search of prey.

The South Vietnamese Army maintained two outposts in
The Valley, and American Special Forces manned another.
Small units of the Viet Cong operated freely throughout the
area. During 1964, the opposing forces had reached a virtual
stand-off. The Allies enjoyed superior firepower, while the
VC were lightly armed but more mobile. The Communists
used the triple-tiered jungle canopy and rugged terrain to
their advantage to fight on relatively even terms with their
adversaries.

Allied intelligence indicated that The Valley was a primary
infiltration point for the North Vietnamese regulars just
beginning to travel south on the so-called "Ho Chi Minh
Trail" in Laos. ARVN and American forces relied on a ten to
one manpower advantage to deny this route to the enemy.
Unknown to Allied command, however, plans were being
put into motion in Hanoi that would not only alter that ratio,

but would dramatically escalate the conflict from a modest counter-insurgency effort to a full-scale war. The A Shau Valley rested precariously on an anvil of vulnerability, and the hammer was already falling.

Chop Kane drove me to the airstrip the next morning, where a Caribou resupply plane waited on the runway. A squad of Vietnamese soldiers was loading the cargo: several dozen huge burlap bags of rice, numerous bamboo coops crammed with live chickens and ducks, three or four massive hogs whose legs had been tied to prevent them from moving around during the flight, and a shipment of ammunition for the Rangers at Ta Bat. I was the lone passenger.

I marveled at the crude but effective method of resupply. The birds and hogs would remain alive at the outpost until needed. Then the soldiers would kill just enough to prepare a meal. It was a simple means of storage that negated the need for complex refrigeration systems.

When the Vietnamese finished loading, I climbed up the open tailgate into the plane. There were no seats, so I perched atop a stack of rice bags and hooked one arm through a webbed cargo strap. There were no windows either. I wouldn't be able to see much, but it was a short flight to Ta Bat.

The tailgate closed, and the twin props roared to life. The olive green plane taxied slowly to the far end of the runway where it then turned into the wind. As the pilot gunned the engines, the Caribou began rolling rapidly down the strip. We lifted off and rose swiftly at a steep angle.

I glanced across at the rows of bamboo coops. The sudden ascent had alarmed the birds. They now squawked and flapped their wings in outrage, sending swirls of tiny white feathers along the deck of the cargo bay. I chuckled at the sight. Nothing like traveling first class, I thought.

Twenty minutes later, the aircraft banked left, floated across a line of rolling mountain peaks and entered the A Shau Valley. By craning my neck to peer through the cockpit windows, I caught a brief glimpse of the terrain below. Its smooth, billiard table appearance was marred only by some intermittent shell craters resembling open sores on the green surface. As the triangular outpost loomed in the distance, the Caribou descended sharply, and then headed straight in toward the runway.

The plane touched down on the crude landing strip of perforated steel plate laid over packed earth, vibrating madly as the engines roared into reverse. Prop wash sent a sandstorm of red dust swirling in the craft's wake. The Caribou bobbed violently up and down on the uneven surface as the pilot literally stood on the brakes. He brought us to a halt about two hundred yards from the end of the runway, then turned and rolled slowly back toward the main compound. The tailgate motors began to whine just before the aircraft lurched to a complete stop. The ramp cracked open and swung quickly down to ground level. A blast of hot, dry air swept into the interior. I blinked rapidly as dust peppered my face, then shuffled to the rear of the plane and hopped down into the blinding afternoon glare.

A hatless American officer with dark hair and black bushy eyebrows was standing nearby with the Vietnamese cargo crew. He strode over to me and glanced at my name tag. I tossed him a salute that he didn't return. "Hello, Oliveri," he said. "Welcome to Ta Bat. I'm Captain Vincent. Come on, I'll show you to your hooch."

I shouldered my bag and followed the captain through the main gate. An ARVN soldier stood inside a log and sandbag guard post just within the entrance. Barriers of crossed logs strung with barbed wire had been swung aside to form a narrow passageway. We turned to the left and clomped alongside a meandering trench network that appeared to be about four feet deep. Clumps of spindly trees grew from small mounds of red earth surrounding the ditches.

Vincent led me to a point where two trenches intersected in front of a dilapidated bunker constructed of wooden logs. It had a flimsy screen door, and there were patches of weeds growing from its dirt roof. A battered tin basin rested on an old ammunition box outside the entrance. Vincent pulled the screen open. "Get yourself settled in. I'll be back for you later. We're having dinner with the camp commander."

I stepped inside, swung my duffel bag down, and glanced around. It was pretty grim. The bunker was octagon-shaped, about fifteen feet in diameter, with a dirt floor. Corrugated metal sheets nailed to the roof formed a crude ceiling. Woven grass mats covered the walls. A narrow alcove served as the entrance, with three broad steps of notched logs and earth fill leading down to the interior. The fragile-looking screen door was the only barrier to the elements.

To the left of the entrance was the "radio room," for lack of a better term. It was just a small area set off by two vertical logs that supported the roof. An "Angry/9" radio sat on a rough plank table against one wall. Static popped and hissed from its receiver. A snake-like power cable led from the radio through a small hole in the bunker wall to a portable gasoline generator outside. A telegraph key and a set of black plastic earphones lay on the table.

A PRC-10 radio was strapped to one of the roof support posts with green web belts. The "Prick-10" was used to contact aircraft and also served as an alternate means of communication with A Luoi, our sister camp four miles to the north. The ARVN 36th Ranger Battalion used the two outposts as a base of operations.

The battalion was split at the time, with two companies of rangers manning each of the locations. Highway 548, an ill-defined dirt road, meandered through the valley, passing close to both Ta Bat and A Luoi. But it was seldom used due to its poor condition. And anyone traveling the road was almost certain to be ambushed. As a result, the two camps were virtually isolated from one another.

Thompson had warned me about the grim conditions, so I was not particularly surprised by what I found. A single cot lay against the opposite wall. It reeked of must. I dropped my gear there beneath a sputtering gasoline lantern that hung from a nail. A battered kerosene refrigerator stood at the far end of the structure. Out of curiosity, I looked inside and found only half a dozen rusted Coca-Cola cans.

Opposite the "radio room" was a small kitchen area. A compact single burner gasoline stove sat on a rough wooden bench. Beside it was a tarnished coffee pot with a long, dented spout. A white metal shelf above the bench held a collection of unmatched aluminum plates, glass jars, square saltine cans and tin cups. Several blackened pots and pans hung from nails embedded in the wall. That was about it. Pretty primitive, but I hadn't been expecting the Hilton.

Vincent returned several hours later, and we strolled across the compound to where Captain Ninh and his staff officers sat beneath a woven-grass canopy. Captain Vincent introduced me to everyone in fluent Vietnamese. Each of the officers smiled and stood to offer a handshake. Then we sat down to dinner as two enlisted men served up heaping bowls of steaming rice, boiled greens and the foul-smelling sauce known as nuoc mam, which was made by fermenting fish for weeks in the hot sun. I helped myself to the rice and greens, but passed on the nuoc mam.

I marveled at the dexterity of the Vietnamese as they easily shoveled mounds of rice into their mouths with chopsticks. I tried using them, but only succeeded in spraying rice across my lap, much to the delight of the group. I grinned sheepishly as a considerate soldier handed me a fork.

Vincent chatted amiably with the Vietnamese as we ate. My knowledge of the language was still rather sketchy, so I just listened quietly throughout the meal. Dai Uy Ninh, the camp commander, and the Bac Si, or medical officer, spoke passable English. They were neat, professional looking and seemed to be well-educated. I was impressed. As the meal progressed they questioned Vincent about General William Westmoreland, who was in the process of replacing General Paul Harkins as commander of U.S. forces in Vietnam. Ninh asked, "Captain Vincent, what kind of man is General Westmoreland?"

Vincent thought for a moment and then said, "Well, Dai Uy, I don't know too much about him other than that he's known as a more aggressive soldier than General Harkins. And he certainly looks like a general."

Ninh held his chopsticks poised over his bowl as he contemplated that. "Do you think more American soldiers will come to our country?"

Now it was Vincent's turn to reflect. He knitted his brow. "I believe that would depend on your government's wishes, Dai Uy."

Ninh nodded in understanding and scooped more rice into his mouth. The Bac Si glanced up from his bowl. "Tell me, Dai Uy Vincent, what do the American people think of our war?"

"Well, Theiu Uy Tranh, I honestly don't think many people know much about it. The ones who do assume my government must know what it's doing."

Tranh pursued the point. "My father fought for the Viet Minh against the French. I know the determination of the Communists. Even now they are building up their strength in the South. Do you think America will stand by us if the war grows?"

Vincent pondered this momentarily. "That is a difficult question to answer. I think yes, but I cannot be sure. In my country the people tell the government what to do. They will make the final decision." Tranh seemed satisfied with that answer.

As we finished our meal, the mess boys brought several pots of strong Vietnamese tea. We drank it plain from small china cups, and the conversation continued in a lighter vein. "Dai Uy," said Ninh, "in Vietnam very few have automobiles. How many Americans do?"

"I'd say just about everyone."

The group seated around the table murmured in admiration. Bac Si Tranh seemed skeptical. "And how many have television?"

Vincent answered, "Again, just about everyone."

Ninh sat wistfully with his chin resting on his hand, mulling Vincent's reply. "I think that this America of yours must be a truly wonderful place."

After the meal, Vincent walked with me back to the bunker. "Listen," he said. "Next time you have dinner with the Vietnamese, make sure you use the nuoc mam. They get insulted if you don't at least try it."

I glanced at him in surprise. "Sorry, Sir. I didn't know that."

Vincent stalked off into the growing dusk without another word. His attitude puzzled me. If sampling the nuoc mam was such an important issue, why hadn't he warned me in advance? I was, after all, very new to this. I had been impressed by the way he handled the Vietnamese and their questions. I would have bet that we were going to get along well. Apparently I was wrong about that.

Our relationship deteriorated steadily. The next morning, Vincent brought me a message to transmit back to Hue. But when I tried to crank up the generator it just wouldn't catch. I tinkered with it in vain for twenty minutes while Vincent fumed. "Didn't they teach you how to work that thing in radio school?" he growled.

"Sir," I said. "Until I got here I never even saw one of them."

Vincent threw up his hands in dismay. "Get on the horn to your buddy in A Luoi. Maybe he can tell you what to do." He stormed off down the trench line.

Damn! I picked up the Prick-10 handset and called Keller, who had since returned to A Luoi. Ken talked me through the starting procedure, and I was finally able to get the generator to kick in. I transmitted the message and then shut down the power. I went back inside the bunker and sat glumly on the cot. Somehow I had gotten off to a bad start with Vincent, and things seemed to be getting progressively worse.

Several days later the generator crapped out for good. Vincent had come over from Ninh's headquarters with a message. I quickly encoded it while he waited and then dashed outside to crank up the generator. It was hopeless. Every time I yanked the starter rope all I got was a sputtering cough. I tried every trick I had learned, but nothing worked. Captain Vincent paced impatiently, growing more annoyed by the minute. Finally he could contain himself no longer. "Ah, hell! I'll have ARVN send it. Get A Luoi and have them call Hue for a new generator."

I was humiliated. Once again I had to call Keller for help. What else could possibly go wrong?

The next morning an L-19 landed at Ta Bat piloted by a new aviator, Lt. Greg Foster. The tall blond flyer had a spanking new generator strapped into the rear seat of his plane. I met him at the runway and we shook hands. Foster hoisted the machine onto the ground. "First time I ever had one of these for a passenger," he chuckled.

I forced a smile. "Thanks, Lieutenant. I really appreciate this."

"Don't mention it." Foster climbed back into the tiny airplane and took off. I lifted the heavy generator onto my shoulder and made my way back to the bunker.

The new power pack worked like a charm. It had taken two weeks, but I had finally gained enough experience to feel that I was beginning to take control of things. But my peace of mind was short-lived.

The American bunker at camp Ta Bat.

Two mornings later I had just cranked up the generator behind the bunker and turned to head back inside. Suddenly I heard a CRAAACK! and dirt shot up from near my feet. Someone was shooting at me! I took off running with bullets raising plumes of wet red dirt at my heels, and dived into the trench, crash-landing with a thud and wrenching my shoulder. Several more rounds snapped by overhead. My white T-shirt was smeared with mud. For some strange reason I found this hilarious and roared with laughter despite the fright and pain of my injury. I guess you never really know how you'll react in a situation like that until it happens. Maybe the laughter was just some kind of nervous release. Later, when I had more of a chance to think about what had happened, I didn't find it quite so amusing.

But now my Italian temper began to get the best of me. Who the hell did that sonofabitch think he was, shooting at ME? I snatched my .45 from the pistol belt I always wore outside the bunker. After low-crawling to the top of the dirt mound beside the trench, I blasted off a full clip across the wire. I had no idea where my target was and I knew that I didn't have one chance in a thousand of hitting anything. However, I felt that I had to do something in retaliation, even if it was a waste of ammunition. There was no return fire.

I had left the generator running, so I limped into the bunker and sent a message to Hue about what had just taken place. Captain Vincent wasn't in camp, so I knew he wouldn't be coming to check on me. But what amazed me was that NOBODY responded. The Vietnamese must have figured that the shooting was just some soldier taking target practice at the small firing range nearby where we occasionally went to test our weapons. I still shake my head in annoyance when I think about that. I could have been lying badly-wounded in the bottom of that trench with no help coming. Unbelievable. I sent the brief report to Hue, but never heard anything back, which wasn't unusual.

I vaguely recalled hearing a story about something similar happening to another operator at Ta Bat. I wondered if it had really been the VC who had done the shooting. Maybe some

ARVN was just pissed off at Americans. An old movie I had seen about the Korean War came to mind. In it, a crusty old sergeant was asked how to tell the difference between South and North Koreans. He chomped his cigar and replied, "The South Koreans are running with you. The North Koreans are running after you." I made up my mind to be cautious with all Vietnamese and trust none of them.

I waited about half an hour before venturing tentatively outside to shut down the generator. There was no further gunfire. Whoever had taken the potshots at me was probably long gone by then. My shoulder ached for several days afterward. But I learned a valuable lesson. Never again would I step outside the bunker wearing a white, easily-visible T-shirt.

After a week, I began to settle into a regular routine. There was little to do other than to send or receive an occasional message or just listen to chatter on the net. Sometimes the enemy would try to jam us by transmitting on the same frequency. It was almost impossible to complete a message under those circumstances, but we continued on anyway to make the culprits think that they weren't affecting us. Then we would simply re-send traffic later when the interference was gone. I spent most of my day reading one or another of the paperback novels stored in a box under my bunk. When I got bored of that, I took a walk around the camp. That soon ended as the weather deteriorated.

Most mornings started out sunny, but angry black clouds often boiled up by midday. Wild thunderstorms punctuated by violent flashes of lightning swept rapidly down the valley. Sheets of blowing rain fell for about an hour and then abruptly ceased. The camp soon became a sea of mud. It was eerie, almost supernatural. The A Shau Valley was truly the most primeval place I had ever seen.

Before long the camp became a sodden mass of mud. Were it not for the steel matting on the runway, no aircraft could have landed at Ta Bat to resupply us. As it was, few did.

I seldom saw Vincent now except when he had a message to send. The captain spent most of his time with Ninh and then bedded down in the ARVN command bunker at night. I began spending more and more time in the commo bunker, living on the C-rations that Doug sent me. I hauled drinking water from the nearby stream in five gallon jerry cans. You had to treat it with a handful of iodine tablets before it was safe to drink, and that made it taste like rat pee.

Personal hygiene was another problem. The ARVN soldiers used an open slit trench as a latrine. They simply squatted over the narrow trough to do their business. I found this to be very uncomfortable. Americans, after all, were used to sitting down to take a crap. Someone had left a battered toilet seat beside the latrine. It was filthy and repulsive, but I decided to try it.

The only way to use the seat was to place it flat on the ground with the hole centered over the trench. As I lowered myself awkwardly onto it, I lost my balance and sat down heavily. I reached out reflexively to break my fall and thrust my hand into a pile of loose shit.

"Aahhh, Christ!" I shook the foul excrement from my hand and gagged in disgust. I tried to remove the mess by shoving my hand into the trench dirt while glancing around to see if anyone had observed the humiliating incident. I pulled up my trousers with my other hand, then made my way rapidly back to the bunker. My face burned with shame as I grabbed my bar of soap and a water can and went to work. From that point on I used the latrine only when absolutely necessary, and then it was in the oriental manner.

At Ta Bat we did our bathing in the stream. The camp was situated on a small knoll overlooking the tiny Rao Lao River. A network of log and earth steps led from the perimeter down to the water. The stream was about eight feet wide at this point and perhaps two feet deep. Twin strips of perforated steel plate lay across the two banks so that the ARVN soldiers could walk out to mid-stream to fill their water cans.

A machinegun nest looked down on the water point. Several weeks earlier, the VC had snapped an ambush on a ranger water party in broad daylight, killing one and wounding two others. Since then, ARVN gunners always manned the position during the day. Somehow that gave me little comfort.

One morning when I could no longer live with myself, I went down to the stream to take a bath. Two rangers clad in faded fatigues were already there, washing clothes or filling water cans. I stripped down to my shorts and walked out onto the steel mat furthest upstream. Then I laid down my towel and stepped off into the gently gurgling water. The stream was icy cool and quite clear. Oddly, it arose somewhere in the hills to the east, tumbled down past Ta Bat out into the lush green A Shau Valley and then turned westward into Laos. It struck me that the VC probably drank from its waters as well.

I had just begun to lather myself when one of the rangers whistled softly to catch my attention. The soldier made a drinking motion with his hand. When I realized what he was trying to tell me, I nodded. They took their water from this spot and washed downstream. I grabbed my towel and moved over to the other steel plank to finish my bath. The soldier flashed a good-natured smile. I winked at him.

I was developing a liking for the rangers. Most were polite and shy, unlike some of the young civilians I had encountered in Hue and Saigon. In their over-sized American helmets, they reminded me of little boys playing army. Most of them seemed in awe of the huge Americans. I sometimes wondered how such benign and passive people could become competent soldiers. Yet, the 36th Ranger Battalion enjoyed an impressive reputation among the U.S. advisors.

When I had finished bathing in the chilly stream, I dried myself and trudged back uphill to the bunker. The radio crackled as I dressed. "Frost Weed Charlie, this is Frost Weed Alpha. I have one routine. Over."

I dashed outside and cranked up the generator. Returning to the bunker, I keyed the handset. "Alpha, this is Charlie. Ready to copy. Over."

A short coded message followed. I copied it, rogered receipt and deciphered it using the current shackle sheet. Someone back in Hue wanted to know how many Americans slept in our bunker. Now what the hell kind of question was that? I called net control again. "Alpha, this is Charlie. The answer to your inquiry is one... I spell, OSCAR-NOVEMBER-ECHO. Over."

"Roger, Charlie. Thank you. Out."

The peculiar request puzzled me. One of the problems with being a radio operator in the field was that you seldom got any feedback on your messages. I knew the information was going back to the intelligence section at the Citadel, but I had no idea what became of it after that. I shrugged. Well, it probably isn't very important.

I went outside to shut down the generator and, out of boredom, kept walking along the wire perimeter. "Old" Ta Bat was in the advanced stages of decay, gradually disintegrating into the red clay of the valley floor. The ARVN had begun construction of a new camp across the runway. In fact, the rangers had already relocated the two 105mm howitzers there. When work was completed, the Vietnamese planned to abandon "old" Ta Bat and move across to their new home. For now, the original camp still held most of the soldier's quarters, two 60mm mortar positions and a single 81mm mortar pit.

I strolled through the open main gate out to the runway. The air was heavy and still. Lansing had mentioned that he liked to take late afternoon walks along the airstrip, but I wasn't feeling that adventurous. This was Indian country, and it seemed foolhardy to me to tempt fate, especially after the incident at the water point. I felt exposed and isolated so far from the bunker. For a moment I studied the heavily-jungled hillsides in the distance. They appeared ominously quiet. Was anyone out there? If so, were they planning to come for us soon? I had to force myself away from that train of thought. It seemed like the longer I remained in the A Shau, the more I came to dread its almost supernatural presence. I cast one last wary glance at the mountains and then walked back to the bunker.

Early the next morning, Vincent stormed through the screen door as I was preparing a cup of tea. "Goddammit, Oliveri... Did you tell Hue you were alone in here?"

I peered at him in surprise. "Yes, Sir. I did. Someone wanted to know how many Americans were sleeping in this bunker. It seemed like kind of a strange question."

Vincent was livid. "You caused me a lot of grief. I got a message through ARVN channels ordering me to move back in here. Dai Uy Ninh is mad as hell."

I stared blankly back at him, not knowing what to say. Vincent shook his head in disgust and left, slamming the screen door behind him. I couldn't seem to please the man, and now he was moving in with me. Damn! A short time later he returned with his gear. We didn't speak very much afterward. Fortunately, he spent most of his days across at "new" Ta Bat, and I didn't see him that often. But there could no longer be any question that the two of us were not very compatible.

One evening, just at dusk, a twelve man ranger patrol slipped out of camp through the main gate and headed north off the end of the runway. I watched from atop a mound of earth outside the bunker until they disappeared into the gathering gloom. Then I returned to the bunker, where the Coleman lantern hissed softly on the table. I pumped up the gas tank, and the lamp flared higher. Rummaging through the box of paperbacks, I found a recent best-seller and lay back on the cot to read.

Moments later a burst of automatic fire shattered the evening calm. I bolted upright. That was close! A fusillade of rifle shots followed almost immediately. I recognized the sharp crack of carbines and the huskier bark of M-1 rifles. The automatic fire had come from at least two Viet Cong AK-47 rifles that were trading rounds with the rangers.

I rushed outside and scrambled to the top of the trench. Just to the north of the runway, red tracers criss-crossed with green ones in the darkness. Three grenades exploded with vicious thumps and brilliant bursts of garish white light. Suddenly a wild round snapped by my head. I leaped back into the trench, raced into the bunker and snatched up my .45 pistol. On the way out again, I grabbed my steel pot and slapped it onto my head. I didn't realize until later that I had it on backwards.

A Vietnamese mortar crew had already reached the nearby gun pit. They slid an illumination round down the tube as I watched. The shell thunked skyward in a shower of sparks and exploded overhead, bathing the perimeter in a lurid yellow glare. The gunners in the pit waited impatiently for further orders. After what seemed like an eternity, but was in reality only a few seconds, the word came at last. "Ban! Ban!" (Fire! Fire!)

Three high explosive rounds rocketed out of the tube in rapid succession and burst in a tight pattern around the ambush site. The exchange of gunfire slowed almost immediately.

The mortar crew fired off another illumination round before resuming its bombardment. Three more heavy shell bursts effectively ended the fight. Within minutes I could make out a line of ghostly shadows approaching the end of the runway. It was the ranger patrol, and they were carrying a wounded comrade. I began to make my way toward the main gate with a squad of heavily-armed Vietnamese. We met three rangers gasping with exertion as they hauled the injured soldier, who had been shot through the hip. Several of us grabbed on to the casualty and helped carry him through the barbed wire gate and down into the dispensary. We hoisted him onto a table.

Caribou resupply aircraft on the runway at Ta Bat.

A medic slit his trousers with a pair of surgical scissors, squinting in the feeble glow of a single lantern. The enemy bullet had drilled a neat round hole through the soldier's pelvis. A thin stream of blood trickled from the bluish circle. It was a painful, if not mortal, injury.

The medic leaned closer to examine the wound in the dim light. A second corpsman tapped me on the shoulder. He pointed to the faintly hissing lantern and whispered with some urgency, "Same-same?"

I nodded and set out for the commo bunker, followed closely by the corpsman. Once inside, I picked up the glowing lantern from beside my cot. Hell. It was almost empty. I handed it to the medic, and we raced back to the dispensary.

To safely refuel a Coleman lantern, you were supposed to wait until the white-hot mantle cooled down. In retrospect, if I had given it any thought, we might have avoided what happened next. But there was no time for delay. The wounded ranger was in terrible pain and might die if we couldn't get some light on him. The corpsman grabbed a small can of gasoline from beneath the table and began pouring it into the base of the lamp. Suddenly there was a dull FOOMF as the fuel ignited. Burning gasoline splattered across the back of my left hand. I screamed in agony.

One of the rangers leaped forward and beat out the splash of flame on the bunker floor with a blanket. I was doubled over, gasping with pain. A corpsman appeared and took a look at my blackened hand. He smeared a dark, greasy ointment on it, and then wrapped it in a loose-fitting bandage. Satisfied that he had done all he could, the medic returned to treating the wounded ranger.

I reeled back to my bunker and sat heavily on my cot. The pain was so intense that I couldn't sit still. I rocked back and forth in a vain effort to find relief. After a few minutes of this, I heard footsteps approaching down the trench line. Captain Vincent stepped into the bunker. He looked concerned. "Are you OK?"

I nodded wordlessly.

"The Bac Si (doctor) sent these over. They'll help the pain." He held out a couple of white capsules. "You know, we might be able to get you a Purple Heart for this since we were in contact with the enemy at the time."

I was hurting too much to give a damn about that and just groaned in reply. In any case, I don't think he ever recommended me for the medal, because I never got it.

"Well, there'll be a medevac in here first thing tomorrow morning," he said. "You'll go back with the wounded ranger."

I grimaced and mumbled a simple thank you.

Vincent left. I gulped the pain killers and stretched out on the cot. The hand seemed to hurt less if I held it on my chest. The capsules eased the pain enough that I could sleep for brief periods. When the throbbing became unbearable, I sat up and raised the hand over my head. This went on most of the night.

Shortly after dawn, a UH-1B "Huey" helicopter swung down the valley and settled onto the runway just outside the main gate. The wounded soldier was loaded on board. I climbed awkwardly in beside him. The sight of the wounded man made me feel a bit embarrassed. He was obviously a lot worse off than I was.

The soldier had an unlit cigarette dangling from his lips. A book of matches lay on the stretcher beside him. I fumbled with it and clumsily managed to light one. I held the flame to his cigarette. "You OK!" I shouted above the whine of the rotors. "Number one!" I patted his wrist and glanced down at the bloody bandage around his hip. He simply stared at me, his eyes glazed over from the combination of pain and medication.

I sat back as the chopper lifted off with a roar. My first field duty had ended as a dismal fiasco due to my inexperience. I felt completely deflated.

When the "Huey" set down at the airfield in Hue, a Vietnamese ambulance whisked the wounded ranger away. The American crew chief helped me step out of the craft and then handed down my duffel bag. Chop Kane was sitting nearby in the commo jeep, waiting to drive me back to the compound. I threw my bag in the back and then climbed into the passenger seat beside the chief operator.

Kane smirked. "Well, Oliveri… you may be a hot-shot radio operator, but you sure as hell ain't much of a field soldier."

I was too tired and in too much pain to let him provoke me. "Thanks, Chop. You're a real class act."

We drove off to the dispensary in the advisors' compound. My first contact with the enemy had ended, but not the way I expected. Unfortunately, it wouldn't be my last.

———

IN THE REAR

I SAT QUIETLY IN THE DISPENSARY located in a small room in the hotel annex. Sergeant Harris carefully peeled off my soggy bandage and examined the injury. There were four sausage-shaped blisters along the back of my hand. Most of the hair had been singed off. Harris said, "Pretty painful, but it should heal OK."

The medic went to work gently cleaning the wound and then dabbed it with salve. He carefully re-wrapped the hand in fresh gauze and gave me some more pain killers. "That's it, kid. Take one of those pills when you need it, and come back every day or so to get that bandage changed."

I thanked him and prepared to leave. As I stepped outside, I spotted Doug coming across the parking lot. He shot a quick glance at my hand. "Hey, dickhead... So you're back, huh?"

I shook my head. "Nice to see you too, asshole. How about helping me carry this stuff upstairs?"

Doug peered at me oddly. "I guess you didn't hear. We're not in the hotel any more. The commo team took over a house down the street. We moved the radio in there too."

I was surprised. Then it dawned on me that I hadn't seen an operator on duty at the Citadel. I hadn't realized that until now.

Doug took my bag, hoisted it onto his shoulder and led me out of the compound. The commo house was half a block west of the hotel on Tran Cao Van Street, not far from Hue University. It was a single story stucco building surrounded by a low concrete fence, as were most of the houses in the city. A tall cement gate topped by a white wooden trellis led into the front yard. An antenna support pole extended through a bushy vine growing across the trellis. The antenna itself dangled above the roof, its far end attached to another pole in the back yard.

Four slate steps led up to a small veranda. I followed Doug inside to a large central parlor. The room was painted light blue. It had a ceramic tile floor partially covered by a wooden bamboo rug. A round cane table dominated the center of the room, surrounded by a set of cane chairs and a couch.

I glanced into the radio room located to the left of the parlor. It was a rectangular area about eight by ten feet. Green wooden shutters covered the twin windows. The radio rested on the corner of an ancient wooden desk. Beneath it on the floor sat the storage batteries that powered the "Angry/9."

Several sleeping cubicles radiated from the central living room. In all, the house was capable of housing eight men. But since someone was always in the field, only a few of the beds were in use. My room was immediately to the right of the parlor, adjacent to the porch. A bathroom lay at the far end, raised about two feet above the rest of the building.

I had no way of knowing it, of course, but virtually all the buildings on Tran Cao Van Street would later be destroyed during the Tet Offensive in 1968.

Doug introduced me to Richard Maxwell, who was on duty in the radio room. The bespectacled operator had arrived only recently while I was in The Valley. He nodded politely, and then went back to monitoring the radio. I rolled my eyes at Doug. Maxwell hadn't seemed very friendly. Doug told me that another operator was due in soon, and when he arrived, Maxwell was slated to go on to Quang Tri. I grinned at that. It seemed like such a long time ago that Doug and I were also scheduled to go up there.

I felt a pang of guilt when Doug told me that Keller had flown out to Ta Bat to replace me. I vowed to make it up to him sometime. Doug caught a ride to the Citadel after lunch. For the time being, I would take a spot in the rotation with Doug, Maxwell and Thompson. There was one good piece of news, though. Our illustrious leader, Captain Schader, was going home the following week. My heart was broken.

I was off duty until the evening, so I decided to walk to the business district on the north side of the river. As I approached the bridge, a cyclo driver pedaled up to me. I shook my head and waved him off. I wanted to walk. I needed time to think. Besides, it was a pleasant, sunny day, typical of the recent weather in Hue. I strolled casually onto the bridge, enjoying the view on either side.

An old Vietnamese man approached from the opposite direction as I reached the middle of the first span. He wore light, loose-fitting pajamas, a cone hat and a pair of rubber sandals. His long, wispy beard was white with age and his hands and feet were bony and gnarled. He resembled a picture I had once seen of Ho Chi Minh. A wild thought crossed my mind. What if it really was the North Vietnamese leader, perhaps on a spy mission disguised as a peasant? I grinned despite my misery. Let's not get paranoid here, I thought to myself.

The old man glanced shyly at me as we passed. Many Vietnamese still avoided contact with the foreigners. I thought I saw apprehension in the man's eyes and reacted quickly. "Chao, Ong," (Hello, Sir) I said, flashing a pleasant smile. I recalled that at one of the briefings in Saigon we were told that Orientals venerated their elders. Many Americans were arrogant and insensitive toward the Vietnamese. I didn't want to be like that.

The old man's demeanor changed in an instant. A broad grin creased his face. He was obviously pleased by being greeted in his own language. He walked slowly backward, continuing to face me and bowing several times. His reaction delighted me. These people are OK, I thought. You just have to treat them with a little respect. I waved to the old man and continued on my way. If he really was Ho Chi Minh in disguise, I chuckled to myself, I had given him no information of value other than perhaps the knowledge that Americans weren't necessarily the devils he might have believed them to be.

At the end of the bridge I turned to the right onto Tran Hung Dao Street. There was a modern Shell gasoline station on the corner. It seemed oddly out of place in the midst of a bustling Vietnamese city.

The Hue marketplace was just beyond the Shell station. Several pagoda-like buildings fronted on the street, with a wide, open-air plaza to the rear. I sauntered through the alley between the structures and into the teeming market itself.

Merchants hawked their wares on all sides. Many had set up small booths to protect themselves and their goods from the elements. Others simply spread their merchandise on the ground and squatted to display it. Several women were selling hot soup and rice, which they ladled into battered crockery for their customers. Acrid smoke from their cooking fires swirled lazily overhead. The stench of rotted fruit and vegetables hung in the air.

I paused at a booth to examine some American-made merchandise, probably obtained through the black market. The proprietor, who was missing a front tooth, held up a red-handled jackknife in his calloused palm. "Numbah one!" he exclaimed. "Hunra' pee!" I had no use for it, and in any case it wasn't worth one hundred piasters. I shook my head and moved on.

At the next booth I noticed a small Vietnamese boy staring curiously at me. The lad was clad in a tee shirt, short pants and a gray pith helmet. He peered at my bandage, his bushy eyebrows raised in wonder. The youngster gestured at my wounded hand, then held his palms up and shrugged, wordlessly seeking an explanation.

I impulsively decided to Hollywood it. I pantomimed pulling the pin on a grenade and throwing it. "VC, VC," I exclaimed, spreading my arms outward to simulate an explosion.

The boy's reaction stunned me. Tears welled up in his almond-shaped eyes. He stepped closer and placed his hand gently on my arm. I was embarrassed and immediately regretted having exaggerated the story. The boy had deeply moved me without saying a word. Here was a youngster who probably had nothing in the world other than the few rags he wore. And yet, he felt empathy for a stranger from a distant land. It was not the reaction I had expected.

I patted the boy's helmet and turned to leave. The encounter had made me very uncomfortable. As I walked back through the alley, the youth trailed close behind. I reached the street and turned back toward the bridge. The lad remained in the passageway, his sad eyes following my every move. When I finally glanced back, he had disappeared into the crowd. Sadly, I never saw him again.

Thompson was monitoring the radio when I returned to the house. He scrutinized me as I came through the door. "What the hell's wrong? You look like you just lost your best friend."

"Nothing. Nothing at all."

Thompson shrugged and returned to the book he was reading. Thankfully, he chose not to pursue the issue. I was in no mood for a discussion. I trudged into my room and lay down on the bed, grappling with a growing melancholy.

As my hand began to feel better over the course of the next week, my spirits rose too. Chop Kane unwittingly helped me with this. The man was such a clod. We were the ones who had to go out in the field while he stayed behind enjoying the comforts of Hue. Yet, he acted like he was making some great personal sacrifice. In retaliation, we made him the butt of our practical jokes.

One of the fringe benefits of living in Hue was having Vietnamese maids who came in daily to clean house and do our laundry. The woman assigned to the commo house was a bony old hag. Her few remaining teeth were stained black from years of chewing betel nut. Thompson and I explained to her through a combination of pidgin Vietnamese and sign language that Kane wanted his underwear starched. We finally convinced her that he would give her two cartons of cigarettes for the job.

"Trung Si (Sergeant) want beaucoup starch," said Thompson, gesturing toward the cabinet containing Kane's shorts.

The woman eyed him suspiciously. "Sau. No sta'. Numbah ten."

Thompson persisted. "Trung Si give two cartons Hoa Ky (American) cigarettes." He held up a pair of fingers to emphasize his point.

The old woman's eyes widened. "Ah… OK! Cigarett-ee. Beaucoup sta'." She gathered up the underwear and left.

Later that day, after Kane got back from the Citadel, the old crone returned. We were all seated in the parlor, desperately pretending not to notice her as she shuffled in. She was carrying a neat pile of heavily-starched underwear, pressed flat and stiff as cardboard. Kane eyed her warily as she made her way toward his room. "Hey," he blurted out. "That looks like my stuff."

He sprang to his feet and followed her into the cubicle. She began stacking the wafer-like shorts in his dresser drawer. "What the hell are you doing?" he roared, snatching a pair from the pile. In the living room we snickered expectantly.

The old woman thrust her jaw at Kane. "You gi' two ca'ton cigarett-ee."

He bellowed in outrage. "You crazy old bitch! I can't wear these!"

We buried our faces in our hands in a vain attempt to stifle our now near-explosive laughter.

The maid's voice rose to a shrill screech. She gestured wildly at Kane. "Two ca'ton Lucky Stri'! You gi' now!"

Chop was livid. "Fuck you, you old whore! Get the hell out of here!"

The woman stormed out of the house, chattering curses at Kane. We could scarcely control ourselves as he stalked into the room, holding up a pair of GI drawers like a paper fan. "Look what that rotten old cunt did to my shorts!"

We collapsed in helpless and uproarious laughter.

On another occasion, I trapped about a dozen mosquitos in a glass jar and released them inside the netting of Chop's bed while he was at the Citadel. The next morning, unsure if this stunt would actually work, I was sitting in the parlor when he emerged from his room with one eye swollen and his face covered with blotchy red bites! I pretended to have a coughing fit in order to disguise my nearly uncontrollable hilarity. He eyed me suspiciously but said nothing. Then he headed over to the hotel for breakfast, absently scratching at the lumps on his face.

Despite the practical jokes, night life in Hue was a bit boring. We sometimes tried to organize poker games at the house, but it was always a problem to get enough players. There was little else to do. Sometimes movies were shown in the second-floor briefing room at the hotel annex. However, that had one drawback. An enlisted man had to walk guard around the building whenever a film was scheduled.

Unfortunately, I drew guard duty the night they ran "Doctor No," a recent release in the States. I had been hoping to see this film. Since arriving in Vietnam, I had become a big fan of Ian Fleming's spy novels featuring the legendary British agent James Bond after reading several of them at Ta Bat.

Author on the veranda of the communications house in Hue.

I had bought an old Thompson submachine gun for ten bucks from a sergeant who had recently returned home. It had just one rusty thirty round magazine, but I liked the feel of the weapon. I strapped on my pistol belt, hefted the Thompson and walked to the hotel.

The movie began promptly at 2000 hours. I started walking my post along the barbed wire perimeter just beneath the screened-in briefing room. I halted at the fence and peered into the darkness. There was an open field between the advisors compound and the Joan of Arc Cathedral complex several hundred yards down the road. The meadow was illuminated only by the feeble glow of the church lights. If there was trouble, it would probably come from there.

I remained on the far side of the building throughout most of the movie, carefully watching for any signs of movement in the gloomy field. Occasionally I circled back to check the main gate. But everything was quiet this night, except for the sound-track of "Dr. No" as the movie ran undisturbed. I pouted each time I caught a fragment of dialogue from the film I had so badly wanted to see.

Ralph Yniguez arrived in Hue that same week. Kane brought him in from the Citadel and introduced him to the rest of us. Yniguez was a short, swarthy Mexican-American from Southern California. He had close-cropped black hair and wore Coke-bottle eyeglasses. In actuality, Ralph Yniguez was a split personality if ever I saw one. First there was the conservative, gung-ho young patriot we believed him to be. Yet, on occasion, Ralph acted like a frustrated beatnik. It was amusing trying to figure out which persona was the dominant one.

Thompson and I checked him out that same afternoon, and immediately worked him into the rotation. It was possible for a new man to take a shift right away, because there was always an experienced operator around if he needed help. Ralph's arrival freed Maxwell for assignment to Quang Tri. He left on the Otter the following day.

The burns on my hand were healing nicely. The blisters had disappeared, leaving only an ugly mass of mottled scar tissue. Stubby bristles were beginning to grow back where the hair had been singed off. I continued to take a regular shift while the hand improved. But I still felt the guilt of Keller having taken my place at Ta Bat.

One afternoon, I took Yniguez to the PX in the compound behind the main hotel. The crotchety supply sergeant who ran it had horn-rimmed glasses and slicked-back hair. He never went to the field, and only opened the PX for three or four hours a day. Yet, he was a non-stop griper. I felt no sympathy for him. We should have had it so good.

Ralph and I walked slowly up and down the narrow aisles, marveling at the variety of goods on the shelves. The Army provided well to discourage its soldiers from pouring money into an active black market. A carton of cigarettes sold for $1. A half-gallon of Gilbey's gin went for $1.50. There was a widely-circulated rumor that some advisors used gin instead of mouthwash because it was much cheaper. We believed it. There were other good bargains to be found as well. Thompson had recently purchased a fine Minolta camera for less than $25. Yniguez and I each picked out a few small items, and then paid the cranky sergeant. We walked briskly back to the commo house.

After lunch the following day, I was off duty, and stepped out onto the porch to cool off. It was a typically hot Hue day, and the inside of the house was stifling. I noticed a soldier by the name of Bateman, who was staying at the house temporarily, standing in the middle of the street. He was engaged in an animated conversation with a Vietnamese woman. She was clad in an orange ao dai, and appeared to be about thirty years old. Even from the porch I could see that she had unusually large breasts for an oriental. She was obviously a prostitute. Bateman was trying to negotiate a price, but without much success.

Bateman was agitated. "Two hundred pee!" He held up two fingers. "Two Hundred!" The woman shook her head.

Bateman glanced up and saw me on the porch. "Hey, man. Come over here and help us out, will ya?"

I walked out into the street. "What the hell are you doing?"

Bateman scowled at me. "This crazy broad wants five hundred piasters for a screw. I say two hundred's enough."

I turned to the woman. "Five hundred pee number ten! We give two hundred."

It was the whore's turn to frown. "Two hunra' cheap Charlie." She reached inside her dress, pulled out one of her breasts, and offered it for our inspection. I nearly dropped my teeth. It was broad daylight, after all, and we were within sight of the hotel.

"All right," I conceded. "Three hundred pee." Give me credit for knowing when I've been out-maneuvered.

The whore responded in a voice tinged with triumph. "OK! Numbah one!"

I shooed the two of them up the walk and into the house, warily eying the hotel as we went. There was no one in sight who might have noticed. Bateman led the woman into a vacant room, leering over his shoulder. "You want in on this?"

I hesitated, concerned about getting caught with a prostitute in the house. But after six weeks in-country, I was feeling pretty horny. My carnal instincts overwhelmed my caution. Besides, what could they do... send us to Vietnam? I leered back at Bateman. "Yeah, I guess so."

Bateman laughed, and he and the woman disappeared into the back room.

I sat in the parlor and drank a couple of beers while we waited. By the time Bateman emerged about half an hour later, I was feeling a little tipsy.

I clomped awkwardly into my room and fumbled around in a drawer for a condom. Then I tottered back to the room where the woman waited patiently. She unzipped my pants. Taking the rubber from me, she helped me put it on, and then lay back on the bed. She was fully clothed, and simply slid the loose dress up above her waist to reveal the bare torso underneath. I made a clumsy swan dive on top of her. She grunted and guided me inside. I began a slow pump.

The whore began cooing a soft string of insincere groans. "Oooh, I lu' you ve'y mu'. You numbah one boom-boom."

"Yeah, right," I muttered cynically. The sarcasm was lost on her. She writhed in simulated ecstasy as I slid my hands up to her breasts. Then she touched her lips lightly to my neck. I continued pumping, but the alcohol had taken its toll. I could feel nothing. Eventually I gave up altogether.

"You finis?" she murmured. I slid off her and stood up, feeling very self-conscious. The prostitute crawled to the foot of the bed and reached down to check for herself. I flushed beet-red. She glanced up at me with a knowing smile. "OK, you. Numbah one GI. We do agai'."

I zipped up my pants and then guided her firmly toward the door. "Come on. Get the hell out of here before the MPs see you." I pressed a wad of piaster notes into her hand. Then I went into the bathroom and took a long shower.

Somebody must have seen what happened and ratted on us. A jeep pulled up in front of the house a short time later, and three MPs piled out. They were wearing white-striped helmet liners and carrying side arms. They stalked inside, fanned out, and began to search the interior. I was sitting on my bed tying my shoelaces when one of the goons burst into my room. "You got a whore in here, buddy?"

I feigned shock. "A whore? Of course not."

He frowned. "I'll just take a look for myself."

"Be my guest." I finished tying my shoe and got out of his way.

The MPs searched the entire house and a shed in the back yard. Finding nothing, they stormed out without another word. I chuckled as they pulled away, but I was pissed. What sonofabitch had let the cat out of the bag? I walked into the parlor where Doug sat with a smug grin on his face. He had remained silently on the couch through the entire incident. I gave him the finger.

We avoided Kane for the next few days. Even though the MPs had found nothing, they had reprimanded Chop, as senior NCO, about the alleged charges. Now he was concerned that his promotion was in jeopardy. I knew how vindictive he could be. We were all on his shit list, that much was certain. I was sure he would eventually find a way to get even with us.

———

HONORS

THE FLIMSY NETTING STRUNG AROUND my bed frustrated the big mosquito. It buzzed in outrage as it bounced along, looking for an opening but finding none. The persistent and irritating noise woke me. I glanced at my watch. It was just past 0800. I had manned the radio until midnight, and then sat up with Doug on the graveyard shift until near dawn. Now bright sunshine beamed through the shutters. I squinted at the light and frowned. I decided reluctantly that I might as well get up.

As I was stepping into the shower, I heard a jeep pull up outside. I had just turned on the water when Chop Kane pounded on the door. "Hey, Oliveri! You in there?"

"Yeah, Chop. Whattaya want?"

"Get your ass out here! The Colonel wants to see you in half an hour!"

I was flabbergasted. "What the hell for?"

"He's gonna give you the CIB!"

"No shit?" I was delighted. Captain Vincent must have recommended me for the highly-prized Combat Infantry Badge after the incident at Ta Bat. I guess he wasn't such a prick after all.

Kane thumped the door again. "Hurry up, you asshole! I'm supposed to bring you there."

"Take it easy, Chop," I pleaded. "I need a quick shower and shave."

My body was still damp as I pulled on a fresh set of fatigues. I took a quick glance at my boots. They could have used a shine, but there was no time. Kane was already in the jeep, leaning on the horn. I raced outside and had to dive into the passenger seat as Chop took off in a spray of gravel. He made a sharp U-turn and then headed out over the bridge toward the Citadel.

When we reached Headquarters, Kane parked the jeep and then hustled me inside. Another soldier, Specialist Ruthenburg, was already there. He, too, was to receive an award. A lieutenant ushered us into the main room where half a dozen staff officers waited. The presentation of the Combat Infantry Badge was still a fairly uncommon event in 1964. None of the advisory team members in the room wore it. Colonel Collins stood before a full-length curtain covering an operations map of I Corps. He was dressed in neatly-tailored and heavily-starched fatigues. The Colonel seemed to be enjoying himself.

Ruthenburg and I stepped up to the curtain and stood at attention. An aide passed the blue and silver badges to Colonel Collins. The portly Senior Advisor carefully pinned them on our fatigue shirts and then shook our hands enthusiastically. After a few congratulatory words, he posed for photographs with us. Word around the advisory team was that the Colonel was openly partial to his field soldiers, since his duties rarely permitted him to leave Hue. I was now convinced of that. It was obvious to me that he enjoyed being with the soldiers who actually had to man the ramparts of his far-flung command.

After a few minutes, the aide reminded Collins that his schedule would not allow him to spend more time with us. The Colonel seemed disappointed, and expressed his regrets. The ceremony began to break up.

Kane and I were soon on our way back to the commo house. I was famished and decided to go over to the hotel for a quick breakfast. When I returned, Kane, Ken Keller and Ralph Yniguez were standing in formation in the parlor. A more ridiculous sight would be hard to imagine. Chop was in his boxer shorts, a beer can in one hand and a Thompson submachine gun in the other. Ken had a steel pot on his head, but wore no boots or socks. Ralph had a Hawaiian shirt wrapped around his forehead. A pepperoni protruded from the holster on his pistol belt. They resembled some half-assed hillbilly militia.

Kane called them to attention, and they threw me a mock salute. "Hey, schmuck," teased Chop. "I didn't know they gave medals for falling on your ass in a shit trench."

"Yeah," Yniguez chimed in. "We heard you were where the bullets were the thickest... in the ammo bunker!"

"Oh, screw you assholes!" I growled, pretending to be angry.

We all laughed. This was our way of making light of the situation. We understood the dangers we faced, and we accepted that as part of the job. But at the same time we all hoped to avoid taking excessive risks. Medals were nice, but not at the cost of injury or even death. It was a curious paradox that we never discussed. This time the gods of war had smiled upon me. On another day that might not be the case. I didn't know it then, of course, but that day was not far off.

———

BACK TO THE VALLEY

BOUT A WEEK AFTER THE awards ceremony, Chop Kane sent me back to Ta Bat again. At first I was a bit apprehensive, but in some peculiar way also anxious to return to The Valley. After screwing up so badly during my first trip there I felt that I had a lot to prove. I doubt Kane cared about any of that. This was probably just his way of getting back at me for the stunts we pulled on him.

At the Citadel, I boarded Lt. Foster's "Bird Dog" to make the courier run to Ta Bat. Foster handed me a flak jacket as I climbed into the narrow cabin. I stowed my Thompson on the floor of the craft. Foster quickly explained how the intercom worked and then jumped into the cockpit. The wind sock near the end of the runway hung almost motionless as the little craft lifted off, its single propeller corkscrewing it through the hot, humid atmosphere.

As we leveled off at about 1200 feet, a sudden downdraft sent the L-19 plummeting earthward. I instinctively grabbed onto the sides of the seat. It was almost like riding in a roller coaster. Foster's chuckle was clearly audible through my headset. The wings continued to waggle with every stray air current as we made our way west. I was just getting used to that and beginning to enjoy the flight when Ta Bat appeared below.

We landed after an uneventful flight to find Ken waiting on the runway. He appeared tired and his uniform was unkempt. His mind was already on a warm shower back in Hue. We had time for only brief greetings before Foster indicated that he was ready to leave. I waved as the L-19 rolled to the end of the strip, gunned its engines and took off, leaving me once again in the heart of the menacing A Shau Valley.

I turned and trudged along the now familiar route through the main gate and then veered left toward the bunker. Nearby, a squad of rangers was demolishing an old bunker in preparation for the move across the runway to "new" Ta Bat. I waved to them as they labored in the hot sun. Then I spotted Captain Vincent striding toward me, hatless and wearing a green nylon jungle suit. I shifted uncomfortably from foot to foot, contemplating what he'd have to say.

"Hello, Oliveri," he said without smiling. "Glad to have you back."

I had my doubts about that, but I played along. "Thank you, Sir. It's nice to be back." At least we were behaving civilly. I resolved not to expect much more.

After the initial chill, our relationship gradually improved. By now I had overcome my inexperience and learned to handle the equipment with some degree of skill. Vincent had reverted to his previous practice of living with the ARVN while I was gone, so we didn't spend much time together. I didn't mind. If he wanted to sleep in the command bunker, that was his business. And besides, I was more comfortable without him around.

Reports of truck sightings on the "Ho Chi Minh Trail" west of camp continued to trickle in with growing frequency, and I transmitted the ominous news back to Hue. I didn't like it. Those trucks were no doubt carrying supplies to enemy forces based in I Corps. I hoped it wasn't to someplace close. As a precaution I began sleeping with my .45 hanging on the end of my cot. The Thompson submachine gun I had acquired was always nearby. Vincent had once remarked that the weapon was virtually useless unless the Viet Cong were actually coming down the bunker steps. I fervently hoped that I'd never have to find out if he was right.

Unknown as yet to I Corps, the trucks we had been reporting represented a major policy shift on the part of the Communists. Early in 1964, the North Vietnamese had sent Colonel Bui Tin south along the "Ho Chi Minh Trail" to reconnoiter supply lines and to report on the combat capabilities of the Viet Cong. It took Tin more than four months to complete his assignment. What he found was not encouraging.

Bui Tin reported back to Hanoi that the VC lacked the capacity to conduct large scale operations. He recommended the movement of regular North Vietnamese Army units into the South. To facilitate this, he also proposed enlarging and improving the "Ho Chi Minh Trail" to accommodate military vehicles.

Because Colonel Tin was a highly respected officer, Hanoi acted quickly on his recommendations. Eleven years later, on April 30, 1975, Colonel Tin was to accept the surrender of South Vietnam from General Duong Van "Big" Minh in Saigon. Minh, in office for only two days, would offer to transfer control of the government to the Communists. Colonel Tin would respond that Minh was in no position to turn over what he no longer controlled. The defeat of South Vietnam would thus become final.

But the end of the war was still light years away in 1964. Colonel Dong Si Nguyen, who later would become North Vietnam's Minister of Construction, was put in charge of the program to improve the trail. His engineer battalions quickly set to work on the vast project, assisted by hordes of civilian workers. By year end, more than ten thousand North Vietnamese troops had successfully infiltrated into the South using the revamped "Ho Chi Minh Trail." The big push had begun, and the A Shau Valley would play a vital part in it.

But for now I had more immediate concerns: rats. Rats were a major nuisance at Ta Bat. They were long, skinny and… well, ratty looking. Unseen during the day, the rodents became positively brazen after dark. They emerged from their lairs as soon as I shut down the lantern and tried to sleep. The pests roamed freely throughout the bunker, rattling cans and disturbing boxes in their quest for food. They even got into the roof, where they scuttled back and forth across the corrugated iron ceiling, sounding not unlike golf balls rolling around on the head of a drum. Fights were frequent, adding a frenzied squeaking to the usual nocturnal cacophony. It became impossible to sleep once the evening "rat races" began.

In an attempt to discourage them, I lit a candle and placed it in an empty coffee can on the dirt floor. That slowed them down briefly. But when the rats became accustomed to the feeble glow, they simply ignored it. Once a rat even scampered across my face as I lay dozing. I bolted upright in disgust, and momentarily thought about grabbing my .45 from where it hung at the end of the cot. I decided against that, which was probably a good idea. I'm sure Vincent wouldn't have appreciated it had I fired up some rat in the middle of the night. I finally came to the conclusion that you had to accept coexistence with the rats of Ta Bat. There was really no other alternative.

Before a week had passed Vincent mentioned that he was leaving in two days. He was scheduled to go home the following week. I was genuinely surprised. I had no idea that he was so close to DEROS (Date Estimated Return Overseas.) When the time came, an "Otter", the only aircraft to visit Ta Bat that week, arrived overhead. I talked it down using the "Prick-10" radio.

"Hello, Otter, this is Ta Bat. Ceiling 500 feet. Wind from the west at ten miles per hour and the runway is dry and secure. Over."

"Roger, Ta Bat. We hear you five-by. Thank you."

The craft touched down at the far end of the runway and taxied to the main gate. Vincent threw his gear aboard and then climbed in. The plane quickly took off into a leaden sky. I watched the olive-drab craft briefly silhouetted against the dreary gray hillsides, and then it vanished into the low-hanging clouds. Captain Vincent hadn't even bothered to say good-bye.

Author *(right)* receives the Combat Infantry Badge from Colonel Collins.

I can't say that I was sorry to see him go. However, his departure left me as the sole American in camp. That was a bit unsettling. I had almost no contact with the Vietnamese commanders, and most of the ARVN enlisted men had already moved across the runway to "new" Ta Bat. If I ever needed help, there were very few armed defenders around me. Infiltrators could have approached my bunker almost unchallenged in the darkness. I felt isolated and badly exposed. It was common knowledge that many South Vietnamese units had been infiltrated by the Communists. The realization that all the VC in the Valley were not necessarily outside the barbed wire perimeter was a bit unnerving.

Several days later I received a coded message from Hue that a new advisor was coming in that night from A Luoi – on foot. My instructions were to prepare a place for him in the bunker. Well, that was easy enough. After sliding the message into my clipboard, I tossed some clutter off the spare cot and opened it up. A sharp slap against the canvas dislodged a layer of fine dust. After setting up the bunk across from mine I shrugged. It wasn't much, but it was the best Ta Bat had to offer. I returned to my own bunk with a book and waited, wondering who the new man was. Hopefully he wouldn't be like Vincent.

It rained heavily that afternoon. The red clay of the valley floor, already saturated from weeks of daily cloudbursts, dissolved into glutinous ooze that sucked stubbornly at your boots. Moving through it drained your stamina. After a while your feet felt like lead weights and you started walking like Frankenstein. I glanced out through the screen door. The afternoon overcast usually burned off after a few hours. Today, however, the skies remained gray and a steady drizzle persisted past dusk.

I returned to my book, pausing once to boil some water for tea on the small gasoline stove. Water trickled intermittently through the makeshift roof and splattered on the dirt floor, creating a small puddle. Otherwise the bunker was relatively snug. Even the rats were quiet for a change.

Around 2100 hours I heard footsteps outside. The screen door swung open and an American clad in a rain-soaked poncho clomped down the steps. He quickly surveyed the interior of the bunker, saying nothing. I arose from my cot. He removed his cap and shook the water from it. "You the radio operator?"

"Yes, Sir. Jim Oliveri."

"I'm Lieutenant Mowrey. Just walked in from A Luoi."

"I've been expecting you, Lieutenant. How about a cup of hot coffee?"

Mowrey's poker face dissolved into a broad grin. "Hell, that sounds great. I sure could use some."

The water on the stove was still warm. I quickly boiled it up while Mowrey shed his wet poncho and stowed his gear. After spooning some instant coffee into a battered tin mug, I poured in hot water and handed the brew to the lieutenant. Mowrey sipped it greedily. "Ahhhh... That's good."

My eyes twinkled. "Welcome to the Ta Bat Hilton, Sir."

Mowrey and I hit it off right away. A Georgia native, Mowrey was of medium height, slim, had light brown hair and was in his late twenties. The lieutenant was easy-going with a good sense of humor, a far cry from the cool and aloof Vincent. One afternoon later in the week, when the weather cleared sufficiently, the Otter brought in some mail. Included was a tape recording from the lieutenant's wife, a real southern belle. After a dinner of C-rations, Mowrey retreated to his cot and listened to it on a small tape player. He plugged in a set of earphones and then sat back, completely engrossed in his wife's message.

I was nibbling on some Saltines, mildly absorbed in my book. Suddenly Mowrey chuckled and switched off the tape. "Listen to this, Ollie," he cackled.

He punched a button and Mrs. Mowrey's soft, feminine drawl droned from the machine. "...I was thinking about you so much last night that I got all sexed up. There's nothing wrong with that, is there, honey? I mean, it's okay for a married woman to feel that way about her husband, isn't it? God, I can't wait 'til you get home. We're gonna have some real great lovin'!"

I snickered in embarrassment. "Damn, Lieutenant... That's pretty personal."

"Yeah, but it's funny, isn't it?"

I laughed in appreciation. I couldn't imagine Vincent doing something like that.

With Mowrey's encouragement, the rangers continued to send regular patrols west to the Laotian border. I Corps wanted more information about the truck traffic moving down the "Ho Chi Minh Trail." Headquarters was concerned that something big might be coming down. Mowrey and I only hoped that it wouldn't be on Ta Bat.

The ARVN patrols all came back with similar reports. Communist trucks continued to roll boldly south, making no effort to conceal their movement. The VC obviously felt secure in their sanctuary across the border. And in reality, they were. Allied forces were prohibited from crossing into Laos. There was a Royal Laotian Army unit operating in the area, but they were poorly equipped and ill-trained, posing no threat to the enemy. In fact, our intelligence indicated that they might even be aiding the interlopers. Rumor had it that the troops of Prince Souvanna Phouma had been heavily infiltrated by the Pathet Lao, or Laotian Communists. Mowrey groused constantly about having to fight a war under such frustrating circumstances. The Special Forces soldiers at A Shau had fewer restrictions. I had even heard stories that the Green Berets had led missions across the border into Laos.

On the 6th of July, the final destination of the enemy trucks we had been tracking became painfully apparent. Twenty-five kilometers southwest of A Shau in the lower portion of Thua Thien Province lay the Special Forces camp at Nam Dong, manned by Captain Roger Donlon and his Green Beret "A" team. Donlon had at his disposal roughly 250 CIDG (Civilian Irregular Defense Group) strike force troops, second rate defenders at best. There was also a small complement of ethnic Chinese soldiers known as "nungs." These fierce fighters were staunchly loyal to the Americans.

There had been trouble during the afternoon between the Vietnamese strikers and the nungs. The dispute quickly escalated into a brief exchange of gunfire. Donlon suspected that Viet Cong agitators were responsible for the disturbance. When the Green Berets finally defused the explosive situation, they tripled the guard around the camp.

At 0230, a furious mortar barrage struck Nam Dong. More than nine hundred VC guerrillas emerged from the darkness and stormed the perimeter. Donlon rallied his meager forces and struck back hard. Despite being wounded numerous times, the Special Forces captain continued to direct the camp's defenses. By 0900, the VC attack had been blunted. With the arrival of daylight, a swarm of allied aircraft descended on Nam Dong to blast the retreating enemy. The camp held, but at the end of the fight it resembled a literal translation of its name. In English, Nam Dong means "five cents."

By the time Team A-726 was relieved, one Australian advisor and two Americans had been killed, along with fifty-seven of the camp's defenders. Sixty-two VC bodies hung lifeless in the perimeter wire. There were signs that roughly double that number had been dragged away by their comrades. Donlon survived his wounds to become the first American soldier to win the Medal of Honor in Vietnam.

The morning after the battle at Nam Dong, Mowrey and I inspected our own perimeter with Dai Uy Ninh. The lieutenant was concerned about Ta Bat's ability to repel a similar attack and said so to the ARVN commander. Ninh smiled confidently. "Lieutenant Mowrey, in a few weeks 'new' Ta Bat will be finished. You will see what a good camp we have."

Mowrey nodded. "I understand that, Dai Uy, but I'm concerned about now. Do you think we could stack up the VC on the wire like they did at Nam Dong?"

Ninh smiled again. "Do not worry yourself, Lieutenant. My rangers are good soldiers.

Mowrey remained unconvinced. I cast a sidelong glance at the rusted concertina wire surrounding the camp and wished I felt as confident as Captain Ninh.

Several nights later, about 1930 hours, Mowrey and I were each stretched out on our bunks reading when the staccato report of an AK-47 burst shattered the stillness of the night. That was close! I dropped my copy of "Rabble in Arms" and glanced at the lieutenant. We both jumped to our feet and grabbed our carbines. While I turned down the Coleman lantern, Mowrey dashed out through the screen door and headed along the trench line toward Dai Uy Ninh's bunker. I stepped outside and, rather hesitantly, climbed up the side of the trench toward our generator where I would be able to see beyond the perimeter.

A wild burst of green tracers darted diagonally across my front in the direction of the main gate. I flopped heavily onto a mound of dirt near the generator and opened fire toward where I thought the enemy fusillade had originated. I burned through ten or twelve rounds before I lost my aiming point in the darkness and held my fire. It's extremely unlikely that I hit anything, but the incoming ceased and blasting away like that, even if it was a waste of ammunition, made me feel better. In any case, the ARVN 105s were now belting out a barrage of heavy shells toward our assailant. If he was still alive, that would certainly have encouraged him to vacate the area.

The ARVN artillery crew ceased fire and the resulting stillness was startling. There was no further gunfire. About half an hour later, Mowrey returned to the bunker. My pulse was just reverting to normal. There had been no casualties, and the rangers seemed to have no immediate plans to go after the sniper. After comparing notes, we crafted an operations report which I then encoded. I wasn't anxious to go outside again and start up the generator. This was, after all, the third time bullets had been directed toward me while I was near there. But it was gratifying to have been able to return fire for once, albeit with little apparent effect. I scrabbled up the side of the trench again and had a difficult time cranking up the generator in the dark. When it finally kicked in I dashed back to the bunker, thankful to get inside and under cover again.

It took a while to get the message through to net control because of bad atmospheric conditions and the usual jamming. When they rogered at last, Mowrey and I talked out what had just happened. We concluded that it had been just some harassing fire to let us know that the VC were still out there. A patrol the next morning found nothing but some spent cartridge cases. As usual, we never heard anything back from Hue in response to our message. My penchant for becoming involved in small firefights seemed to be growing. When I had more time to think about it later, I decided that, given a choice, I would prefer small unit actions like this one to something akin to the Nam Dong experience.

A week later I was recalled to Hue, and Ralph Yniguez came out to replace me. Mowrey seemed genuinely disappointed that I was leaving. We'd only been together less than two weeks, but we'd shared some dramatic moments. When the Otter arrived with Ralph on board, the lieutenant walked with me to meet the plane. Mowrey threw my gear aboard and wished me luck. I promised to keep in touch, thinking that I would probably return soon. But my next trip to Ta Bat would be a very brief one, and by then Mowrey would be in a different sector of I Corps. I never saw the likable officer again. I deeply regret that.

———————

NAM DONG

THINGS QUIETED DOWN CONSIDERABLY AFTER the battle of Nam Dong. Radio traffic was minimal as Doug, Keller and I manned net control through the rest of the week. Kane arrived at the house one morning and spotted me in the radio room. "Oliveri, I volunteered you to go out on an operation tomorrow with the 3rd Regiment. You'll be Major Crittenden's operator." His eyes glinted with self-satisfaction. We were still on his shit list, and apparently I was to be the first to feel his wrath.

I feigned unconcern. "Where to, Chop?"

"I don't know, but you'll be out at least a week. I hear rumors that this could be a big one."

Once he left I discussed this development with Doug and Keller. "If it's big," I theorized, "it must have something to do with Nam Dong."

"Maybe," said Doug. "But isn't that in Quang Nam Province? Da Nang should be handling it, not us."

Keller shook his head. "Nah, it's in Thua Thien. But I haven't heard of anything big going on."

I shrugged. "Well what the hell else can it be? Man, I'm not looking forward to dragging my ass out there, I can tell you."

They sympathized with me – to an extent. I'm sure they were both happy that they didn't have to go in my place. Unable to come to any sensible conclusions, we had a beer together, then Doug and I turned in, leaving Keller on duty. The two of them would have to work twelve hour shifts while I was away.

The next morning I cleaned and oiled my pistol, and then packed my duffel bag. Keller offered me his carbine in exchange for the heavier Thompson. If I was going to be moving around quite a bit the little rifle would be much easier to carry.

I was supposed to meet Crittenden in the hotel that afternoon. At 1500, I slung the carbine over one shoulder and my bag over the other. Keller stepped out of the radio room to shake hands and wish me luck. I made some half-hearted wisecrack, then walked briskly up to the compound. As I crossed the parking lot Crittenden emerged from the back door of the hotel. He was dressed in light jungle fatigues and smiled when he saw me. We had met once previously and recognized each other immediately.

"Hello, Oliveri. How are you?"

I slid my bag to the pavement and saluted. "Fine, Sir. Nice to see you again."

Major Forrest Crittenden was a veteran infantry officer. As a young 2nd lieutenant he had earned renown and a Purple Heart at the battle for Pork Chop Hill during the Korean War. His career had slumped since then. Now Vietnam was his opportunity for promotion. It was, in fact, every American officer's opportunity.

As we chatted, a jeep pulled into the compound and ground to a halt nearby. Crittenden waved to the driver. He turned back to me and said, "This is Hiep, my driver. He'll be taking us out to Nam Dong."

Oh, shit, I thought, nodding absently to the Vietnamese. It WAS Nam Dong. Damn! Crittenden clambered into the front seat beside Hiep while I climbed into the back. The somber driver made a sharp U-turn and headed back out of the compound. At the corner, he steered south onto Highway 1.

Major Crittenden twisted about in his seat. "We're going to spend the night at Phu Bai. Then we'll roll out just before dawn."

I nodded my acknowledgement as the jeep bounced along the uneven road. It took us forty minutes to cover the fifteen miles to Phu Bai. Upon arrival at the ARVN compound there we joined a large convoy of waiting vehicles. I whistled in admiration. This was some powerful force preparing to move out to Nam Dong.

Crittenden led us into a nearby single-story stucco building. Inside was an open barracks area where a platoon of Vietnamese soldiers was preparing to spend the night. They had set aside a couple of cots for us. I dumped my gear on one of them, then returned to the jeep. I set the radio on net frequency and squeezed the handset.

"Frost Weed Alpha, this is Frost Weed Fox Trot. How do you hear me? Over."

Doug's voice came back loud and clear. "Roger, Fox Trot. This is Alpha. I hear you three-by. Do you have any traffic? Over."

"This is Fox Trot. Negative. Just doing a commo check. Fox Trot out." Well, at least we had communications.

I strolled back to the barracks and sat on my cot. Crittenden came in moments later accompanied by Hiep. The major had brought a knapsack full of sandwiches from the hotel. We talked casually while we ate. Crittenden offered a sandwich to Hiep, who shook his head. Our driver then went off to find the ARVN mess. Queer bird, I thought, watching him leave. Never smiles. Hardly even says anything.

I turned back to Crittenden, who was telling me what he knew of our mission. The 3rd Regiment had been called in to assist with a major sweep around Nam Dong. Intelligence had indicated that the VC attacking force might have remained in the general vicinity to lick its wounds. The intent was to catch them before they had sufficiently recovered to move back across the border into Laos. Crittenden and I would remain inside the outpost with the headquarters group.

Around 2100 hours, I checked the jeep and the radio again. Everything seemed ready. Satisfied, I decided to get some sleep. I stretched out fully clothed on the uncomfortable cot. I laid the carbine on the floor beside me, but kept the .45 strapped to my waist.

Hiep was staying with us, so we rearranged our three cots in a small alcove at one end of the building. Just across the aisle, several squads of ARVN soldiers were settling in. Weird-sounding oriental music blared from a transistor radio. The female vocalist wailed mournfully against a backdrop of gongs, chimes and cymbal crashes. It reminded me of a night I had spent in Chinatown several years previously. I grimaced. It was going to be tough to get any rest with that racket. I turned on my side away from the noise and eventually drifted off into a fitful sleep.

Major Crittenden shook me awake just before 0400. "Let's get ready," he muttered.

Hiep brought in some steaming tea. I took the small china cup from him and sipped gently. "Cam anh (Thank you), Hiep."

The driver nodded silently, his face expressionless, as usual, then went off to prepare his own breakfast. I rummaged in my bag for one of the little green C-ration cans containing scrambled eggs and chopped ham. Definitely not one of my favorites, it tasted like congealed axle grease, but it was all I had. I took a tiny P-38 can opener from my pocket and cranked it around the can until the lid popped loose. Then, with a fork from my mess kit, I ate the cold meal, jealously imagining the hot food that would be served shortly at the hotel.

The convoy prepared to move out shortly after I finished my makeshift breakfast. Crittenden was off somewhere discussing plans with his counterpart. I picked up my bag and weapon, figuring to meet him at the jeep. As I walked outside, I absently put my finger on the trigger of the carbine. The rifle barked sharply, discharging a round into the path directly ahead. I halted in my tracks. What the fuck? I knew I hadn't chambered a cartridge. I never did that unless there was a need to do so. That was SOP. How the hell could that have happened? I glanced around. In the bustle and confusion of the moment no one seemed to have noticed. I shrugged and continued on to the jeep. Once there, I removed the magazine from the carbine. Satisfied that the rifle was now indeed clear, I slapped the clip back into the weapon.

The accident gnawed at me. I was certain that the carbine had been unloaded when I turned in. Yet, as far as I knew, only the major, Hiep and I had been near that rifle. I made up my mind to keep a careful eye on the ARVN driver.

The convoy moved out at 0500. The first gray streaks of approaching dawn were just beginning to brighten the skies to the east. Hiep switched on his running lights as we took our place near the center of the column and began bouncing along Highway 1. When we reached the junction with Highway 14, we turned off and headed southwest for Nam Dong. Behind us, the crimson rim of the morning sun edged slowly above the horizon.

Highway 14 was a thoroughfare in name only. In reality it was nothing more than a crude dirt road leading up into the highlands. During the rainy season it deteriorated into a muddy morass, virtually impassable to motorized vehicles. Fortunately, it was now relatively firm beneath the grinding wheels of our convoy.

I glanced forward and back along the length of the undulating column. If you had to drive into enemy territory, the middle of the convoy was the best place to be. VC ambush teams usually struck at the front or rear of a moving column. Nevertheless, I kept the carbine on my lap pointed out to the left. For the rest of the morning I seldom took my eyes off the heavy vegetation beside the road where danger might lie.

It was a slow, rugged ride. The road was badly rutted and the jeep lurched violently whenever we hit a particularly deep furrow. Choking and blinding dust churned up by the dozens of heavy vehicles ahead swirled into our faces. It took three hours to cover the forty-five kilometers to Nam Dong, but we arrived without incident. The sun was well above the horizon as we jolted up the narrow path leading to the front gate. The main body of the convoy began to deploy along the sides of the road. Crittenden instructed Hiep to drive on into the camp itself.

In the two weeks since the battle, Captain Griffin and his "A" team had done a remarkable job of rebuilding Nam Dong. Almost every structure had been destroyed or badly damaged during the attack. Yet, now there was scarcely a sign of any of that. Not knowing better, I would never have guessed that a major fight had taken place here recently.

The jeep rolled into the outer perimeter, passing a newly resurfaced helicopter landing pad on the right. We pulled up to the inner gate where Hiep stopped. Griffin and several of his men were waiting for us there. It was at this very spot that Captain Donlon had personally shot three members of a VC demolition team as they attempted to blast a path through the barbed wire.

Griffin approached the jeep. "Good morning, Major. Welcome to Nam Dong."

"Thank you, Captain. I'm glad to be here." Crittenden gestured toward me. "This is my radio operator, PFC Oliveri."

I smiled at the Green Beret officer and tossed him a casual salute. "Nice to meet you, Sir."

Griffin nodded pleasantly. "You're both welcome to stay in the team house while you're here. We've got plenty of room."

"Thanks," said Crittenden. "We appreciate that."

Crittenden instructed Hiep to park the jeep, then went inside. I waited until the driver left the vehicle and began walking back down the path to find his unit. Something about Hiep still troubled me. I shrugged. Whatever it was would have to wait. I could smell fresh coffee.

After a welcome breakfast of hot biscuits, I returned to the jeep. Griffin sent along a Vietnamese signalman to help me set up communications with Hue. The "Angry/9" radio in the vehicle transmitted its signal via a "long-wire" antenna strung between two poles. It had a series of insulated connectors along its full length of about sixty feet. The connections used depended on the frequency we were broadcasting with at any particular time. I carefully unrolled the wire on the ground and snapped together the proper number of connectors.

The ARVN signalman provided two bamboo poles, each about twelve feet in length. I secured one end of the antenna to a pole while the soldier dug a shallow hole. When that was done we raised the support with the antenna attached and slid the base gently into the ground. I crammed some rocks around the pole to brace it while my helper shoveled dirt into the hole.

In order to work properly, the long-wire antenna had to face broadside to the compass point I wanted to reach. Thus, the position of the second pole was critical. I turned to the signalman and pointed out beyond the gate toward what I thought was the general direction of Hue city. "Hue? Hue?"

The ARVN nodded vigorously. "OK! Numbah one!"

I secured the free end of the antenna to the second pole and positioned the entire rig on the ground so that the wire faced the right direction. The signalman dug another hole, and we repeated the process with the second pole. When everything was firmly in place, I reached up and snared the antenna lead-in wire. As my assistant watched, I attached it carefully to the terminal on the radio.

Now came the test. If we had done everything properly, I should be able to make contact with net control. I started the jeep for power, walked around to the radio mount on the side of the vehicle and flipped a switch. The "Angry/9" crackled to life. Coincidentally, Keller was in the midst of sending out a net call. I listened patiently as the individual stations responded. The signals were all very strong. That in itself was unusual. I knew from experience that poor atmospheric conditions often made it difficult for some stations to reach Hue. Evidently Nam Dong was situated in a good reception zone.

When the others had all cleared the air, I picked up the telegraph key and tapped out a series of "Vs" to alert Keller. I requested that he give me the strength and readability of my signal. Ken answered immediately on voice. "Frost Weed Fox Trot, this is Alpha. I hear you five-by. How are you, goombah? Over."

I grabbed the black plastic mike. "This is Fox Trot. Everything's number one. Be advised that I hear all Frost Weed stations loud and clear and can relay if necessary. Over."

"Roger your last, Fox Trot. Appreciate hearing that. Request to know your location. Over."

"Ah, this is Fox Trot. I'm at that place I was worried about. Over."

"Alpha, roger. Sorry about that. You take care of yourself. Over."

"This is Fox Trot. That's affirm. Thanks for your concern. Hope to see you soon. I have negative further. Out."

I switched off the radio and shut down the jeep engine. I was pleased. It seemed that communication with Hue would be no problem. Unless Crittenden had traffic to send, I'd simply check in with net control several times a day for messages. Otherwise my time was my own. I thanked the signalman with a smile and a hearty "Cam Anh!" He grinned, nodded vigorously, and then headed back to his duties. I went off to report to the major.

Crittenden was pleased. "That's fine, Oliveri. I have nothing to send yet. You can take a look around if you like."

I recovered the camera from my bag and began a walking tour of the camp. Nam Dong was loaded. There were several fresh companies of ARVN troops to augment the forces already sweeping the surrounding countryside. In addition, two heavy 155mm howitzers now sat inside the perimeter. The huge tubes lay astride massive black tires. Steel coils the size of a man's thigh bracketed each gun barrel to absorb the fearsome recoil of the great shells. The howitzers fired sporadically at suspected VC concentrations to the southeast throughout the morning. I circled the big guns and walked toward the northeast perimeter.

Nam Dong essentially consisted of two perimeters. The Vietnamese strike force lived in crude huts within the outer perimeter. The American Special Forces team occupied the inner ring, where most of the main camp buildings were located. The outpost sat in a valley surrounded by rugged 3000 foot mountains. Isolated as it was, Nam Dong was very vulnerable, as we had learned just a short time previously. Roughly 5000 members of the Katu montagnard tribe lived in the valley, many of those in nearby Nam Dong village. A stream flowed through the hamlet, also known as Ta Rau.

A new command bunker was under construction near the wire. At the moment it was nothing more than a yawning hole in the ground. The Green Berets called it "the swimming pool." Nearby was the "fire arrow," a wooden device in the shape of an arrowhead. Tin cans mounted on it contained jellied gasoline. In the event of a night attack, the camp's defenders would light the fire arrow and swivel it toward the enemy positions. Support aircraft could then guide on the arrow to more accurately locate their targets. This gave the camp an extra measure of control over friendly fire in the darkness.

Just beyond the outer perimeter the terrain dropped away gradually to form a gently rolling bluff. Nam Dong's airstrip lay about two hundred yards down the side of the small plateau where I now stood. On the far side of the runway was a heavily overgrown strip of ground reaching up to a low ridgeline about five hundred yards from the wire. The main VC assault had originated from this point, rolling rapidly across the airstrip and up the hillside into Nam Dong's defenses. A small herd of water buffalo now grazed peacefully in the area where hordes of Communist troops had fought and died only a few short days previously.

Two mortar positions straddled the main gate. There was another in the northwest corner of camp. Just beyond that sat the Special Forces mess hall and shower room. What a far cry from Ta Bat, I thought. These green beanies really knew how to live.

Next to the mess hall was the partially-finished communications bunker. The quarters for the nungs, ethnic Chinese soldiers loyal to Special Forces, occupied the southwest corner of camp along with an 81mm mortar pit. The southeastern sector was taken up by the camp dispensary and another mortar position.

As I walked, I noticed a spent rifle slug laying in the dirt, likely a remnant of the recent battle. I picked it up as a souvenir. By the time I completed my brief tour of the camp I had several more in my pocket. I wondered if they had been brought here on the trucks we had reported from Ta Bat.

I returned to the jeep and found Crittenden and Hiep there. "We're going out to check on the battalion," said the major. "Be back in a couple of hours."

I unhooked the lead-wire from the radio and wrapped it around the antenna pole. Hiep climbed into the jeep and cranked up the engine. Crittenden waved as they lurched out toward the main gate and rattled down the dusty road. I turned away as a cloud of red dust swirled up behind them.

Author with jeep at the Nam Dong Special Forces camp.

I walked into the team building where Griffin and several of his non-coms sat chatting. Just inside the front door was a small armory, its doors closed and chained. To the right was the team room, with the sleeping quarters just beyond. The men were seated around a small wooden table. I quietly pulled up a chair so as not to disturb their conversation.

One of the men, Sergeant Parmelee, glared at me. He seemed a bit old to be a Green Beret, and his long hair appeared somewhat unsoldierly. "What's this PF doing here?" he muttered sarcastically, referring to my rank.

I smiled at first, thinking he was just teasing me.

Parmelee turned to Griffin. "I thought you had to be a sergeant to come out here," he grumbled.

Captain Griffin frowned. "Shut up, Al."

They resumed their previous conversation while I silently fumed. At one point Parmelee got up and unlocked the armory door to check on something. I glanced inside and saw a huge cache of weapons stacked neatly throughout the small room. There were carbines, M-1 rifles, Thompsons, even BARs. I whistled in admiration. "Man, you've got enough guns in there to start a war!"

Griffin chuckled at my unintentional pun. "You're right. That's our reserve. We use them to arm recruits for our strike force."

I stepped to the door and peered inside. Parmelee was examining a weapons inventory. "Say, Sarge," I said. "If you ever have to get rid of some of those carbines, I sure could use one. Had to borrow the one I've got now."

Parmelee looked up and then called derisively to Griffin, "Hey, Captain... This PF needs a carbine."

Griffin shrugged. "So give him one."

Parmelee snatched a rifle from the rack and tossed it to me. Then he grabbed two thirty round "banana clips" from a shelf and held them out. "Here you go, PF. Just don't shoot yourself in the fuckin' foot."

I hefted the weapon and grinned. It was one of the highly-prized fully automatic models. I was delighted. "Hey... thanks a million, Sarge!" For a rifle like that I would overlook a lot of ridicule.

Parmelee nodded. "Don't mention it, kid." He slapped me roughly on the back. It was not until we had left Nam Dong before I finally realized that Sergeant Parmelee never again called me a "PF."

Later that afternoon, Captain Griffin asked me if I would be willing to take a guard shift while I was in camp. I quickly agreed. It sounded like it might be an interesting task, and I was in an adventurous mood. Griffin assigned me a shift from 2300 to 2400.

While we talked, I noticed the Australian warrant officer attached to the team sitting nearby and listening to our conversation. A balding man in his forties with salt and pepper hair, he didn't seem very happy about what he was hearing. The Aussie studied me with furrowed eyebrows and a scowl on his face. Evidently he wasn't too confident that I could do a satisfactory job, because he subsequently came to check on me twice during my guard stint. I guess Sergeant Parmelee wasn't the only one who felt uncomfortable trusting his personal safety to an inexperienced PFC.

At 2300, I shouldered my brand spanking new carbine and began my tour of the quiet camp. I stopped first at the main gate to be sure that it was chained and locked. I loitered there briefly, trying to imagine the hellish events that had taken place at this very spot just a short time previously. Then I continued along the perimeter, completing a full circuit of the camp in about 15 minutes. I repeated the trip half an hour later. Both treks along the wire were uneventful. I performed several more guard shifts before leaving Nam Dong, all unsupervised, I'm pleased to say, by the once-skeptical Aussie.

The 3rd Battalion's operation proved to be a dismal failure. For five days Crittenden handed me nothing but negative contact reports to transmit back to Hue. Despite hundreds of ARVN soldiers in the field, the VC were not to be found. They had either abandoned the area, or were determined to avoid contact with the powerful force now operating out of Nam Dong. Whatever the reason, we had drawn a complete blank.

Crittenden instructed me to dismantle the commo set-up on the morning of the sixth day in preparation for returning to Hue that afternoon. Hiep loaded the jeep while I rolled up the antenna. Major Crittenden called me into the team house when we had finished. We thanked the Special Forces soldiers for their hospitality and shook hands all around. I made a distinct point of showing my gratitude to Sergeant Parmelee. Unknown to us at the time, Captain Griffin's "A" team was scheduled to be withdrawn shortly, and the outpost would soon be turned over to the Vietnamese Special Forces. Nam Dong had survived its moment of glory and would play little further part in the war.

We joined up with the column and rolled out of Nam Dong just after 1400 hours. The convoy ground slowly back up Highway 14 toward Phu Bai. I cradled the new carbine on my lap throughout the return trip.

We pulled into the advisors compound late in the afternoon, faces and uniforms covered with red road dust. Hiep parked the jeep and then went off to find a ride back to his unit. Crittenden dismissed me before entering the hotel. "Well, Oliveri, I want to thank you for your help. It was a pleasure working with you.

"Thanks, Major. I enjoyed it."

"Would you mind if I asked for you again on our next operation?"

"No, Sir. Not at all."

"OK, then. You take care. I'll see you again."

"So long, Major." I hoisted my bag onto my shoulder, grasped the two carbines by their slings and started up the street to the commo house.

Potter was on duty when I walked through the door. "Whattaya say, partner? Welcome home."

"Thanks, Doug." I dropped my bag and laid the two carbines on the table. "What's new around here?"

"Same old shit. We've been working twelve hour shifts since you left. Haven't had time for anything else."

"What about Chop? Couldn't he help you out?"

Doug stifled a snort. "Come on, man. You know better than that. He just hangs around the airfield all day. You should have seen him yesterday, armed to the teeth, hoping to tag along on some 'Eagle Flight.' The guy thinks he's Sergeant York!"

I laughed at the analogy. "Well, I'll take a shift tomorrow so I don't have to listen to you guys cry. Ken working tonight?"

"Yeah. If you do the morning shift we can switch off."

"No problem." I pointed to my new rifle. "How do you like the carbine I got from Special Forces?"

Doug's eyes widened in admiration. "Hey, is that an automatic? I never saw one of those before."

"It's a souvenir of Nam Dong," I said wearily as he examined the rifle. "What a hell of a place that was. I'm glad to be back, even if it means putting up with you clowns." With that I carried my gear into the bedroom, stripped off my dusty fatigues and headed for the shower.

———

R & R

I N LATE JULY A USO troupe arrived in Hue to entertain the troops. The show took place in the screened—in utility room above the dispensary. There were about seventy raucous members of the detachment in the audience as Colonel Collins introduced the performers. The act consisted of an aging singer, who had somehow squeezed herself into a too tight black sequined dress, and a three piece band. The musicians were clad in civilian clothes and looked bored. I settled back, not expecting very much. A makeshift spotlight snapped on, illuminating the group.

The singer turned out to be quite good. For the next half hour she belted out the hit tunes of the day, including those of the Beatles, the Everly Brothers and Dean Martin. The spectators appreciated the performance, cheering lustily after each song. Finally the woman announced that she would close the show with "something very special" for one lucky soldier. To my horror, she pointed directly at me and told me to come up front.

I recoiled in embarrassment. But she persisted until several other soldiers, hooting uproariously, pushed me out of my seat into the aisle. I made my way reluctantly up to the microphone. The singer threw her arms around me, then ran her fingers across my crew cut hair. Up close I saw that her makeup couldn't conceal the age lines in her face. She made an exaggerated fuss over me as the audience urged her on. At last, accompanied by a drum roll, she planted a big wet kiss on my cheek. The onlookers cheered wildly. I flushed beet-red.

View of the Nam Dong airstrip from the camp.

When I finally escaped back to my seat a sergeant in the row behind leaned forward and tapped me on the shoulder. "I knew she was gonna pick you," he chuckled. "They always look for the youngest guy."

I smiled sheepishly. I was exactly one week shy of my twenty-first birthday.

I arose early the next morning to allow time for a leisurely breakfast before relieving Keller at 0800. Doug was already up and dressed, so I dragged him across to the hotel for breakfast. Only a few advisors were inside. With little to do, the two young Vietnamese waitresses stood chatting near the rear of the room. They glanced toward us as we sat down. The taller one giggled. I was amused. I knew the girls loved to flirt with the huge, friendly Americans, so I winked at them. The smaller one smiled, and then lowered her eyes as she approached our table. She had long black hair reaching half way down the back of her orange ao dai.

I said, "Chao, Co" (Good morning, miss). She tittered shyly. "How about two poached eggs and some coffee?"

"Two po' egg; ca'fay. Okay."

Doug ordered the same. Our waitress skittered into the kitchen and returned ten minutes later with our breakfast. We ate the eggs greedily while the waitresses pretended not to watch. I took two vitamin tablets from a bottle on the table, and washed them down with sips of coffee. When we finished, I stood up and patted my stomach.

"Number One!" I announced, and winked at them again. Their eyes twinkled as we made our way to the door. Yep, I thought, when you're not in the field, this "hardship tour" isn't so bad at all.

On July 27th I bought a case of beer at the PX to celebrate my birthday. Doug, Ken and Chop Kane joined me in the living room that evening to drink and trade insults. Until that day I hadn't been old enough to legally vote or drink liquor, but not too young to risk my life in combat. I can't recall if I bothered to think about that at the time, but if I had I'm sure I would have smiled wryly at the irony of the situation.

Several days later, Yniguez choppered in from Ta Bat. He was scheduled for R&R, and was booked on a flight to Nha Trang in three days. Lieutenant Mowrey also came in for a break from the field. With no advisor now at the outpost, there was no need to send another operator out there.

Every American soldier was entitled to a week of Rest and Recreation (R&R) during his tour in Vietnam. There were several schools of thought on how best to take advantage of that. Some impulsively seized the first opportunity to flee to a resort city such as Da Lat or Nha Trang. Or, if they could afford it, they might hop a MATS (Military Air Transport Service) flight to Bangkok or Hong Kong. Others jealously hoarded their R&R until nearer the end of their tours, gambling that an opening would be available when they felt they needed it most. Still others split their time into two shorter trips.

To tell the truth, I hadn't given much thought to R&R yet, but when Kane uncharacteristically offered me the chance to go to Nha Trang with Ralph, I jumped at it. The following day, Chop had orders cut for the both of us to fly out on the Otter. "A birthday present," he called it. I gave up trying to figure him out. There was simply no understanding this man of so many inconsistencies. I almost felt sorry for all the terrible things we had done to him. Almost.

Keller drove us to the Citadel the next morning to catch the Otter. The courier plane would take us down to Da Nang, where we would then try to find space on the first available craft going into Nha Trang. I had heard a lot of good things about the city. Nha Trang was considered one of the most desirable resort areas in South Vietnam, rivaling Da Lat, a favorite of upper level Republic of Vietnam government officials. Nha Trang had perhaps the most beautiful beach in all of Southeast Asia. There were also some excellent restaurants there. If one wished to escape the war without actually leaving the country, Nha Trang was the place to go.

We arrived at Da Nang to find that the next available to Nha Trang wasn't until the following morning. We would have to stay the night at the advisors' hotel. Naturally, I wasn't upset about that, remembering the pleasant time Doug and I had spent there just three months previously. We were so green then, I thought with a snicker. It seemed like a lifetime ago. "Chili-burner," I said to Ralph, "I think you're gonna like this place."

We enjoyed a movie at the hotel that evening, then relaxed in the enlisted men's club until midnight. There was a huge breakfast in the dining room the following morning before we boarded a waiting Caribou for the next leg of our journey.

I didn't like flying. In fact, my very first flight had been aboard the commercial jet to San Francisco several months earlier. But since arriving in Vietnam, I had flown in virtually every type of aircraft in the American military fleet, ranging from the tiny L-19s to the cavernous C-123s. There was simply no way to avoid flying. By now I had learned to live with it. I closed my eyes and dozed fitfully throughout the flight.

We landed at Nha Trang on a gorgeous, sun-drenched morning. There was an advisory hotel in town, but we didn't go there. Military personnel on R&R stayed at special cabana-like quarters right on the beach. A truck dropped us at the office where we checked in and drew separate rooms. The building was a long, single level complex of connected cubicles. A cement footing ran the length of the structure, shielded by a corrugated sun roof. A vacationing soldier could walk directly from his quarters right down to the water's edge.

Ralph and I stowed our bags, put on swim suits, and then trudged across the hot yellow sand to the shore. We stretched out on oversized bath towels, sweating profusely in the brilliant sunlight. I showed Yniguez the scars on my back and warned him about over-exposing himself to the sun as I had on the beach in Hue. He nodded politely, but I could see that he wasn't too interested in my advice. Where Ralph came from they were used to the hot sun.

I made sure to rub on plenty of lotion, and also rigged up a makeshift umbrella using a second towel and some sticks I had found in the closet of my room. I was determined not to make the same mistake again.

The view from the beach was breath-taking. We were at the center of a bowl-shaped coastline that curved sharply out to sea both north and south of where we sat. The shore rose gradually inland until it reached the pea-green mountains dominating either end of the bowl. Directly across from us, about half a mile offshore, lay a small island. It was volcanic in appearance. I had never seen Hawaii, but I guessed it must look very much like this.

Up the beach, several young Vietnamese boys were wading in the sparkling surf. As was their custom, they wore no trunks, electing instead to swim in the nude. Three teen-age girls stood near the water's edge, fifty yards to the south. Unlike the boys, each wore a bright, two-piece bathing suit. Ralph and I looked at each other and shrugged. Too bad. After all, we were here to have a good time.

An hour of bright sun and hot sand was about all we could stand. Dripping with perspiration, we dashed down to the water and dove into the gently-rolling breakers. Refreshed, we returned to our rooms to clean up for dinner. I couldn't help looking back at the beautiful scene we had just left. Ralph noticed it too. It seemed incongruous to find a place like this in the same country where Ta Bat existed. Maybe we were just two dumb GIs, but the irony wasn't lost on us.

Once inside, I glanced at my body in the mirror and noted with some satisfaction that I had acquired only a modest red tinge. I took a cool shower and then dressed in civvies. Someone had told us to try a little French restaurant in town. It was actually run by Vietnamese, but it supposedly offered the best steaks in Nha Trang. Quite frankly, we were a little skeptical. In Vietnam you could never be sure if you were going to get good aged beef or stringy water buffalo. It was often a crap shoot.

The steaks turned out to be excellent. A frail old oriental waiter hovered nearby throughout the meal, seeming anxious to please us. We delighted the old man with lavish compliments that I'm sure he couldn't understand, and then chuckled at his gap-toothed smile. The war seemed so far away at this point that I felt more like a tourist than a soldier.

We lingered over the meal, sharing some laughs over a bottle of fine French wine. After paying the bill and leaving a handsome tip for the good-natured waiter, we strolled back to our quarters. I had some letters to write, but Ralph, warmed by the wine, set out in search of female companionship.

As I was sealing an envelope about an hour later, there was a gentle knock on the door. I swung it open, expecting to find Ralph, and was mildly surprised to see a young "boom-boom girl" standing outside. She was heavily made up, and a little on the chunky side, but she had a pretty face. I blurted out, "What the hell are you doing here?"

"Ral' sen' me," she replied. "Me numbah one cowboy girl."

"Well, I'll be damned," I muttered. "That crazy Mexican." I grasped her wrist, led her gently inside, and slammed the door with my foot.

Early the next morning, I pounded on Ralph's door. "Get up, you drunken whore master!" I kept thumping the door until a disheveled Yniguez finally appeared wearing only GI drawers. He was a sight. Ralph cradled his head in his hands, shooting bleary-eyed daggers at me through trembling fingers.

"Take it easy, amigo. I got a splitting headache."

"Tough shit," I cackled, totally lacking in sympathy. "You wanna play, you gotta pay. Come on... let's go get some breakfast."

"Wait a minute while I find my friggin' pants." Ralph threw up a hand to shield his eyes from the light, as Dracula might, and then vanished back into the room.

I called through the open door. "By the way, thanks for the present last night."

Ralph reappeared, struggling to pull on a pair of khaki shorts. "What? Oh, yeah. Forgot about that. Don't mention it."

"She was pretty good. Even gave me a massage."

Ralph snorted. "If you're finished bull-shitting, let's walk over to the hotel."

"OK... if you think you can make it." Ralph snorted again.

Entering the advisors' compound, we were stunned to find it an anthill of activity. Squads of American enlisted men swarmed about the installation, filling sandbags and then carrying them up to the roof where other soldiers were building fortifications. We gaped at the scene in astonishment, unable to comprehend what was happening. Ralph finally approached a sweating specialist and tapped him on the shoulder. "Say, Mac... What the hell is going on?"

The beefy soldier eyed Ralph as if he were insane. "Haven't you heard? The North Vietnamese attacked one of our destroyers last night."

We were taken aback. It was August 3rd, 1964. The previous afternoon while we were enjoying our steaks, the Navy reported that three North Vietnamese patrol boats had emerged from the mouth of the Red River and launched a sudden attack on the U.S. destroyer Maddox, cruising just ten miles offshore. In a brief but violent skirmish, all three boats fired torpedoes, none of which found the American warship.

The Maddox turned toward the sea, its guns blazing. A shell struck one of the enemy boats, stopping it dead in the water. Within minutes, a swarm of jets from the U.S.S Ticonderoga roared overhead and began strafing the remaining North Vietnamese craft. One vessel sank almost immediately, and the other was crippled. The unharmed Maddox withdrew with a clear-cut victory.

A second and more controversial incident occurred two days later. The Maddox was joined on station by the destroyer C. Turner Joy. Sometime after 2000 hours, the two ships again reported contact with enemy boats. But in the darkness, and with the weather deteriorating, it was impossible to determine with any degree of certainty if the blips on the American radar screens were indeed attacking patrol boats or merely just electronic clutter. Lacking visual confirmation, the matter remained somewhat questionable. Nonetheless, precipitated by this shadowy incident, the first bombing of North Vietnam was just hours away.

President Lyndon B. Johnson asked Congress to approve a resolution of support for U.S. retaliation against the North Vietnamese. Thus was born the "Tonkin Gulf Resolution", which authorized the president to take any necessary measures to defend American forces, and to prevent further aggression. A major escalation of the war was about to take place.

On the night of August 5th, carrier aircraft from the U.S. Seventh Fleet attacked four Communist patrol boat bases and an oil depot in the southern "panhandle" area of North Vietnam. American jets flew 64 sorties against the selected targets. Two planes were shot down. One pilot was recovered safely and returned to his carrier. The second, Lieutenant Everett Alvarez Jr., was captured, and became the first American aviator held as a prisoner of war in North Vietnam. Two days later, Congress officially passed the Tonkin Gulf Resolution.

On August 4th and 5th, Ralph and I conducted a determined search for space aboard any aircraft flying to Hue. We somehow managed to get on a Caribou the first day. As its engines sputtered and roared to life, we sat back in the cargo slings and waited for the tailgate to close. From our vantage point, we saw a jeep lurch out onto the runway and then race to the rear of our aircraft, where it screeched to a halt. An overweight sergeant jumped from the vehicle with a clipboard in his hand. He examined the papers, and then stuck his head into the cargo bay.

"PFCs Oliveri and Yniguez... are you in there?"

I glanced at Ralph. We both knew what was coming. Eligibility for seating on any aircraft in Vietnam was determined by rank, and we were at the bottom of the chain. "Right here, Sarge," I called out.

"You're being bumped," he replied. "Sorry 'bout that." He didn't look sorry.

"Ah, for Christ's sake," I muttered.

Ralph poked me in the ribs. "What the hell are you bitching about, gringo? Now we get to stay an extra day." My mouth snapped shut.

A second jeep pulled up as we hopped down onto the steel matting. A captain and a lieutenant brushed past us and clambered into the plane. The tailgate whined shut behind them, and the Caribou taxied onto the runway, from where it quickly took off into a gentle headwind. The jeep vacated by the two officers took us back to the R&R hotel, and we were able to re-register for another night.

We checked in again at the airfield the next morning. With all that was going on, the strip was a beehive of activity as officers and enlisted men sought transportation back to their units. We finally found a C-123 going up to Da Nang, and decided to fly there. With a little luck, we might then be able to catch the Otter to Hue. Ralph and I fidgeted in our seats as the plane warmed up, half expecting to be bumped again. Ralph, I think, was hoping for it. I was ready to go back, but I'm sure he wouldn't have minded spending another night in Nha Trang. It didn't happen. This time, no jeeps raced onto the runway, and the plane took off on schedule.

We stayed the night in Da Nang, and then met the Otter the following morning as it prepared to leave for Hue. We were fortunate; the Otter was completely booked except for two vacant seats. I wound up sitting next to Captain Monahan, the I Corps chaplain. I said, "Good morning, Sir," and slid into my seat.

Monahan glanced up from the magazine he was reading. "Oh, good morning, Oliveri. Nice to see you."

I felt uncomfortable. Two weeks before, I had been on duty in the radio room when Monahan walked into the house. The good reverend peered at the Playboy centerfolds we had taped above the radio and said, "I suggest you take those down."

I felt like I had just been caught playing with myself. Fortunately, an incoming call spared me from further embarrassment. Monahan left without another word, but he didn't look happy. And now here I was sitting beside him on the flight back to Hue. Out of the corner of my eye, I caught Ralph snickering in the seat behind me. I wanted to strangle him. I felt much better when we finally reached Tay Loc, and I was able to steer clear of Chaplain Monahan.

Keller and Doug were glad to see us. The compound was still buzzing about the bombing of the north. Thompson had been working out of Quang Tri, but was visiting for several days. He had generously volunteered to take a shift while we were away. Tony told us that the garrison at Quang Tri had been placed on full alert following the air raids. There was serious concern about a possible North Vietnamese reprisal across the DMZ. Units from Dong Ha in the east to Lang Vei in the west quietly increased their readiness and waited.

Nothing happened. After several days, the tension began to dissipate. The Americans didn't follow up their punitive raids, and the Communists limited their response to verbal protests. The I Corps advisory team gradually returned to its normal routine. The crisis had passed.

———

A SHAU

KANE WAS FINALLY PROMOTED TO Staff Sergeant. Doug and I spotted him in the hotel dining room the morning after he received the orders granting him another stripe. It was an absurd sight. Chop was seated at a table by himself with a shit-eating grin on his face. He was staring lovingly down at his sleeve, where his new insignia had just been sewn on. Kane seemed oblivious to everything else as he sat gently caressing the long-awaited patch. He looked utterly ridiculous.

I shook my head. "Do you believe this guy?"

"He must have gone dinky-dau," cackled Doug. We left with Chop still at the table admiring his new stripes.

A new advisor was assigned to Ta Bat in mid-August, and Yniguez flew out to join him. Shortly afterward, now-Staff Sergeant Kane cornered me in the living room of the commo house. "Hey, Oliveri. Major Crittenden's going out on an operation in the A Shau tomorrow. He asked for you and I said OK."

The bastard didn't even smile. I guess he thought he was finally getting even with me for my practical jokes. Actually, I had been expecting to hear from Crittenden again, so this was no big surprise. And I knew from my experience at Nam Dong that the Green Berets usually lived quite comfortably. This might not be too bad.

The next morning, I cleaned and oiled my weapons, and gathered my gear. At 1000 hours I slung my new carbine over one shoulder and my bag over the other. Doug drove me to the airfield. As we rolled onto the Nguyen Hoang Bridge, a Buddhist funeral procession approached from the opposite bank. Doug pulled over to let them pass. The mourners trudged slowly along, many of them carrying hand-lettered prayer signs. They marched to the halting rhythm of clashing cymbals. Several years later, during the Tet Offensive, the VC were to smuggle weapons into Hue concealed in the trappings of sham funeral processions. Now, however, the mourners passed peacefully on toward the cemetery while we watched curiously. When the span was finally clear Doug stepped on the gas and continued on to Tay Loc.

Crittenden was waiting on the fringe of the runway with a small group of ARVN soldiers. An empty Caribou loomed behind them with its tailgate down. Most of the Vietnamese troops had already been airlifted to A Shau. This was the final contingent. I said good-bye to Doug and walked over to join them. Catching Crittenden's eye, I saluted smartly. "Good morning, Sir."

The Major returned my salute with a smile. "Hello, Oliveri. Glad you could make it."

"Thanks, Major." I glanced around for his driver. "Did Hiep already go on ahead, Sir?"

Crittenden frowned. His response was terse and measured. "I guess you didn't hear. Hiep was arrested. They found out he was a VC collaborator."

"You're kidding!" I was thunderstruck.

"No, I'm not. He's in jail somewhere up north of here."

I couldn't believe it. Here I had spent a week with the man and all the while he was actually a VC. I guess my instincts about the shooting incident at Phu Bai had been correct. I KNEW I hadn't loaded the carbine that morning. Hiep must have done it. Maybe he had hoped to disrupt the operation with an "accidental" shooting, or perhaps even hit the jackpot by getting Crittenden shot. Jesus, it made sense!

I sat silently during the short flight to A Shau, fighting back waves of paranoia. If I dug deeply enough, I could think of many seemingly innocent people who might reasonably be considered VC suspects. There was Charlie (wasn't he aptly named?) the old cyclo driver who cruised the area near the advisors compound. He often pedaled me across the bridge to the marketplace. It was sometimes said, perhaps in jest, that he was a VC sympathizer. And the little barber who cut my hair in the hotel lobby. He never uttered a word as he worked with his clicking scissors and keen-edged straight razor. Razor? Damn, I'd have to give that some more thought. I'd always found getting a haircut relaxing, so I usually visited the barber about every week to ten days while I was in Hue. Maybe not any longer. I recalled a story I had heard about three VC who had been killed one night near Da Nang when ARVN soldiers snapped an ambush on them. One of the victims was the advisors' barber. And Bui, the young Vietnamese college student Keller had befriended. He often came down to the house from nearby Hue University and Ken would help him study English. Who knew what he was really up to? After all, we had confidential information in the commo house. I had never liked him anyway. And… and…

The Caribou's sudden descent interrupted my train of thought. I gazed across the aisle. Crittenden sat quietly studying me. The Major flashed me a fatherly smile and nodded his head gently. He understood. I felt a pang of affection for the wise old soldier. Without saying a word, he had persuaded me to forget about Hiep for the time being. There was far too much else to worry about at the moment.

The plane touched down, rumbled briefly along the steel-matted landing strip and coasted to a halt. We disembarked into the brilliant August sun.

A Shau was a fairly large outpost. The triangular headquarters compound containing the Team A-113 Special Forces command post and the sway-backed ARVN HQ building lay on the north side of the installation, its apex pointed in the general direction of Ta Bat. Fifty yards south of the base of the triangle was another long, rectangular compound. Eight large barracks and half a dozen smaller structures stood within its confines. The Vietnamese strike force called this home. A narrow dirt walkway connected the two emplacements. The camp runway jutted off at a slight angle below the ARVN compound.

The mountains seemed closer and higher than they had at Ta Bat. Dark green jungle grew all the way up to and over even the tallest of the peaks. Looking west from the camp gave one the illusion of standing at the bottom of a huge, emerald-colored pottery bowl with broken and jagged edges.

Crittenden and I grabbed our gear and headed up the path toward the command post. A tall American officer with dark crew-cut hair was striding toward us. He was hatless, and wore a pair of aviator sunglasses. He grasped Crittenden's shoulders with both hands. "Forrest," he said with sincere warmth. "How the hell are you?"

Crittenden smiled. "Just fine, Harry. It's been a long time." He turned toward me. "Oliveri, say hello to an old buddy of mine, Major Harry Ching." I offered my hand. Crittenden later told me that he and Ching had served together in Korea.

"Good to have you with us," said Ching. "We want you both to stay in the team house while you're here. We've got a hell of a cook."

Crittenden beamed. "That's damn considerate of you, Harry. We appreciate it."

We stepped inside the team building. The interior was relatively dim. I blinked my eyes until my vision adjusted to the light. A husky master sergeant stood to our right with one foot resting on a cane chair. Several other Americans sat around a metal table. I recognized Sergeant Moore, a tall black man with red hair who had passed through Hue on several occasions while I was on radio watch at Tay Loc. The group eyed us curiously as we entered the room.

Ching introduced us to master sergeant Standing, the team's intelligence specialist. While Crittenden and Ching chatted, Standing took me aside. "Listen, Oliveri. Patience and Cotter are out in the field. You and the major can use their bunks while they're away."

After I thanked him, Standing led me through a doorway strung with thin strips of white plastic fringe. He was like a concerned mother hen as he stepped into a cubicle and pointed out a metal-framed bed with Sgt. Patience's name on it. I stowed my bag and weapon beside it.

A Shau was beginning to look pretty good to me. The Green Berets even had their own generator to provide electricity, as well as a large refrigerator to make ice and keep their drinks cold. Anyone was welcome to help himself to a beer or soda as long as he dropped a dime into a bucket atop the cooler. The "B" team back at Da Nang kept the stock replenished regularly.

Crittenden sent me over to the strike force compound to set up our radio inside one of the barracks buildings. Someone had already erected poles and strung the long-wire antenna. All I had to do was to plug in the correct number of connectors. I tuned the radio to net frequency and called in. There were no messages. I shut down the generator and then looked around. ARVN soldiers were laying down sleeping mats and blankets on the dirt floor. Several others were building fires outside to cook rice. We had brought along two companies, but there was still plenty of room inside. No one was bunking down near my radio, and I hoped that meant it would remain undisturbed.

That evening Crittenden and I ate dinner with the team. The food was excellent. Special Forces units always seemed to come up with outstanding cooks. The Green Berets liked to portray themselves as some sort of super soldiers, and doubtless felt they deserved the best. I secretly questioned whether they were all that good, but they certainly knew how to make outpost duty quite comfortable.

After the meal, Sergeant Moore set out to fire a harassment and interdiction (H&I) mission from the 81mm mortar pit just outside the team building. Moore's standard procedure was to launch H&I at random almost every night just before dusk. The team had carefully calculated the distances to some strategic terrain features. Any attack against the outpost would most likely originate from these points. By firing the big 81 at these positions near sundown, Moore and his crew hoped to disrupt any potential assault by catching the enemy troops as they massed.

I wandered over to the pit to watch the mission. Moore struggled with the heavy steel tube, grunting audibly as he manhandled it into position. When he was satisfied with the placement of the mortar, he crouched down and sighted the weapon, using the pre-positioned aiming stakes embedded in the perimeter of the pit. Moore studied some numbers written in a small brown notebook and adjusted the elevation knob to correspond with them. The ARVN mortar crew stood nearby, armed with several deadly-looking shells. When Moore was ready to fire, he stood straight up over the mouth of the tube. The crew passed three of the steel-finned projectiles to him, and Moore slid them down the barrel in rapid succession.

POWK! POWK! POWK! The mortar spewed streams of yellow and white sparks up toward a darkening sky. The shells soared along a parabolic arc to the target, a grassy clearing about a thousand meters, or one kilometer, west of camp. If the VC were planning an attack, this would be a logical jumping-off point.

WHOOM! WHOOM! WHOOM! The roar of the impacting shells reverberated down the valley. Moore finished resetting his sights even before the echoes died away. This time the target was a protruding tree line just over fifteen hundred meters to the northeast. The enemy force would almost certainly place its heavy weapons in there. Moore dropped three more rounds into the gaping mortar. Once again, the shells arched skyward.

By now the twilight had deepened considerably. When the rounds landed, the flashes were clearly visible. Three more explosions boomed ominously across the valley floor. I winced, imagining the shards of hot shrapnel ripping through the vegetation. Those blasts would probably have flattened anyone moving inside the tree line.

That was the end of the mission. Had there been enemy troops in those areas, they would surely have dispersed by now. If so, the H&I fire would have served its purpose. Unfortunately, we would probably never know for certain.

Twilight descended quickly upon the camp. To the west, the setting sun sank behind the surrounding peaks, briefly bathing them in liquid gold. In contrast with the deep purple shadows at the base of the mountains, the effect was startling. I paused to admire the sight. Vietnam is really a gorgeous country, I thought. Too bad death doesn't appreciate beauty. A slight smile curled my lips. Doug would call me a half-assed philosopher for thinking that way. I pulled myself away from this surrealistic scene and moved off to the team house.

At A Shau, every American shared guard duty. During a two hour shift, we were responsible for walking one complete circuit of the perimeter each hour to check the guard positions and the general integrity of the defenses. The Green Berets had little faith in the ability of the Vietnamese to perform this task. ARVN soldiers had a well-deserved reputation for sleeping on guard duty. This was especially so among the ranks of the A Shau strike force, second rate troops recruited from the local populace. They were unreliable at best, and the Americans refused to trust their personal safety to them. I drew a shift from 0100 to 0300. I turned in early, hoping to get a few hours of rest before going on duty.

Ten minutes before my watch began, Standing tip-toed into my cubicle and shook my shoulder gently, being careful not to disturb anyone else. "Rise and shine," whispered the team sergeant. Most of the others lay sleeping quietly in their racks. It was silent except for an occasional grunt or the squeak of a bedspring. I lifted a hand to acknowledge Standing, and he shuffled back to the kitchen.

I pulled on my boots and then stepped out of the sleeping bay. Standing had poured two cups of coffee from the battered pot that usually bubbled all night long. I muttered a grateful thank you, impressed with the treatment we were receiving, and slumped onto a wooden kitchen chair. I spooned some sugar into the steaming brew and sipped it. Bitter and very strong. I reached for the sugar again. Standing leaned against the refrigerator, absently watching me.

"Pretty quiet tonight," offered the chief non-com. "But keep an eye on that north bunker. Those humps have been missing the gong."

I nodded. I knew from experience that each guard position was equipped with a metal hoop strung from a bamboo pole. The guards at the main gate rang their gong roughly every fifteen minutes. The soldiers at the other positions were supposed to return the signal sequentially to confirm that they were awake and alert, and all was well. Apparently the machine gunners in the north bunker had been missing their cue. This was not an uncommon experience. The Americans found it maddening.

I gulped the last of my coffee and rose laboriously from the chair. I strapped on my pistol belt, and then slung the carbine over my shoulder. Nudging the screen door open with my foot, I stepped out into the darkness. A swarm of mosquitoes, attracted by the lights of the team house, buzzed annoyingly around my head.

It was a fairly clear, moonless night, but visibility was relatively good. With no city lights to eclipse them, thousands of stars twinkled brilliantly in the black sky. Their vast numbers and startling clarity were stunning. To the west, a few high clouds hung like a thin shroud above the horizon. In another five or six weeks, thick clouds associated with the rainy season would begin to roll into the valley, obscuring the skies for extended periods. Eighteen months later, the VC would take advantage of the cloud cover's ability to limit air support and attack A Shau. The camp's defenders would hold out for three days against an overwhelming force before finally abandoning the outpost. A Shau would never reopen again. The area would become a prime infiltration route for North Vietnamese forces entering South Vietnam.

Now however, I walked to the main gate and nodded to the guards. The Vietnamese were clad in tailored camouflage fatigues and brown berets. They seemed reasonably alert. Both had M-1 carbines slung on their shoulders. I jiggled the chains on the gate and found them tightly padlocked. The only keys to that lock were safely hung in the team house. "Number one!" I exclaimed pleasantly to the guards.

"OK! OK!" The guards grinned happily, pleased with the simple compliment. I started to move away from the gate. If all went well, I should complete a full circuit of the camp in about fifteen minutes.

Walking A Shau's perimeter in the dead of night was a nerve-wracking experience. Shadows darted ominously. Every sound seemed amplified by the extreme quiet. Dry red clay crunched beneath my boots with every step. I felt painfully exposed. My mind conjured up images of gun sights targeting on my back. It was a very uncomfortable thought. Although the night was cool, dampness began to spread from my armpits as I passed behind the concrete generator building.

View of the A Shau Special Forces camp.

CLANNNNG! I crouched reflexively at the sound of the gong at the main gate. I glanced around sheepishly, hoping no one had seen. I took a deep breath to settle some jangled nerves before resuming my journey along the wire.

Answering gongs rang out in a ragged sequence from the guard positions. I noted with annoyance that the north bunker directly ahead hadn't responded. I swore softly and quickly covered the remaining twenty-five yards to the log emplacement.

The position sat on a slight rise at the very apex of the triangular perimeter. It had an unobstructed field of fire northward in the direction of Ta Bat. The .50 caliber machinegun inside could pivot in a wide arc more than 240 degrees left and right. I stepped cautiously down into the sandbagged entrance. The interior was deathly quiet. I paused momentarily, waiting for my vision to adjust to the stygian blackness. Then I noticed the outlines of two bundles sprawled in a corner of the bunker. Jesus! Here they were supposed to be on guard, and instead they were curled up in sleeping bags!

"Hey!" I hissed. "Wake up!"

A sleepy murmur responded to my outburst. One of the bundles began to stir.

"Number ten, dammit!" I kicked at the other figure. The two Vietnamese scrambled out of their sacks. They looked embarrassed. "Now stay awake in here," I growled. I'm sure they couldn't understand my words, but they knew what I was saying. Both of them nodded their heads vigorously.

I grimaced in disgust, then spun around and groped my way toward the doorway. I knew they'd probably go right back to sleep as soon as I left. I made a mental note to tell Standing about it. Maybe he'd report them to the camp commander, who'd probably do nothing. What a joke.

The compound outside seemed relatively bright compared to the interior of the bunker. I resumed my trek, moving steadily south along the wire. I passed behind the team building and then cut across to the main gate again. All was quiet. I trudged back to the kitchen and stepped gingerly inside, careful not to disturb the sleeping Americans.

I used the half hour remaining between rounds to write a letter. When finished, I dropped it into a wire basket that held outgoing mail. Incoming letters also went in there, but they never remained very long unless the recipient was out in the field.

My second tour of the camp was uneventful. To my surprise, the north bunker responded promptly to the gong, so I didn't bother to check on the occupants again. I awakened Sergeant Moore, my relief, at 0250. When I was certain that he was up and around, I went back to bed and fell asleep almost immediately.

The next night I drew the first watch from 2300 to 0100. Rather than trying to grab a little rest first, I stayed up chatting with the team members until most of them had drifted off into the sleeping bay. With little else to do, I decided to start my first tour a bit early. I made a quick circuit of the perimeter and finding nothing out of the ordinary, returned to the team house. Only Jones, one of the medics, remained seated in the kitchen. The young sergeant, just a year or two older than me, was writing a letter to his parents. He was wearing only a pair of fatigue pants cut off at the knees and rubber sandals. We conversed sporadically as he wrote.

Just after midnight, I picked up my carbine and headed out the door again. I went directly to the front gate, where everything seemed to be secure. Then I turned to begin the now-familiar trek along the wire.

CRACK! CRACK! Two shots rattled from the northeast corner of camp. I halted in my tracks. What the fuck was going on now? I spotted muzzle flashes near the perimeter as two more reports echoed across the compound. I started to move cautiously in that direction, then hesitated, not quite sure what to do.

Jones bolted past me, sandals flapping as he ran. He gestured madly with his weapon. "Watch the gate! Watch the gate!"

I whirled and leveled my carbine at the entrance. I could see nothing but the two guards at the gate, staring wide-eyed into the darkness behind me. Inching sideways, I finally bumped up against the sandbag wall surrounding the mortar pit. I still had no idea what was happening.

Major Ching burst from the team house, roaring for his interpreter. "Ho Chi... Find out what the hell they're shooting at!"

More shots crackled along the wire. By now the camp was filled with running men who jabbered in excitement as they darted about. Minh, the interpreter, now stood in the center of the compound comically dressed only in his undershorts. He called out to Ching, "He say he hear a noise and he shoot at it!"

The Major reacted with exasperation. "Well, tell him to knock it off!"

Minh chattered a shrill phrase and the shooting stopped. Ching turned to the men milling about the area. "Anyone see or hear anything?" Nobody had.

I continued to cover the gate while some of the others checked the guard positions. Ten minutes later, after finding nothing, the group began to disperse. As far as we could tell, there had been no incoming fire. Jones shrugged as he walked past me on his way back to the team house. "Sometimes these characters get a little trigger happy."

At first light, the mystery was solved. The guards on the northeast wall spotted the carcass of a water buffalo just beyond the outer perimeter. The animal had evidently wandered into the wire from the nearby village during the night. It had somehow managed to avoid the minefield outside the fence, but the nervous sentry's bullets had found and killed it. There would be hell to pay with the villagers this day. Sergeant Jones later referred to the incident as "a goat fuck."

I joined several other team members at the breakfast table. We chuckled about the buffalo while we enjoyed a meal of crackers with Australian butter topped off by lots of hot coffee.

Standing came into the room. "Major Ching wants a weapons check in twenty minutes." He glanced at me. "Here's your chance to fire an AR-15."

Ching was clearly concerned. The previous night's incident had proved to be a false alarm, but the major knew that the installation at A Shau was badly exposed. Harry Ching wanted to be sure that his men were ready for anything.

We assembled in the northwest corner of camp with a wide array of weapons. Besides their personal AR-15s, the Special Forces soldiers had a vast inventory of BARs, Thompsons, light machineguns and M-79 grenade launchers. Major Ching even brought along the team's 57MM recoilless rifle. They threw some cans and bottles outside the perimeter and then began firing at them. Standing handed me his rifle. "Here. Try this."

Only the U.S. Special Forces carried the AR-15, later known as the M-16. The little black rifle was light, had a modest recoil and was very comfortable to shoot. It had a well-deserved reputation for causing devastating wounds with its tiny, high-velocity ammunition. I looked forward to firing it.

I took aim at one of the cans and squeezed off two rounds. Both passed harmlessly above the target. I glanced down at the weapon. The AR-15 had unusual raised sights. I realized that I would have to aim lower than I might have with my carbine. My next few shots sent the can spinning wildly across the ground. I really liked that little rifle. It made my weapon seem antiquated by comparison. I removed the magazine and inspected it more closely. Glancing up, I noticed Ching watching me. He had the recoilless rifle on his shoulder. "Wanna take a crack at this?" he grinned.

I shook my head emphatically. "No thanks, Sir. I think I'll stick to these popguns."

He laughed heartily and then turned back to the perimeter. One of the team members loaded a shell into the 57. Ching pointed the barrel westward, peered intently through the eyepiece and pressed the trigger. A tremendous thunderclap erupted from the weapon. I was momentarily stunned by the powerful concussion. The round rocketed off toward the hills, where it exploded with a distant thump. The big rifle's violent back blast stirred up a huge cloud of choking dust that swirled wildly around us.

A stentorian voice rang out despite spasms of dust-induced coughing. "JEE-ZUS CHRIST, Major! Please don't fire that mother-fucker again!"

We all roared with glee despite our discomfort. When everyone had finished firing, we cleared and inspected the weapons before carrying them back inside the team house.

Later that morning I walked over to the ARVN barracks for a radio check. Hue had no traffic for us, so I returned to the team house. Crittenden and Ching were seated at the table engaged in a quiet discussion. The major gave me a brief nod when I reported that there were no messages. I sat down on the bamboo couch and began flipping through a magazine.

Sergeant Monaghan, the demolitions expert, swept through the plastic fringe and clomped into the kitchen. He spoke softly to Ching and then glanced over at me. "Hey, Oliveri... I'm taking out a short patrol. Wanna come along? We'll be back in a couple of hours."

I turned to Crittenden. "OK with you, Sir?"

The major casually waved his hand. "Sure. Go ahead. There's nothing else happening anyway. Just be careful. I don't have another radio operator." I rolled my eyes. Well, at least he was concerned for my safety, even if not for the reason I might have hoped.

Monaghan grinned. "Come on... get your weapon. You got any canteens?"

I shook my head. The stocky sergeant went back into the sleeping bay and returned with two canvas-covered water bottles. "Here. Put these on your belt."

I carried the canteens back to my cubicle and hooked them into the eyelets in my pistol belt. Then I added two thirty round magazines for the carbine and three clips for the .45. I buckled on the entire conglomeration, grabbed my cap off the bed and went out to rejoin Monaghan.

The sergeant was waiting by the mortar pit with several nungs and a squad of Vietnamese soldiers. When he saw me emerge from the team house he turned and waved his arm like a cavalry officer. We began to move out down the path to the Vietnamese compound, passing through to the airstrip. Monaghan led us to the right and followed the runway to the end. We then marched steadily west toward the ridgeline, gradually spreading out until there was a five yard interval between each man. The nungs moved up to take the point. Monaghan and I dropped back until I was fifth in line, directly behind the Green Beret sergeant.

We carried a lot of firepower for a small patrol. Most of the Vietnamese had big M-1 rifles hanging almost comically from their tiny shoulders. One carried a Prick-10 radio. Although he hadn't said it, Monaghan may have asked me along because he felt that I could take over as radio operator in an emergency. Another soldier had an M-79 grenade launcher. Near the rear plodded a two man machine gun crew. Monaghan was armed with his AR-15 rifle as well as a big .357 magnum pistol. I was carrying my automatic carbine and the .45. We were really loaded for bear.

We soon reached the base of the hills and began climbing. It was hot on the hillside, but not excessively so, I thought. Within minutes, however, my shirt was soaked through and my eyes stung from perspiration. My legs began to cramp painfully. Too much time behind the radio, I mused ruefully.

Monaghan glanced back at me. "You OK?"

I nodded grimly. There was no way I was going to let these guys know that I was hurting.

About halfway up the hillside we reached a small trail running parallel to the ridgeline. The point man stepped cautiously out onto the path and veered to the right. The rest of us followed. The going got easier once the trail leveled off and we stopped climbing uphill. I reached for one of the canteens. After swirling some tepid water around in my mouth, I spat it on the ground. Then I drained half the bottle. Damn, it was hot! I wiped the sweat from my brow with the back of a forearm.

The vegetation formed a triple canopy overhead. Dense elephant grass interspersed with other underbrush rose to chest height. Taller shrubs and small trees reached up to about twenty feet. Still larger trees topped out about fifty feet above us. It was deathly still along the trail. The only sound came from the soft buzzing of some insects. I was instinctively aware of the need for noise discipline. I found myself whispering whenever it was necessary to converse with Monaghan.

We caught occasional glimpses of the camp through small gaps in the emerald wall of vegetation. I was astonished to see how every detail of the outpost was clearly visible from this point. When we passed behind the team house I looked down again and saw someone, obviously an American from his height, walking across the compound. No wonder we're patrolling up here, I thought. Can't just sit back and let Charlie watch everything going on below.

We continued steadily along the trail. Monaghan kept glancing back to check on me. My legs trembled with fatigue and there was a distinct coppery taste in my mouth. But I stubbornly nodded my head to let him know that I was OK.

The nung on point suddenly held up his arm and we halted.

Monaghan motioned for me to get down. I scuttled crab-like into a small hollow beside the trail. It stank of rotting plant matter. I pointed the carbine up the trail but saw nothing.

I was impressed with the discipline being shown by these soldiers. No one appeared overly excited. There was no talking or coughing. They just dropped in place and waited. I used the opportunity to drain my first canteen while Monaghan edged up forward to see what had halted us.

There was a shell crater beside the trail directly ahead. It seemed relatively fresh. Probably from one of Moore's H&I missions, I thought. The jungle had an astonishing ability to quickly overgrow artillery damage, much as we would replace a divot on a golf course. This hole would disappear before long, yet at the moment it showed no signs of healing. But there was something else. The lead nung knelt beside Monaghan and pointed out a splash of earth that had been ejected from the crater. It contained a partial sandal print. Someone had been up here, and not long before.

My senses sharpened as quick jolts of adrenaline coursed through my veins. I forgot about my fatigue. Monaghan motioned for us to proceed, but cautiously. We inched slowly forward, weapons held at the ready. My palms were moist, so I alternately wiped each one on my pants legs. My eyes scanned the damp jungle as we moved. I hoped that we weren't walking into an ambush.

We continued on ahead without incident for about fifteen minutes. Finding nothing further, Monaghan decided that we had gone far enough and should return to camp. After a brief rest, he got the patrol turned around and we began working our way back down the hillside. It was much easier going downhill, and we reached the end of the runway in less than thirty minutes. As we walked along the airstrip, Monaghan slapped me on the back and chuckled. I guess he was as relieved as I was that we hadn't run into anything further and were now apparently out of danger.

When we re-entered the compound Monaghan went off to report to Major Ching. I'm sure the Green Beret commander wasn't happy to hear what we had found. The sandal print was an additional piece to the worrisome puzzle that Ching's team was working diligently to solve. Meanwhile I headed for the sleeping bay where I laboriously removed my gear and stowed it. I was feeling quite self-satisfied for having completed the grueling patrol, but physically and mentally exhausted from the hard climb and the stressful experience on the trail. However, I was extremely grateful that it hadn't been much worse. I dropped onto the rack and quickly fell asleep.

The next day we had a very distinguished visitor. Green Beret Captain Roger Donlon, the hero of Nam Dong, flew in to confer with Major Ching. Donlon was still suffering from wounds inflicted the previous month when his camp, the one I had recently visited with Major Crittenden, was nearly overrun by a force of 900 Viet Cong. The word was that the pale and quiet man before us was in line to receive the Medal of Honor for his actions that night.

As Major Crittenden and I entered the team house, Major Ching gestured toward his guest. "Forrest, this is Roger Donlon."

Crittenden offered his hand and said, "Roger, it's a privilege to meet you. I understand you're up for the CMH."

Donlon nodded wordlessly and shook hands with both of us. I was thrilled to meet the man whose actions we had heard about and found so unbelievable. To think that we had played just a very small part in the relief of his camp was extremely satisfying. In December of 1964, Captain Roger Donlon became the first American to win the Medal of Honor in Vietnam when President Lyndon Johnson presented the award in a ceremony at the White House.

Ching swung a couple of chairs alongside the table and motioned for us to sit down. He then told about the night Nam
Dong was attacked. The distant flashes of bursting shells at
Donlon's camp had been clearly visible from A Shau. Ching
had ordered a full alert. The team had spent a nervous night
monitoring the radio for battle reports and watching the light
show to the south.

Donlon said nothing during Ching's monologue. We all
knew the story of Nam Dong by now, and he had little more
to add. But he seemed interested to learn that Crittenden and
I had recently been there, and asked several questions about
the camp. Finally, Ching's interpreter, Minh, came in and put
an end to the discussion. "The Caribou is ready to take off,
Major Ching."

"OK, Ho Chi," said Ching. "Thank you."

Captain Donlon and another officer shook hands all around.
Donlon was scheduled to leave within days for the States. We
walked with the two visiting Green Berets to the main gate.
Donlon waved and then trudged laboriously across to the
landing strip where the Caribou waited. The crew chief stuck
out his hand to help the young captain up the ramp. Once
the tailgate closed, the aircraft quickly took off for the return
flight to Hue.

During the days following our encounter with Captain
Donlon, contact with the enemy was sparse. I had little to
do but send an occasional situation report for Major Crittenden. One particular afternoon Crittenden gave me a routine
message to transmit back to Hue. When I got to the radio
and started sending, I found that the atmospherics were very
bad that day. On top of that, the enemy was jamming our frequency, as usual. It was next to impossible to get a message
through. I tried putting on a headset and using Morse code
(CW). I began to make some progress that way, but it was
very slow.

After an hour passed and I hadn't returned, Crittenden came down to look for me. When I saw him I whipped off the headset. "Communication is really bad, Sir, but I'm making progress. I'll stick with it until they get it."

He nodded appreciatively and headed back to the team house. I returned to work. Eventually Hue rogered, so I shut down the radio and took off. Hoping to avoid boredom and the building heat, I decided to take a nap. I stretched out fully clothed on Patience's bed. A gentle breeze flowed through the open shutters, helping to cool the room. I soon nodded off.

Some time later I awoke with a start. I had been having a recurring dream again. My body felt cool and clammy despite the heat. Cold drops of perspiration clung to my underarms. I sat up laboriously and massaged my eye sockets with clenched fists. The arteries in my temples pulsed violently in tempo with my pounding heart.

The dream had become a nightmare, and it was always the same. First there was total darkness punctuated by wildly-colored flashes of light. Then a strong sensation of vertigo followed, during which I struggled desperately to halt my fall by clutching at threads hanging tantalizingly just beyond my grasp. I was sure that the dream signified my death. But how it would take place and when was unclear, concealed in the murky blackness. I guess that bastard supply corporal in Saigon had gotten far deeper into my mind than I realized. Now I couldn't shake off a growing sense of foreboding. Somehow I knew that I wouldn't survive to go home. I sighed heavily and stood up.

I could hear the low murmur of voices in the team room. The camp seemed relatively quiet, with normal activity restricted by the heat. Two flies were circling just overhead, engaged in a curious buzzing squabble. I swiped at them with my rumpled fatigue hat and they disappeared.

Stepping into the kitchen, I found Ching, Standing and another sergeant chatting. I sat on the bamboo couch and picked up a magazine. I had just begun to flip the pages when Major Crittenden stuck his head in the door.

"Harry... You in there?"

Ching turned. "Yeah, Forrest. What's up?"

Crittenden seemed disturbed. "You, uh, better come down to the ARVN compound," he stammered. "They just got a message from your patrol. One of your men is down."

Ching bolted from the room and dashed off toward the gate. Standing and the other sergeant exchanged apprehensive glances. They had both served for several years with Patience and Cotter, the two who were on the operation.

A haggard Ching returned fifteen minutes later. "Patience is dead," he announced grimly. "Sniper got him through the heart. A med-evac is on the way now to pick him up."

"Goddamn it!" roared Standing. He slammed the table in helpless fury. The usually self-reliant Ching seemed uncertain what to do next. Finally he turned and trudged slowly out through the door.

I peered uneasily at Standing. The team sergeant sat quietly with his elbows on the table and his forehead resting on his cradled hands. I exhaled softly and slipped the magazine back into the rack. I felt like an intruder and wished I could be someplace else—anyplace else. It was an awkward moment. I muttered, "Sarge, I'm sorry." I couldn't think of anything else to say.

Standing looked up in surprise as if he had forgotten that I was in the room. "Thanks, Oliveri." He dropped his head back on his hands. After a short pause, he spoke again without lifting his eyes. "You know, me and Patience were good buddies. We knew each other in the States before we even joined this team. Our families are back in Fort Bragg now. I'm

gonna have to see his wife next month when we go home."
He paused. "What the hell can I tell her? Damn!"

I wished I could think of something comforting to say, but
nothing appropriate came to mind. "Listen," I mumbled, "I'll
move out of his cubicle. I don't think I should be in there now
anyway."

Standing's head shot up. His eyes flashed. "No, damn it!
You stay there. He's dead, and there's not a thing you or me
or anyone else can do to change that." Immediately regretting
his outburst, Standing's voice softened. "Stay there, Oliveri.
Patience wouldn't have minded."

I stood up, wishing to give the sergeant some time to
himself. For want of a reason to leave, I made a pretense of
going down to check on the radio. As I stepped through the
door, I met Crittenden coming up the path.

"You heard about Sergeant Patience?" he asked. I nodded.
"This operation's wrapping up," he continued. "We'll be going
in tomorrow."

I can't say that I was disappointed. I had no desire to stay
in the dead sergeant's quarters. It just didn't seem right.
Someone would have to pack up his gear, and I really didn't
want to be around for that. It would be best for all concerned
if we just went back to Hue.

The remaining team members spent a quiet night in
camp. There was little talk, and none of the usual laughter
and grabass. Several of Patience's closer friends sat silently nursing cans of beer, alone with their pain. Some of the
others turned in earlier than usual. A Shau itself lay hushed
in the tropical darkness. I spent an extremely restless night in
the dead sergeant's bunk, unable to sleep and suffering from
extreme pangs of guilt.

After breakfast the next morning, I packed my bag and then
carried it out into the team room. The Otter was due in at

noon. I checked the ARVN barracks to be sure that the radio was taken down and properly secured for the trip, then returned to the team house. Major Crittenden emerged from the building carrying his gear. I said, "I'll be right with you, Sir." He nodded and continued on to the airstrip

Standing was seated at the table. The team sergeant looked haggard. I said, "Sarge, I'd like to thank you for everything. I hope we'll meet again."

Standing flashed a wan smile. "Thanks, Oliveri. I just hope to hell it isn't in this God-forsaken place."

I walked down to the runway where Crittenden and Ching were standing together. Within minutes, the Otter appeared in the distance, its wings waggling in a slight updraft. The plane made one pass over the camp and then glided in to a soft landing. The pilot taxied over to where we waited, pausing only long enough to toss out a packet of mail to Ching. The major winced when he saw Patience's name on the top envelope. Crittenden and I climbed aboard and waved solemnly to the Special Forces commander. The Otter's engine roared. We began to roll down the runway. As we lifted off, I twisted around in my seat for a last look at the camp. I would never see A Shau again. What a wild place, I thought. I had met some good people there, but I wasn't sorry to leave. And to tell the truth, we hadn't accomplished very much. The operation had yielded only a few stragglers. Our mission would go into the books as a failure, but that was the nature of the war in Vietnam during the summer of 1964.

———

QUICK TRIP
TO TA BAT

K ANE SENT ME BACK TO Ta Bat during the beginning of
September to relieve Yniguez. It would be my third and
final visit there. My brief week at the outpost proved to
be a wild one.

Just prior to my arrival, a resupply Caribou had met disaster at Ta Bat. The aircraft touched down on the undulating runway, quickly unloaded its cargo and then taxied to the
far end of the strip. The pilot gunned the twin engines. The
craft began to pick up speed as it prepared to take off. Then,
for some reason, the plane lost power. Recent rains had left
pools of water on the surface of the runway. That may have
contributed to the problem. By the time it reached the end
of the airstrip, the Caribou had generated just enough lift to
clear the ground.

The plane clawed to a height of about fifty feet. Then it suddenly stalled and began to float back to earth like a deflated
balloon. The Caribou smashed into the jungle several hundred
yards beyond the runway, finally careening to a shattering halt
in the dense undergrowth. A squad of rangers quickly rushed
down the landing strip toward the crash site. Within minutes
they bulled through the thick wet underbrush and reached
the downed aircraft.

Fortunately, the Caribou's gentle descent had spared the
crew from serious injury or death. By the time the Vietnamese

got to them they had extricated themselves from the wreck. The rangers fanned out to form a defensive perimeter around the stunned survivors and the shattered craft. As yet they did not know if the plane had been brought down by hostile fire.

The aircraft appeared to be a total loss. One wing had snapped off at the fuselage, and the prop was snarled in the ten-foot high elephant grass. The tail section pointed skyward at an odd angle. The nose of the craft, decorated with a Playboy bunny, projected from the undergrowth. There had been no fire. The quick-thinking pilot had cut the engines just before impact, thereby preventing an explosion that might have killed them all.

Several of the Vietnamese guided the aviators back to camp while the remaining rangers maintained security around the plane. Within two hours, A Vietnamese Air Force H-34 helicopter dropped down through the overcast to pick up the crew. When I arrived several days later the wreck was still sitting in the jungle. It would remain until the end of the week when it was dismantled and lifted out by a huge "Skyhook" helicopter.

I soon found Captain Cooper, the new advisor, to be an enigma. Stocky and dark-haired, he was a West Point graduate whose military specialty was armor. I couldn't understand why someone with his background was advising an infantry battalion. Cooper must have wondered the same thing. According to him, he was merely a temporary replacement until a permanent advisor became available. He expected to be relieved shortly.

My brief week at the outpost indeed proved to be a wild one. For some reason, nothing of ours had been moved across the runway to "new" Ta Bat. As a result, I found myself back in the same old leaky bunker again. I had no idea that I was about to find out just how leaky it really was.

A typhoon sideswiped the northern provinces early in the week, causing considerable damage along the coast before curving out into the South China Sea. The Special Forces camp at A Shau was so heavily damaged that it had to be completely rebuilt. It would be weeks before the outpost became fully operational again. We lost communications with net control for more than twenty-four hours when Hue's antenna blew down. For the most part, Ta Bat was spared from the high winds by its sheltered location in the A Shau Valley. But we did have heavy rain lasting for more than two days. Under this deluge, the camp quickly dissolved into a morass of red mud. Parts of the airstrip lay under eighteen inches of water. The normally tranquil creek doubled in width and turned a dark brown as the silt-laden storm runoff boiled through. We had been given an early and unwelcome preview of the approaching rainy season.

Shortly after the skies finally cleared, the first Caribou arrived with supplies, including two cases of C-rations. Captain Cooper and I were quite grateful for that, to say the least. Our food supply was virtually non-existent and we had been living on boiled rice and tea. It seems a bit hard to comprehend now, but we were really looking forward to opening some of those little green cans that we normally so despised.

Toward the end of the week trucks began moving down the "Ho Chi Minh Trail" again. I reported the ominous news to Hue. Cooper and I had a long discussion about this development in the evening. I was concerned, recalling what had happened at Nam Dong two months previously.

"I wouldn't worry about it," said Cooper. "There's too much firepower in this valley. The VC would never go up against it."

I didn't share Cooper's confidence. Complacency could get you killed pretty quickly out here. The Otter arrived the next morning with Yniguez on board. My final week at Ta Bat had come to a close.

CONFLICT

KANE HAD MOVED INTO THE hotel while I was at Ta Bat. Sergeant Haight, the billeting non-com, finally tired of Chop's incessant griping and found space for him on one of the upper floors. A sour old SFC named Trano, who was temporarily detached from Da Nang, took over Kane's former room in the commo house. I guess someone at headquarters didn't like the idea of a group of junior enlisted men living unsupervised there.

During my first night back in Hue, Doug, Keller and I were sitting in the living room enjoying a couple of beers while listening to a music tape. It was just past 2100. Sergeant Trano, who had been in bed, suddenly burst into the room wearing only his shorts.

"I want that music turned off now," he growled.

We looked up in surprise. Doug said, "What was that, Sarge?"

"You heard me. I want that fuckin' music shut off now."

Potter glanced quizzically at us and then back at Trano. "OK, Sarge. Didn't know it was bothering you."

Trano snorted and returned to his room. Doug reached across the recorder and turned down the volume. Keller and I looked at each other and shrugged. We resumed our conversation in a more subdued tone as the tape continued to play softly.

Trano stormed back into the room. "Now you three listen to me," he snarled. "If that music isn't turned off right now I'll have your asses in front of the Colonel tomorrow morning."

I rather doubted that. The Colonel certainly had more important things to worry about than our tape recorder. But Keller got up and pushed the recorder's STOP button. "Take it easy, Sergeant Trano. It's off."

Ken had the watch. He turned his back on Trano and stepped into the radio room. Doug and I shook our heads in disgust. With our little gathering now broken up we had no other choice than to go to bed. But I couldn't sleep. I was fuming about Trano. Who the hell was this arrogant ass to throw his weight around like that? Before he did he should have gotten down in the mud and the blood with us. We were the ones who had to risk our necks out in the field while he had a nice cushy job in the rear. He might as well have been back in the States. To my mind he was just another rear-echelon asshole. I had absolutely no respect for the man.

I arose early the next morning before the others and was cleaning my carbine in the living room when Trano emerged from his cubicle. "Morning, Sarge," I said icily. He ignored me.

I nonchalantly pointed the carbine just beyond his ear and yanked back the operating rod. I released the bolt. It slammed home with a sharp clang. Trano flinched. Without saying a word, I had delivered a clear message. He glared angrily at me, and we locked eyes in a brief psychological skirmish. Then our unwelcome visitor turned and stormed out of the house.

It was entirely out of character for me to behave that way, but I didn't care. I wasn't about to let some jackass like Trano intimidate us, not after all we'd been through. Back in the states or even in Da Nang I would never have acted that way toward a senior non-com. But it was different here. In truth, Vietnam was no place for a garrison soldier like Trano. Young draftees like Doug, Tony, Ken and I hadn't been in the Army long enough to experience much else other than duty in the field. Trano should have known better. It was a lot more dangerous to behave like he had out here where almost every man was heavily armed. Being a prick could have its consequences. I'm not sure Sergeant Trano realized that until the moment my rifle bolt slammed home. My only regret was that he might find some way to give us grief because of what I'd done. That never happened. The cranky old sergeant's temporary duty ended two days later and he returned to Da Nang where he was undoubtedly more comfortable in the "chickenshit" environment there. We weren't sorry to see him go.

Shortly after the incident with Trano, Doug and I walked across the bridge and made our way to the local tailor shop. The proprietor was a heavy-set, dark-skinned entrepreneur from India who specialized in supplying custom-made cheap western clothing to the Americans. We called him "the Indian." He catered to his customers by keeping careful records of their measurements and providing quick delivery. Somewhat surprisingly, perhaps, there were many other merchants from his country living in Hue.

Doug and I both needed a couple of light-weight civilian shirts to wear off-duty. Since the Indian already knew our sizes, we had only to select the material we wanted from the huge bolts of cloth in his shop. The shirts would be ready in two days.

As we left the Indian's we ran into Sergeant Harris, the team medic. He greeted us cheerfully. "Hey, where are you guys headed?"

"No place special," answered Doug.

"I'm on my way to the 'Lotus,'" said Harris, referring to a nearby bar frequented by the Americans. "Wanna join me for a beer?"

I glanced at Doug. He shrugged. "Sure."

We walked about a block to the bar and went inside. The interior was poorly lighted and reeked of either stale beer or urine. Two overhead fans spun slowly, barely cooling us as we looked around. Several hostesses wearing thick gobs of makeup sat before a cheap-looking bamboo counter. Their tight-fitting ao dais were dyed various shades of pink, purple, red and green, giving the group the appearance of a faded rainbow. For two bucks you could take any one of them into a private room in the back. They eyed us as we took seats at the end of the bar. One slid off her stool and slinked over to Harris.

"Hey, Joe," she cooed. "You buy me 'Saigon Tea?'"

Harris chuckled. "Nah. Not today, Co." He motioned to the slit-eyed bartender. "Ba Muoi Ba for me and my friends."

Ba muoi ba meant "thirty-three" in Vietnamese. That was also the brand name of a notorious oriental beer. I didn't care much for it. Ba Muoi Ba smelled bad and tasted worse. Rumor had it that it contained formaldehyde. I didn't doubt it. But since this was Harris' buy I said nothing.

The bartender reached beneath the counter and produced three bottles of luke-warm "33." He pried off the bottle caps and slid three grimy glasses across the bar. One quick glance convinced us to drink from the bottles. Harris tossed a packet of piasters on the counter, then took a long pull on his beer. The bar girls watched his every move with broad, insincere smiles plastered on their faces. Harris glanced across at them. "Ah, what the hell. Bartender, give them a drink!"

The girls beamed. It was their job to get customers to buy them drinks. Of course, the bartender never actually served them alcohol. It was usually some concoction containing mainly tea, thus the name for the drink. The girls were paid for the number of drinks they hustled. Normally the Americans disliked being cheated, but Harris was in a good mood that day. After buying another round in return, Doug and I headed for the door, leaving Harris happily chatting with the bar girls.

I had the 1600 to midnight shift. Keller sat in for me while Doug and I scooted up to the hotel for a quick dinner. When we returned it was already past 1800. I sent out a net call, but no one had any traffic. The I Corps area was quiet.

———

FAREWELL TO
THE COLONEL

O CTOBER PASSED IN RELATIVE QUIET. Several new operators arrived, and we took turns breaking them in. Without realizing it, Keller, Thompson, Doug and I had become the team veterans, seemingly overnight. The four of us would have to handle the bulk of the field assignments until these replacements gained some badly needed experience. I certainly empathized with them. I hadn't forgotten how difficult my first two months had been. If I could help them avoid suffering anything similar I was glad to do it.

One night a group of us walked over to the annex to see a movie. Before the film began, Colonel Collins came in to make an announcement. "Men," he began, "Since Sergeant Patience was killed, our forces in I Corps have in turn killed one thousand VC. That's an outstanding accomplishment, and I want to thank each of you for your part in achieving it."

I secretly questioned whether the Colonel's numbers were accurate, but I took him at his word. Having been at A Shau when Patience was killed, I took a special interest in hearing that we had made the enemy pay dearly for his death. In my more quiet moments, I wondered how much more it would take before we were finally satisfied.

At the end of October, two months of political turmoil culminated in widespread riots and protests against the regime of Premier Nguyen Khanh. On November 1st, Ambassador Maxwell Taylor urged Khanh to flee the country. That same day, Tran Van Huong became the new premier of South Vietnam. Khanh chose to ignore Taylor's advice, and remained in Saigon. In the wild world of Vietnamese politics, he was destined to become premier yet again.

The monsoons gradually took hold during early November, and would maintain a watery grip on I Corps until April. In the early stages Hue remained relatively warm, with the cooler weather still several months ahead. But now the typical morning dawned gray and bleak. It drizzled much of the day, often with a period of steady rain late in the afternoon. Sometimes the sun burned through for a few hours, but never lingered long enough to dry out the persistent dampness. The city was dank and clammy, permeated by an odor of decay. In such weather, even people began to rot.

I was irritable. A painful fungus growth in my crotch had kept me awake most of the night. Harris at the dispensary gave me some ointment, but it didn't help much. Nothing did in these conditions.

Keller and I were sitting on the porch of the commo house one gray afternoon quietly watching a steady drizzle fall when Chop Kane pulled up outside in the team jeep. He dashed up the walk and slid into a vacant bamboo chair. Tiny raindrops formed a sheen on his uniform. "The Colonel's going home tomorrow," he announced. "There's gonna be a formation at 1100 in the hotel parking lot so he can say good-bye to the team members. Who's got the morning shift?"

"I do," responded Keller. He and I had been alternating shifts with the replacements while Doug was in Hong Kong on R&R.

I leaned forward. "Hey, I'll go. I like the Colonel."

"Okay," replied Kane. "Don't forget." With that he arose and raced back to the jeep. Chop made a sharp u-turn through a pool of muddy water and then headed back up the street toward the hotel.

The following morning dawned overcast and dreary. A soaking drizzle continued to trickle from the skies. I dressed in a set of fresh fatigues and prepared to walk to the hotel, wondering if the rain would threaten the ceremony. Just before 1100, as if on cue, the drizzle ceased. Within minutes hazy sunlight shone weakly through the thinning cloud cover. I pulled on my cap, glanced skeptically at the skies and stepped off the porch.

Perhaps two dozen soldiers were assembled in the hotel parking lot. They stood silently in a loose formation of three ranks with their backs to the street. I entered the main gate and took my place in the rear row. Nobody spoke. We waited quietly until Colonel Collins emerged from the hotel promptly at 1100 accompanied by two aides. Someone called the waiting group to attention.

The Colonel strode to the front of the first rank and faced the men, the silver eagles on his collar glinting in the pale sunshine. He paused before every soldier, thanking each for his service to the advisory team. The men saluted him in return. Several offered brief comments. Collins proceeded along each row repeating the process. When he reached me I saluted smartly. "Good luck, Sir."

The ceremony had obviously touched Collins. When he spoke, his voice was constricted with emotion. "Thank you," he exclaimed. "Thank you very much."

The Colonel shook my hand and then moved on down the line. When he had bid farewell to the last man, he clambered into his jeep and was whisked to the Citadel airfield where an aircraft waited to fly him to Saigon. As Collins' vehicle disappeared around the corner, someone dismissed the group. The parking lot cleared within minutes. After heroically struggling to break through the cloud cover, the over-matched sun vanished as quickly as the departing advisory team members.

I trudged slowly back to the commo house, suffering a mild bout of depression. The miserable weather certainly didn't help my mood. My own departure still seemed so far off as to be almost unimaginable. And things were growing progressively worse. The prophesy of that jackass supply corporal in Saigon continued to haunt me, especially at night when ominous dreams still disturbed my sleep.

I forced myself to turn my thoughts to Colonel Bissett, the new senior advisor. Bissett was a man of medium height and build, considerably smaller in stature than Collins. He appeared cool and somewhat aloof, the complete antithesis of his popular predecessor. It remained to be seen what type of soldier he was.

Back in the states, meanwhile, the presidential election campaign was in full swing. Another leader, Lyndon Johnson, was about to bury Barry Goldwater in one of the greatest political landslides of all time. The prevailing opinion among the advisory team members favored Johnson's re-election. As one career sergeant put it, "No way I want Goldwater to get in. That prick will toss atom bombs around here like firecrackers. Man, all I want is to finish my year and go the hell home." Most of us echoed his crude sentiments.

When Johnson was finally assured of four more years, he prepared to shift the war into high gear. The change would not be long in coming.

As we got deeper into our tours, Keller, Doug, Tony Thompson and I gradually began to think of ourselves as somewhat elite. It wasn't something we discussed openly or flaunted, but simply an attitude of quiet confidence that manifested itself in our professional performance, a performance seemingly immune to petty distractions and even dangerous situations.

Supposedly only the best ended up in Vietnam, but in reality we knew that wasn't true. We had met too many assholes to believe that. In any case, we were becoming rather clannish, never getting as close to the new team members as we did to each other. It was just too painful to think about possibly losing a friend, so we tried to avoid that by not making any new ones.

In mid-November, Chop Kane began to break up the clan. Thompson went to Quang Tri where he was assigned to the ARVN 2nd Regiment as Lt. Mowrey's commo man. Quite frankly, I would have been happy to get that assignment myself and have the chance to reunite with Mowrey. I envied my friend.

The weather deteriorated steadily through the latter part of the month. Thick overcast and steady drizzle kept daytime temperatures in the low sixties, almost arctic compared to what we had become accustomed to during the dry season. On Thanksgiving Day, the clouds parted and a brilliant sun briefly warmed the city, imparting a more cheerful atmosphere to the holiday.

We enjoyed a full turkey dinner later that afternoon in the hotel dining room. It was not necessarily the way we would have preferred to celebrate, but it wasn't too bad. Those Americans who could be spared came into the city for the day. Helicopters carried complete meals in insulated containers to those remaining in the field. Doug, Keller and I had no idea that this was to be our last opportunity to enjoy a meal together in Vietnam. Two days later, Kane sent Keller and me to Quang Tri.

———

QUANG TRI

T HE DETACHMENT CARRY-ALL MADE SEVERAL trips each week between Hue and Quang Tri. Keller and I boarded the vehicle in the hotel parking lot around 1000 hours. We threw our gear into the back of the van and then found seats inside. We were the only passengers. The chubby, balding sergeant who drove the vehicle pulled out as soon as we settled in. He called out over his shoulder that he expected to make Quang Tri by noon.

Keller glanced at me with a twinkle in his eye. "Well," he said, "at least they can't send us any further north." I chuckled. We both knew full well that the next stop beyond Quang Tri was the DMZ.

About fifteen miles out of Hue, Highway 1 crossed a culvert bridge over a shallow ravine. As we approached we saw ARVN military police (QCs) on the road warning traffic to slow down. A wrecker was operating on the bridge, blocking one of the two lanes. It was lifting the chassis of a military truck from the bottom of the ravine. This created a bottleneck by forcing the opposing lines of traffic to share the one remaining lane.

Keller and I jockeyed for a better view as the van inched forward. The truck had evidently hit a mine and plunged over the side of the ravine. When we finally inched our way onto the bridge, the wrecker crew had just finished attaching a cable to the shattered vehicle. A crowd had gathered at the side of the road, and children chattered in excitement as the wrecker boom lifted the smashed truck several feet from the mud. We were unable to see anything further once the carry-all passed across the far end of the bridge and continued on its way.

A short distance further up Highway 1 we passed an old steam-engine train headed south on the railroad tracks that ran parallel to the road. The rickety locomotive, most likely abandoned by the Japanese at the end of World War II when their army left Indo-China, belched a plume of black smoke as it hauled six or seven battered freight cars toward Hue. It was the only train I saw during my stay in Vietnam.

We pulled into the advisors compound at Quang Tri about an hour later. The small American team there lived in a double row of one-story barracks constructed of plywood paneling topped by sheets of corrugated iron roofing. The structures resembled beach cabanas I had seen back on Long Island. The alleyway between the buildings contained two concrete troughs set in the ground just beneath the roof over-hang. During the monsoons, rainwater cascaded in torrents from the metal roofing into the troughs, and then ran off into the nearby rice paddies.

To my eye, the compound itself seemed isolated and exposed. On one side was a large open soccer field used oc-casionally as a helicopter landing pad. To the rear of the bar-racks lay a network of rice fields roughly three hundred yards in width. Several small thatched huts were visible just beyond the edge of the paddy water. Farmers tended the rice shoots during the day, often working in shin-deep water alongside plodding water buffaloes. There was no telling how many of them also carried old SKS rifles and two or three rounds of ammunition after dark.

The city of Quang Tri itself was little more than a squalid shanty town, its streets crammed with the usual complement of shabby bars that catered to Americans and Vietnamese alike.

Cheap shops stocked black market goods, mainly American soaps, toothpaste, canned food, soda and inexpensive electronic equipment. Other merchants dispensed soup and rice dishes from shallow store fronts, the Vietnamese equivalent of western fast-food restaurants. The city was actually a miniature version of Hue, complete with its own moat-encircled citadel. But Quang Tri lacked the beauty and charm of the ancient imperial capital.

Keller and I found the sergeant in charge of quarters. We inquired about Thompson, only to learn that he was out in the field. We also discovered that living space was at a premium in the tiny facility. There were no vacant rooms. The sergeant shrugged. We would have to share quarters with someone. He offered to squeeze second beds into two of the narrow cubicles. It would be a very tight fit, but the non-com didn't seem too concerned. "Sorry 'bout that," he said with a mocking grin. We knew he wasn't.

The sergeant's attitude annoyed me. We had seen this sort of thing many times before. I could understand why some of the field soldiers referred to these "back-office" types as "REMFs," or "Rear Echelon Mother-Fuckers." They never had to go out into the bush and were rarely, if ever, exposed to enemy contact. Some of them completed their entire tours without ever hearing a shot fired in anger. I resented their condescending attitude toward those of us who had. Was it a feeling of inadequacy that caused this sergeant to treat us that way, because we had experienced the field duty that he had not? Or did he jealously regard us as just some over-rated "glory-hounds" who needed to be brought down a peg? Whatever the reason, there were many like him. And I, in spite of the danger I faced in my job, was quite happy not to be counted among them.

As for the problem with quarters, I wasn't all that much concerned. Since half of us would probably be out in the field at any particular time, I didn't think privacy would be much of a problem. I was right about that.

The asshole sergeant thought he was screwing me by assigning me to share Thompson's room, but I was actually delighted. However, when I saw the cramped eight by ten foot cubicle, I knew that my friend wasn't going to be very happy about the arrangement. The thought brought a wicked grin to my face.

Keller drew quarters with Maxwell, who was on duty in the radio shack. After dropping off our gear in our new rooms, we set out to find our fellow "Frost Weed Bravo" member.

The commo shack was a small stucco shed about eight feet square situated on a concrete slab at the rear of the compound. There was just room enough inside for a table, two benches to hold radio equipment and a couple of chairs. Perhaps three men could fit into the room, but like everything else in the compound, it was a tight squeeze.

Maxwell was waiting at the door, seeming very glad to see us. He had received a message from Doug that we were on our way. We shook hands enthusiastically.

I edged inside to the radio and picked up the handset, flicking the "transmit" switch with my other hand. The Angry/9 emitted a whirring hum. "Frost Weed Alpha, this is Frost Weed Bravo. Over."

Doug's disembodied voice blared from the speaker. "Roger Bravo. Alpha here. Is that Romeo Oscar Oscar (Radio Operator Oliveri)? Over."

"That's affirmative, Alpha. Just wanted to let you know we arrived safely. Anyone miss us yet? Over."

Potter's chuckle was clearly audible as he replied. "Only the cowboy girls. How are things up along the Delta Mike

Zulu (DMZ)? Over."

"Not bad so far, Alpha. Maybe we'll get to see you for Christmas. Over."

"Roger, Bravo. You keep in touch now. Over."

"That's a copy, Alpha. Give us a call if you need any expert technical advice. Bravo out." I put the mike down gently and turned off the transmit switch. I was going to miss Doug.

Maxwell could scarcely conceal his delight at our arrival. He had been working twelve hour shifts seven days a week before we got to Quang Tri. Thompson was the only other radio operator assigned there, but he was out in the field with Lt. Mowrey most of the time. Whenever he came in for a few days, Tony would generously offer to take a shift in order to give Maxwell a break.

One of the reasons Kane had given for moving Keller and me to Quang Tri was to put Frost Weed Bravo on the air around the clock. The net was expanding. But wretched atmospheric conditions, particularly at night, made reception difficult. Stations in the northern sector of the net often had difficulty reaching Hue. With Communist activity increasing throughout the area, I Corps needed Quang Tri functioning after dark as a backup for net control. Since we were closer to the more distant outposts, theoretically we should be better able to communicate with them. The idea was good, but in reality, it didn't always work out that way.

Keller, Maxwell and I quickly devised a schedule employing three eight hour shifts. By the first week of December, we had settled into a new and more workable routine.

Thompson came in from the field shortly after our arrival and we had a minor reunion. After laughingly threatening to throw me out of his room, Tony told us a wild story. Some time earlier he had ordered a device from Sears Roebuck to convert his carbine to full automatic. When it arrived, he installed it quickly before going out on an operation.

ARVN had located a VC unit near Cua Viet in northeast Quang Tri Province. For once, they moved rapidly against the enemy, likely at the urging of American advisors. The 2nd Regiment assembled a powerful force of armored personnel carriers, jeeps mounted with .50 caliber machineguns and various other vehicles. The convoy moved out during the night, inching cautiously into position just before dawn. At first light they advanced against a small village suspected of harboring Communist guerrillas. A VC unit temporarily quartered in the hamlet was taken by surprise, but reacted quickly.

Thompson was riding with Lt. Mowrey as the allied force accelerated up the dirt road leading toward the enemy hamlet. Their jeep was near the middle of the column. Suddenly they were startled by the ear-splitting crack of a rocket bursting against the side of the lead APC. The convoy immediately ground to a halt.

Confused shouting erupted all along the length of the column. More rocket blasts and volleys of AK-47 fire added to the chaos. Several ARVN soldiers were caught in a cross-fire and killed. Veteran non-coms shrieked at their troops, frantically urging them to use their weapons. Frightened soldiers slowly began to put out return fire. The enemy fusillade slackened almost immediately.

Thompson dived out of the jeep and scrambled into the brush at the side of the road. Brambles tore into his forearms and shins, inflicting jagged scratches and angry red welts. But adrenaline was coursing through his veins. He felt nothing.

Twenty yards ahead and to his right a black-clad VC soldier wearing a cone hat arose from the undergrowth, preparing to fire an RPG-2 rocket. Thompson raised his carbine and squeezed the trigger. There was a hollow click. Tony yanked on the operating rod and chambered another round. Again the weapon failed to fire.

The Viet Cong launched his rocket. Smoke swirled around his head as the missile sped toward its target and exploded with a thunderclap. He pivoted slightly and spotted Thompson. Their eyes met momentarily, and then the enemy soldier disappeared back into the thick elephant grass. Tony's heart pounded wildly in his chest.

The VC ambush was a delaying tactic. A squad had formed a rear guard that attacked the column while the main body fled from Cua. Now they too began to melt away. Heavy fire continued to crackle from the South Vietnamese, but their targets were gone.

Thompson edged back to the road and saw Mowrey on the far side of the jeep. The lieutenant was shouting and gesturing at his counterpart, urging him to send his troops in pursuit. But the ARVN captain was in no hurry to yank the tail of the tiger. He momentarily ignored the American's advice. While the two argued, Thompson tossed the carbine into the back of the jeep with disgust, grateful that he still had his .45.

Several crucial minutes passed before Mowrey was finally able to spur the Vietnamese officer to action. Once the captain agreed to engage the VC, he made a great show of shouting orders at his subordinates, who then dashed off with their instructions. The troops began to move. The APCs and jeeps swung around toward the side of the road. At a signal from the commander, the entire line darted forward into the underbrush.

It was now full daylight. The lethal-looking vehicles bucked and plunged across the uneven ground. Each left a narrow trail of flattened saw grass in its wake. The jeep now carrying Mowrey and Thompson followed behind the advancing skirmish line.

The attack force rolled quickly past the small village. Just beyond its outskirts lay several crude earthen bunkers. The well-concealed mounds, topped with grass, appeared to have been occupied recently. An APC smashed into one of them, shearing off its top with a bone-jarring impact. ARVN supporting infantry dropped grenades into the opening, where they exploded with muffled thumps. There was no movement inside the bunker.

The task force snarled onward in a shallow U-shaped formation. Suddenly three black-clad figures bolted from the undergrowth midway between the points of the U in a desperate attempt to escape the onrushing strike force. The .50 caliber machineguns and lighter .30s on the APCs opened fire almost simultaneously. Orange tracer sticks flicked out toward the fleeing VC. For an instant, the bullet stream flailed the ground at their feet. Then the heavy slugs rose up and shredded the doomed men. The pursuers rolled over and past the shattered bodies.

The attackers were now overcome with blood lust. Gunners whooped and cheered as their vehicles bounced along, unhindered now by any return fire. They began to trigger long bursts indiscriminately in all directions. Here and there they flushed small groups of the enemy from cover and mowed them down like targets in a shooting gallery. Thompson found himself caught up in the excitement of the moment. It was almost like a cavalry charge, he thought. All they needed was someone to blow a bugle.

The line continued to plunge ahead until it reached a dense tree line. Unable to penetrate further, the vehicles slowed and then turned about. They retraced their path, alertly watching for live VC. There were none.

ARVN infantrymen swarmed across the battlefield. They trussed up the enemy bodies with commo wire and carried them back to the main road suspended from "chogey sticks." Just like a big game hunt, thought Thompson wryly.

Once the foot soldiers had completed their work, thirty-two VC corpses lay stacked at the side of the road. Everyone was elated. At this stage of the war, it was one of the largest enemy body counts yet recorded in I Corps. The news reverberated all the way to Saigon. *Stars and Stripes,* the military newspaper, even sent a reporter to cover the great victory. The battle received extensive coverage in the next issue. It was an experience Thompson would never forget, and one that made the timid Vietnamese captain a national hero.

———

FLIGHT TO KHE SANH

T O QUALIFY FOR COMBAT PAY, radio operators needed six days each month subject to the threat of hostile fire. As a result, we often volunteered to fly resupply or spotter missions to earn the extra $55. Most of the time it was easy money.

I Corps was relatively quiet in December. By mid-month we were becoming quite restless. The rainy season was in full swing, and bright days were few and far between. Maxwell and I took advantage of one dry morning to drive up Highway 1 to Dong Ha. Lieutenant Greg Foster flew the province "milk run," and we planned to meet his L-19 aircraft there. I knew Lt. Foster from Hue and had flown with him on several occasions. He had, after all, helped me out at Ta Bat by flying in that new generator to replace the one I had been unable to start. Foster was a regular guy, only a year or so older than me, and I liked him a lot.

We waited at the airstrip for about an hour before Foster descended from the leaden skies, his tiny plane dipping and waggling as it passed through some capricious air currents on the way down. After he was safely on the ground, Maxwell and I walked out to greet him. "Hey, Lieutenant," I shouted. "Where the hell have you been?"

Foster hopped down from the cockpit and removed his helmet. "A little respect for an officer, if you please."

I made a rude sound. "Yeah, very little respect."

The pilot laughed. He seemed genuinely pleased to see us. "How are you bums doing? I was wondering when I'd run into you guys up here. Hey, Ollie... screwed up any generators lately?"

I laughed at the good-natured insult and shook his hand.

A Vietnamese courier was waiting beside a jeep at the edge of the runway. Foster handed him a packet of mail for the advisory team. The ARVN soldier accepted it without a word, clambered into his jeep, and then drove off.

Foster glanced up at the overcast sky. "Listen," he said, "I've got to get out to Khe Sanh before the weather changes. Either of you want to come along for the ride?"

"Hell, yes," I answered, knowing full well that I needed a couple of flights to qualify for December's combat pay. I turned to Maxwell. "Do you mind, Max? We shouldn't be too long."

"No problem," yawned Maxwell. "I can crap out here for a while." He glanced back at the jeep, scoping out the back seat as a promising site for a nap.

I climbed into the rear seat of the "Bird Dog" behind Foster. While he prepared for takeoff, I spread a flak jacket on the seat and settled in on top of it. The little L-19 had no armor. If we encountered any ground fire, the flak jacket would prevent me from taking a round in the balls. At least I hoped so. I slipped on a set of headphones as Foster revved the engine. We began rolling down the runway and quickly lifted off into a mounting overcast.

Foster followed Highway 9 west. About fifteen minutes out of Dong Ha, the pilot keyed the intercom. "Hey, Ollie... You see those elephants down there?"

I squinted through the left window at the green terrain passing below. "No. Where?"

"Hang on a second." Foster banked the aircraft and threw it into a long, curving glide. "Right down there to our left."

I focused on the ground a thousand feet below. I saw nothing but green jungle. "I don't see anything. Are you busting my chops or what?"

Foster pulled out of the sideslip. "Aw, for Chrissake! You guineas must be blind. Something in the genes, I think." He resumed a westerly course, still muttering in mock anger.

I chuckled. "Elephants, my ass," I mumbled, making sure to key the mike so Foster could hear me. I still wasn't sure if he was giving me the business or not. In military jargon "seeing the elephant" was a metaphor commonly used to describe a soldier's first combat experience. I wondered if Foster was just breaking my balls.

We continued west toward the Special Forces camp at Khe Sanh. When the runway appeared below, Foster gestured downward. His voice crackled over the intercom. "Hey, Mr. Magoo... can you see that?" I gave him the finger.

We circled the camp once, and then descended rapidly toward the landing strip. From the air, Khe Sanh closely resembled A Shau. There were similar towering hills to the west. A narrow river, the Rao Quang, ran past the outpost, much as the Rao Lao did at camp A Shau. I was struck by the almost uncanny resemblance.

Foster throttled back on the engine, a maneuver that always made me uncomfortable. It seemed like we had lost power and were in an uncontrolled dive. We coasted downward, the only sound coming from the soft whooshing of air flowing over the wings as we glided toward the landing strip.

Foster brought the Bird Dog in for a gentle touchdown. The main gates of the camp were on our left roughly at the midpoint of the runway. Lt. Foster cut his engine and halted just opposite the barbed wire entrance. Several Green Beret noncoms approached the craft. One of them called out, "How ya doing, Lieutenant?"

Foster waved. "Okay, Coffey. Everything number one here?"

The sergeant nodded. "Yeah, not bad." He peered expectantly into the cockpit. "You got some mail for us?"

Foster reached down and then tossed out a tan leather packet. "Here you go."

Coffey grinned. "Thanks, Lieutenant." He passed up some outgoing letters. " You coming in for something cold?"

"I'll take a rain check. Got to get my passenger here back to Dong Ha. I'll see you in a couple of days."

"Roger. You take care now." The Green Berets turned and headed back into the camp, anxious to open the mailbag.

Foster was in a hurry. Fog was beginning to build up along the ridgeline, and a fine drizzle had started to fall. He wanted to get clear of the area before conditions worsened. As it was, we would have to fly lower than normal to stay beneath the thickening clouds. That wasn't a good thing. It would make us a better target. I absently checked the position of the flak jacket beneath my butt.

We took off into a steadily descending overcast. About five minutes out of Khe Sanh, Foster's voice crackled in my earphones. "We're taking some ground fire." He sounded cool and detached.

I swung my head back and forth in confusion. I hadn't seen or heard anything. Then I spotted it. Far below, a bright orange pinpoint seemed to float lazily up toward us, accelerating as it approached. Finally the tracer round snapped by, about twenty yards off our left wing tip.

The earphones sputtered again. "Not even close!"

Bullshit! It was close enough. I hunched lower in my seat and squeezed my legs together, wishing there was something more substantial than a flak jacket under my ass.

"I'll check the coordinates," said Foster. "Maybe Khe Sanh can put a couple of rounds on him."

He swung the plane into a compact turn while he examined his map, and then radioed a report back to the Special Forces camp. I would have preferred to have gotten the hell out of there, but my opinion didn't count. I was just along for the ride. The mortar crews at Khe Sanh would mark the target, but they couldn't fire until we cleared the area for fear of hitting our craft.

Foster turned back on course to the east. Behind us, I imagined the 81s barking salvoes at the unseen sniper. Hope they ruin your day, Charlie, I thought with satisfaction.

We continued on to Dong Ha without further incident, descending toward the runway just ahead of the approaching bad weather. As the little plane touched down, I spotted our jeep. Maxwell was sacked out in the back seat, with his brown and green jungle boots protruding from the vehicle.

I popped out of the craft, happy to be back on the ground. Foster hopped down beside me. "Thanks for flying 'Foster Airlines,'" he cackled.

I glared at him. "Yeah, right. Elephants...ground fire. Next time I'll go with someone else."

Foster chuckled again and set about securing the tiny plane. He had decided to spend the night in Quang Tri rather than risk continuing on to Hue in the worsening weather. When the pilot was satisfied with the disposition of his craft, Maxwell drove us back to the compound. It had been a long day.

I was feeling tired later when I took over my watch, so I brought a big thermos of coffee into the radio shack. The net was quiet. I used the time to write a few letters and catch up on my reading. After a while my eyes began to feel heavy and my head started to droop. I drank two cups of coffee in an attempt to stay alert.

Just before midnight a tremendous roaring explosion sent me springing to my feet. I dashed outside to see what the hell had happened. A huge fire blazed brilliantly on the far side of the rice paddy behind the compound, illuminating the distant figures of running men and a towering column of smoke. I stared in disbelief at the spectacle.

The sergeant on CQ duty suddenly burst into the alleyway. "Everybody up! Alert! Everybody get up!" Lights began to snap on. I ducked back into the radio shack for my carbine.

The compound was a beehive of activity. Armed men rushed to the perimeter, ready to defend the installation if necessary. Excited soldiers whispered nervously about sappers or a mortar attack. Or perhaps this was just a diversion to draw attention away from something else. We waited apprehensively for whatever might yet develop.

An hour later the fire on the far side of the paddy burned itself out. Nothing further happened. Word finally came down that an ARVN truck had triggered a mine up the road. It had been a big one, possibly devised from a dud artillery shell. Three Vietnamese soldiers were dead and the truck was a total loss. With the threat of an attack seemingly past, men began to drift back to their beds. I took one last look at the smoldering wreck and then returned to the radio shack to complete my watch. Thankfully the remainder of the night was quiet, but I needed no further coffee to stay awake.

Two weeks later, Lt. Greg Foster's plane disappeared while flying near the A Shau Valley, possibly as a result of enemy ground fire. I never heard if any wreckage was found or if Foster was rescued. But none of us ever saw him again. Recently I checked the database of the names on the Vietnam Memorial, but Greg Foster isn't listed. According to the criteria for inclusion on "The Wall," accidental deaths in the combat zone qualified. If Foster was lost in a crash not related to enemy fire, he should still have been listed. Or, considering how the "fog of war" can cloud many issues, maybe he didn't perish after all. I've never been able to clarify that and it remains an unresolved mystery to this day.

———————

HOLIDAYS

CHRISTMAS WAS APPROACHING. IN MID-DECEMBER, I received a welcome surprise. Orders arrived from Saigon promoting me to Specialist 4th Class. It was an unexpected but much appreciated advancement, so I rushed off to the PX to find new insignia. The promotion also meant an increase in pay of about $30 a month.

I decided to call Doug in Hue to find out if he had also gotten the same orders. I reached for the land line and cranked the handle. Now you have to understand that the telephone system in Vietnam was horrendous. First you had to know the code name for the facility you wished to contact. The Quang Tri compound was "Wolf," and I wanted to reach "Eagle," the switchboard in Hue. Sometimes the call had to be routed through a series of switchboards. It was an extremely tenuous arrangement. The call could be easily disconnected at any number of points. Switchboard operators frequently checked open lines by plugging into them and saying "Working." If there was no response they broke the connection. Sometimes a caller was cut off even if he did respond. I had been disconnected several times in mid-conversation. It was maddening.

The switchboard answered, "Wolf."

"Wolf, this is the radio room. Can you get me Eagle?"

There was a brief pause and then I heard a distant click in the receiver. "Eagle."

"Eagle, this is Wolf. Let me have the radio room."

The line crackled softly three times until Doug picked up. "MACV Radio, Specialist Potter."

"Hey, Douglas, it's Jim. Specialist Potter? Don't tell me they promoted a loser like you!"

Doug cackled. "Yeah, the orders just came in this morning. How about you?"

The operator cut in. "Working."

"Working," I replied, thinking that we had better make this fast. "Yeah, I got mine too. Congratulations."

"Thanks. That should make us…"

"Working."

"Working, goddammit! Doug did you…:

Click.

"Doug? Doug?" That was the extent of our conversation. I put down the phone and sadly shook my head. It was pointless to get angry over this.

Christmas week brought mixed emotions. We all came in from the field for a couple of days, one of the rare but enjoyable times that the entire team was together. Yet, this would be my first Yule away from my family, and I was feeling homesick. The penetrating heat of the dry season was gone, but it still seemed too warm for Christmas. There was probably snow back home by now, I thought. To get everyone into the spirit, we planned a big party for Christmas Eve.

Ken and I went to the PX and bought beer, soda, pretzels and a box of foot-long cigars that smelled like they were made from equal parts of stinkweed and horse manure. Maxwell and Thompson purchased some hard liquor and other snacks. We set up everything in our tiny room. It was going to be cramped, but we'd manage. We were all determined to make this a holiday to remember.

Just after sundown, we began to gather in the cubicle. We used Tony Thompson's recorder to play a tape I'd recently received from my friend Richie, featuring many of the latest hit songs in the States. He used a clever disk-jockey style, complete with folksy chatter and one-liners. "...And this song is dedicated to our boys in Vietnam," it went. "Stay alert, guys, and don't let any Viet Cong through the lines!" That drew a hearty laugh. If only Richie knew that there were no lines over here. The bastards were everywhere. That thought quickly flew out of my mind. There would be no time for negativity this night.

We enjoyed the tape so much that we played it over and over again. I opened the box of cigars and handed out a few. We lit up the unusual stogies and puffed away until the room filled with swirling clouds of rotten-smelling smoke. For some reason I found that hilarious and broke into a hearty laugh.

Keller opened a letter from his wife and read parts of it to us. We all savored this personal connection with home and normalcy. If anyone had a right to feel down tonight it was certainly Ken, the only married man in the group. Yet here he was trying to cheer up the rest of us. I felt a glow of affection for the tall, lanky Ohio native. Thompson and Maxwell took out Christmas cards they had received from home and passed them around. It was a bittersweet moment, but we all felt better for sharing it. I guess maybe we were becoming a little maudlin, because Keller finally cracked a joke to break the mood.

A knock on the door interrupted our raucous laughter. I opened it to find two Australian warrant officers, Dave Walner and Anthony Morrissey, standing in the hallway. Walner roared, "Merry Christmas, mate! Can we come in?"

I was delighted. "Hell, yes! Come on in and have a cigar! They stink so bad none of us want to smoke them anyway!"

We all liked the happy-go-lucky Aussies. They were always friendly and full of fun. Although considered officers, many of

them were actually career enlisted men, and felt more comfortable among us than with the American brass. Walner and
Morrissey squeezed onto Tony's bunk, opened cans of beer,
and joined in the uproarious laughter. I sliced up a pepperoni
I had gotten in a package from home and passed it around.

There was another rap on the door. Tony opened it this time
and found a young Marine corporal and a black PFC from the
motor pool outside. "We heard you guys laughing," said the
Marine. "Sounds like you're having a good time in here."

Tony gestured toward the others. "Come on in!"

Between guffaws I bellowed across the room, "Hey Tony,
you better leave the door open!"

Thompson brought out a fruitcake his family had sent him
and sliced it up with his bush knife. Nobody back home ever
actually ate fruitcake, but here it was a welcome delicacy.
I took a piece and thought it was the best thing I had ever
tasted. I guess Christmas can do that to you.

Before long, several more lonely advisors drifted in to share
the holiday cheer. I looked around the room in disbelief. It
was wall-to-wall people. I never would have imagined that
our tiny cubicle could hold so many. Soldiers sat everywhere
with their arms around each other's shoulders, drinking beer,
nibbling on the modest Yule fare, and just enjoying the fun.
For one night, at least, the horrors of war were forgotten. At
one point we spontaneously broke into a chorus of "Silent
Night." It was one of the most poignant Christmas moments
I have ever experienced, before or since.

I reached over and grasped Ken's hand. "Merry Christmas,
buddy."

He nodded gently. "You too, man. Let's hope the next one
will be in a better place."

"Amen to that."

As the party in Quang Tri reached its peak, Viet Cong terrorists were carrying out an attack against U.S. personnel in

Saigon. Two Communist agents disguised as ARVN soldiers drove an explosives-laden vehicle beneath the Brinks Hotel, where American officers were housed. A timing device triggered a powerful blast at 1745 hours, just when the building figured to be most crowded. Army personnel suffered two dead and fifty-eight wounded.

The explosion reverberated all the way to the White House. Ambassador to South Vietnam Maxwell Taylor recommended that President Johnson approve an appropriate retaliation against the North. But the president turned him down. He did, however, indicate that he was seriously considering the commitment of U.S. combat troops to Southeast Asia. There were still just 23,000 Americans in South Vietnam, but the onset of a massive build-up was only scant months away.

The week between Christmas and New Years was relatively uneventful except for a visit from the actor Raymond Burr of *Perry Mason* fame. Burr spent an entire evening in the detachment club chatting with the troops and seeming to enjoy himself immensely. He was just a regular guy, and we appreciated that.

Ken, Maxwell and I resumed working eight hour shifts. I dared to begin thinking more frequently about going home. When I first arrived in Vietnam, a year had seemed so long as to be unimaginable. But now, with only four months left, the end of my tour was actually in sight. If I could just manage to stay in Quang Tri, the last few months would be comparatively easy duty.

Our detachment had a New Years party planned in the compound bar. The Quang Tri facility was too small to have separate clubs for the officers and enlisted men, so we shared one. Nobody seemed to mind. The festivities were scheduled to begin that evening at 2200 hours. Maxwell had the shift to midnight, with Keller slated to take over until 0800 when I was due to relieve him. With this schedule, I was the only one who would be able to enjoy the entire party.

But I was in no rush to get there, and strolled into the club about half an hour late, when things were already going full blast. I said hello to the guys and found a seat at the bar. It was New Years Eve, and I was in the mood to celebrate.

An Army captain I knew vaguely eased onto the stool beside me. "Hello, Oliveri. How are you?"

I turned toward him and smiled. "Not bad, Captain Rennert," I replied, pleased with myself for having remembered his name. "How about yourself?"

"So far, so good. Can I buy you a drink?"

Normally I wasn't much of a drinker, but I didn't want to appear impolite. "Sure. Thanks."

I ordered a rum and coke from the obnoxious Vietnamese bartender, who always seemed to have a sneer on his face. I wasn't about to let that sour little fart spoil my night. He slid my glass across the counter with a scowl. I just smiled at him, although I wanted to wring his scrawny neck. This holiday meant nothing to him. Tet, his New Year, was still a month away.

The multi-colored juke box behind the bar was blaring away. I stared at its lights reflecting in the mirror behind the bar. Rennert leaned forward to make himself heard above the pounding music. "Oliveri, if you don't mind my asking, have you ever considered making a career of the Army?"

I put down my drink. Now THAT was a hell of a question. I paused before answering. "To be honest with you, Sir, I have thought about it."

Rennert perked up. "And?"

"It's not for me. I just want to finish my enlistment so I can get on with my life. Why do you ask?"

Rennert pointed to the blue and silver CIB above my left breast pocket. "You've already got something many a career man would give his left nut for."

I ran my finger along the horizontally engraved rifle. I never talked about it, but I was very proud to wear the Combat Infantry Badge. "You're probably right about that, Sir. But I wouldn't stay in as an enlisted man. What could I expect... twenty years and a staff sergeant's stripes?"

Rennert shrugged. "There's OCS."

I shook my head. "Not for me. I'd have to extend. I'm not ready to do that."

"That's too bad. I think you'd do well."

"Thanks, Captain. But to tell you the truth, I don't think I could handle it. The constant traveling, not knowing where you're gonna be tomorrow." The liquor was beginning to loosen my tongue. "I've seen too many lonely and unhappy soldiers, especially during the holidays. It's just not the life for everyone."

Rennert stared into his glass. "Well, I can't argue with that. I've spent a few Christmases away from my wife and kids." He picked up a pack of cigarettes from the bar, tapped one out and lit it. "But military life does have its rewards."

"That's true. I've already gotten a lot out of it." I swirled my drink with a little plastic straw. The ice tinkled softly. "In fact, I'm glad I came over here. I'm just beginning to realize that now. But it's not something I'd like to make a career of."

"You might be making a mistake."

"How so?"

"The Army needs bright young men. There's a real future in the service for someone like you."

I chuckled. "I don't know about that. There were times when I wasn't real good at my job. I was a disaster when I first got here. It took me a while to become competent."

Rennert furrowed his eyebrows. "But you did. That's the important thing. With your record you could probably call the shots."

I laughed sarcastically. Rennert was beginning to annoy me. "You sound like my recruiting sergeant."

Rennert flashed a sheepish grin. "Yeah, I guess I'm full of shit, huh? Sorry, I didn't mean to stick my nose in your business."

I felt a pang of remorse. Rennert was just another lonely soldier away from home looking to make conversation. My annoyance began to slip away. "No sweat, Sir. Tell you what... let me buy you a drink."

"Sure." He seemed genuinely appreciative.

I signaled to the morose Vietnamese. "Bartender! Give my friend a refill."

Some time later I excused myself and went to the latrine. Something I couldn't quite identify was nibbling at the back of my mind. Without realizing it, Rennert had touched a nerve. Throughout my first six months in-country I had kept myself focused on returning home. Now things were becoming a bit more complicated. I wasn't thinking only of going home now. In the short time I had been here my emotions had run the full gamut – fear, boredom, anger, exhilaration, amusement and shame. But through it all ran the common thread of satisfaction. I believed in what I was doing, and honestly felt that I had contributed something worthwhile here. I wondered if I would ever do anything else to compare with it.

To be perfectly frank, I had never felt so alive as I had since arriving in Vietnam. The constant exposure to danger made every experience seem far more intense. I recalled something I had read during my short stay in college about how it is impossible to truly live until you have faced the probability of death. That philosophy now seemed firmly embedded in my psyche. Still, it disturbed me that I could not sort out these chaotic thought processes. The prospect of returning home without finishing the job filled me with a vague sense of unease. The more I wrestled with the problem, the more complex it became. If a solution existed, it was still beyond my capacity to find it. Perhaps I never would.

I washed my face in the chipped porcelain sink and stared at the streaky reflection in the mirror. "Hello, lifer," I muttered. I shook my head and looked away. "Shit."

I dried my hands with a paper towel and then walked back into the club. Sipping my drink while the juke box blared, I slid back onto the stool beside Rennert. We resumed our conversation in a lighter vein, and I also became engaged in some banter with Walner and several other team members. Before I realized it, the clock over the bar reached midnight. At the stroke of twelve, the two dozen men crammed into the tiny club shook hands all around and wished each other a Happy New Year. Someone bellowed "Fuck Vietnam!" We all roared with laughter.

I awoke the next morning twenty minutes before I was due to relieve Keller. It was too late for breakfast, but the thought of food made my stomach cringe anyway. My head pounded, and I felt disoriented. Had I really downed all that rum and Coke? I burped softly, and became sickened when a hideous sweet taste filled my mouth. I had no way of knowing then, of course, but I would never be able to drink that particular concoction again.

I staggered to the latrine to clean up. You couldn't drink tap water in Vietnam, unless you were willing to risk contracting any one of a multitude of tropical maladies. Consequently, there was a large bottle of treated water on the back of the sink to be used for hygienic purposes. I splashed some into a paper cup and used it to brush my teeth. My mouth tasted like talcum powder mixed with dog shit.

I stumbled to the radio shack, taking exaggerated, tentative steps as if I had just learned to walk. Ken glanced up as I opened the door. He stretched and then yawned. "Man, you look like hell."

I frowned at his apparent lack of sympathy. "Tell me about it." I peered around the room through red-rimmed eyes. "Is there a bucket in here?"

"A wastebasket. What do you want it for?"

"Are you kidding? Some time this morning I'm probably gonna puke in it."

Ken chuckled. "You wanna play, you gotta pay." He got up to leave. "Oh, yeah. Happy New Year."

I made an obscene gesture as he went out the door, and then sat down heavily. What a way to start the New Year, I mused. Have to make a net call... as soon as the room stops spinning.

———

GENERAL WESTMORELAND

TONY THOMPSON NEEDED A RIDE in from Dong Ha, so Keller and I drove the seven miles to the airstrip to pick him up. It was mid-morning when we rumbled into the ARVN installation, where Tony was waiting for us outside one of the white stucco buildings. Keller halted the jeep, and Thompson threw his gear inside. "Mind if I drive?" he asked.

"Be my guest," answered Ken, who then scrambled into the back seat. Thompson shifted gears, and we took off with a grinding roar.

Half way to Quang Tri, Thompson suddenly stomped on the brake pedal. I pitched forward and nearly cracked my forehead on the windscreen. "What the hell are you doing?" I squawked.

Thompson was staring at the road apron to our right. I turned back to see what he was looking at. An ill-defined spur ran parallel to the road for about twenty-five yards, ending in an open cul-de-sac. Knee high grass grew in the narrow space between the highway and the side road. Thompson shifted into low and pulled off onto the shoulder.

Three VC bodies lay sprawled in the sparse grass to our left. My eyes widened at the sight. I stared wordlessly for a moment, and then turned to Thompson. "How the hell did you know they were here?"

Tony seemed puzzled. "I didn't. Somebody back at Dong Ha said something about an ambush last night, but I had no idea where it happened. Weird, isn't it?"

We climbed out of the jeep and walked hesitantly toward the dead guerrillas. The corpses were gray-tinged and appeared shrunken. The eyes of the one nearest us were still open and stared in different directions, a result of the terrible trauma that had robbed them of their synchronization. The corneas were an opaque milky color. It was a ghastly sight straight out of a Grade B horror movie. A second victim's thick black hair was slicked back and caked with red mud. They couldn't have been dead very long. There was still none of the putrid stench of decomposition we had come to know so well. They had probably been killed during the early morning hours and subsequently dumped here.

We stood gaping at the poor bastards. No one else was around. It was unnaturally still. A gentle breeze whispered through the brittle stand of saw grass, and flies circled the bodies, buzzing softly as they flitted from one corpse to another. I glanced up at some angry black clouds scudding overhead. The sky was an eerie gray dome. A chill rippled up my spine. It was such a surreal moment that none of us could think of anything to say. We returned to the jeep and departed without another word. All three of us felt much relieved when we finally reached the compound.

The incident was forgotten several days later when we learned that General Westmoreland himself was coming to visit us. There had been rumors that "Silver Arrow," as the Commander of U.S. forces in Vietnam (COMUSV) was known, planned to stop at Quang Tri, but we had been skeptical. Hardly anyone paid serious attention to most of the scuttlebutt circulating around I Corps. But on the morning of Westmoreland's projected arrival, Colonel Bissett drove up from Hue in a small convoy to await his superior. The vehicles parked in a tight semi-circle on the soccer field adjacent to our compound.

We waited expectantly. Everyone found an excuse to loiter nearby, hoping to catch the big show. I put fresh film in my camera, and then clipped it to my belt. Around noon, we heard the distant whap-whap-whap of approaching Hueys. A murmur of excitement rippled through the small crowd.

It was a bright, partially overcast morning. Three olive-hued helicopters emerged from the haze south of the compound. One craft settled gently onto the surface of the soccer field while the others circled above, machine guns bristling like stingers from their open side doors. They darted back and forth above the lone Huey idling in the open meadow below, their engines snarling in anger with each pass.

General Westmoreland hopped down from his helicopter, accompanied by an entourage of aides. An ARVN major and several Vietnamese in civilian clothes followed close behind. Colonel Bissett met them at the gate and snapped off a smart salute.

The rest of us stood in a loose formation outside the barracks. I took several long range shots of the general and his group entering the compound. As they approached, I saw that Westmoreland was tall and slim, with sharp, piercing eyes. His green uniform was heavily starched and tailored. Even without the imposing four stars on either collar he was an impressive sight. Jeez, I thought, he sure LOOKS like a general. I recalled how Captain Vincent had once said almost the same thing.

Westmoreland strode over to a small knot of waiting advisors. The American personnel snapped crisply to attention, but our two Australian warrant officers remained casually at ease. That surprised me. I clicked several pictures of the odd scene.

I glanced to my right to locate the others. Just at that moment, General Westmoreland pivoted and strode across the open ground directly toward me. Before I realized what had happened, he was three feet in front of me with his hands on his hips, staring straight into my eyes. Taken by surprise, I jerked to an inept position of attention. I swiveled my head around to face the general, but my body remained oriented awkwardly toward my friends. The camera dangled unattended at my side. Out of the corner of my eye, I glimpsed Tony Thompson laughing at my discomfort.

Westmoreland peered down at my name tag, then across to the Combat Infantry Badge above my left breast pocket. "Where did you get your CIB, Oliveri?" The question was almost a command, warranting an immediate response, I thought.

I blurted out, "In the A Shau Valley, Sir!" I was extremely uncomfortable standing in such an unnatural position, but I didn't want to move while Westmoreland was questioning me. Perspiration trickled maddeningly down my back.

The general's eyes bored into mine. "Were you at Ta Bat or A Luoi?"

"Ta Bat, Sir. I spent some time at the Special Forces camp, too." I was mildly surprised to find that Westmoreland was so familiar with The Valley. Well, I thought, he IS the commanding general.

Westmoreland nodded but said nothing further. After looking me over once more he turned away and then continued down the line, pausing to speak with several others as he made his way across the compound. I was finally able to relax. My back ached from standing in such an awkward position. I glared over at Tony, who slapped his leg with glee.

Within fifteen minutes of his arrival, Westmoreland was back aboard his Huey. The craft lifted off with a roar, its rotor wash propelling a blizzard of dust and debris across the compound. The gunships continued to circle their charge as it gained altitude. We watched until the entire formation vanished once again into the lingering haze.

I stalked after Thompson. "Goddammit, Tony, you almost made me laugh in the General's face!"

Thompson held his side and hooted uproariously. "I couldn't help it!" he gasped. "You looked so friggin' ridiculous!" He snapped to attention with his head swung sharply to the left in an exaggerated imitation of my stance.

"Very funny," I snorted. I could feel my ears reddening. "Har, har."

We walked off to the mess hall together. Tony and Maxwell snickered occasionally throughout lunch. Even I eventually saw the humor in the situation. I finally joined in the laughter, although mine was somewhat half-hearted.

Following lunch, I took the afternoon radio shift. After checking in with net control, I cranked the land line and called Doug in Hue.

"Say, partner... did you hear about "Silver Arrow?""

"Yeah. He came through the Citadel."

"What did you..."

There was a loud click, and another voice burst into our conversation. "This is 'Wolf.' Who's on this line?"

"Specialist Oliveri, Sarge."

The switchboard monitor gave a satisfied grunt. "I thought it was you. You know you're not supposed to discuss confidential material on an open line."

I sighed. "C'mon, Sarge. Give me a break. Everyone in I Corps knows who was here today."

"Well, you've been around long enough to know better. I'm gonna have to write you up for a security violation."

Now I was really pissed. "Ah, for the... OK, OK. Do what you have to do. Hey, Doug... are you still there?"

"Yeah, I'm here."

"I'll talk to you later."

"Roger."

I slammed down the phone. What chicken shit! I was really beginning to appreciate becoming a short timer. And Rennert wanted me to stay in the Army. Fat chance of that happening. I was now more determined than ever to finish my enlistment and go home.

Three days later I was assigned to Lang Vei. I don't know if it had anything to do with the land line incident, but I wouldn't be surprised. Lang Vei was probably supposed to be my punishment. At that point I couldn't have cared less. At least I wouldn't have to deal with any more rear area assholes. And besides, I knew that Captain Ed Walsh and Warrant Officer Dave Walner had been sent out there recently as advisors to the ARVN 3rd Battalion, 2nd Regiment. How bad could it be working with those two? I figured that I could do a couple of months there while standing on my head. I was dead wrong about that.

———

ASSIGNMENT: LANG VEI

THE C-123 SET DOWN ON the undulating runway at Khe Sanh as gently as a plane that size could. Lang Vei had no airstrip, so all passengers, supplies and mail had to be routed through the nearby Special Forces camp. When the aircraft finally rolled to a stop and opened its cavernous cargo bay, I grabbed my gear and hopped down onto the perforated steel plate surface. It was a gray, overcast morning. I looked around. Khe Sanh hadn't changed much since my brief visit there with Foster some months before. A brief pang of guilt coursed through my body. I hadn't thought about my missing friend for a while.

Captain Walsh and Warrant Officer Walner were waiting for me by their jeep on the apron of the landing strip. Walsh waved a big paw as I emerged from the plane. I made my way over to him and saluted. "Nice to see you, Sir."

Walsh grasped my wrist in his massive hand and pushed my arm down. "Come on, Oliveri," he growled. "You know better than to salute me out here. And don't call me 'Sir', either. If it makes you feel better, call me 'Dai Uy'."

I grinned. "You got it, Dai Uy."

A smiling Walner stepped forward and shook my hand. "Welcome to the team, mate. And I'm 'Dave', by the way."

Walsh flashed an evil grin at Walner and said to me, "We asked for a good radio operator, but unfortunately, they sent you."

I chuckled. "Thanks, Dai Uy."

Walner sighed. "Seriously, mate... we really need a good radio man."

I chuckled again. "I hope you're not still saying that a week from now."

Walsh and Walner turned back to the jeep. They had been at Khe Sanh for several hours visiting with Captain Charles Allen and his A-323 team of Green Berets. Now they were anxious to get back to their own camp. "Let's go," said Walsh. "We'll give you a tour of Khe Sanh next time."

Walner drove while Walsh rode shotgun in the front passenger seat. I had the back of the jeep to myself. It was about six miles to Lang Vei. We skirted the northern edge of the runway, then swung south onto a narrow dirt road that ran through broad coffee groves owned and tended by a small group of Frenchmen. Khe Sanh's soil and climate were ideal for growing coffee beans. The plantation owners made an excellent living by using cheap Vietnamese labor to export their crops east to Quang Tri and Hue, or west to Savannakhet in Laos. They worked hard, but loved this beautiful, primitive land. Like their fathers before them, most had spent their entire lives in Vietnam.

It took us about ten minutes to pass through the groves of thriving coffee trees. When we finally reached Highway 9, the main road running from Dong Ha on the coast all the way into Laos, Walner turned west.

The outpost at Lang Vei was situated in the extreme northwest corner of South Vietnam, twenty-three kilometers south of the DMZ, and just a few kilometers from the Laotian border. It was literally at the end of the line. Beyond Lang Vei there was nothing but jungle until you reached Laos or North Vietnam, save for two or three squad-sized listening posts.

We passed through the tiny village of Khe Sanh itself. There was a small but busy marketplace on the north side of the road. I caught a glimpse of merchants cooking food or hawking their wares, including bottles of soda, canned goods and even some military equipment. Dead rats hung from strands of wire threaded through their heads. For a couple of piastres, villagers could pluck a couple for the evening meal. A thought flashed through my mind. I wondered how many times I had already unknowingly eaten rat meat for dinner. I didn't dwell on the subject. Further up the road, several official-looking buildings straddled the highway. We sped past a couple of sprawling villas, probably those belonging to the Frenchmen.

Lang Vei was about two and a half miles from Khe Sanh Village. When we reached the outskirts of the camp, I saw that a steep spur led up to the main gate. Walner shifted into low. The jeep labored up the incline, gears whining in agony. We swept past a bored-looking guard into the confines of the outpost. Walner swung to the left, drove another fifty yards, and then lurched to a halt behind a log bunker. "Well," said Walsh, "here's your new home."

We walked around to the front of the structure. The bunker was rectangular, about thirty feet long by fifteen wide. A thatched portico extended over a stairwell leading down inside. Half a dozen water cans and two galvanized trash cans sat neatly beside the steps. Some wiseass had hand-lettered a wooden sign that hung above the doorway. It read, "El Barrio." The slum. Undoubtedly Thompson's work. There were four narrow casement windows set into the base of the bunker just above ground level, and they provided some welcome light to the interior. Stacked sandbags formed a sort of window well, providing some protection for the fragile glass. I was impressed. By Special Forces standards, the bunker was quite crude. But it was downright luxurious compared to the rat hole at Ta Bat. Walsh led us down the steps. There was a small wooden table just inside the entrance. I dumped my gear on the floor and looked around.

General Westmoreland *(left, with back to camera)* visits the cadre at the Quang Tri advisory compound.

Massive wooden beams ran the length of the structure, supported by equally stout logs set vertically into the dirt floor. Shiny corrugated metal sheets covered the roof and walls as had been the case at Ta Bat. To the right was a utility area. The radio sat on a wooden shelf against the far wall. Its cables snaked outside through the single small window on that side. A kerosene-powered refrigerator stood to the left of the Angry/9. Beside it was a triple-tiered metal storage rack filled with cans of food and other supplies.

The sleeping area was to the left of the entrance. Four portable cots hugged the walls. The furthest was vacant, and Walsh gestured toward it. "That's your bunk," he said. "You might as well stow your gear. If you want, you can take a look around the camp."

I tossed my gear and the carbine onto the empty cot, but kept my pistol belt strapped on, as I almost always did in the field. Then I stepped back outside to see what Lang Vei had to offer.

The outpost was situated on a small plateau overlooking a tiny montagnard village. The montagnards were primitive mountain people known as "moi", or savages, by the ethnic Vietnamese. ARVN regarded them with contempt. The montagnards near Lang Vei were part of the Bru tribe. In recent years, American missionaries had arrived, and were working diligently to educate the Bru and to create the written language they had never had. To the missionaries the war was a major inconvenience that made their task that much more difficult.

Lang Vei was known in I Corps as "The camp in the clouds." It sat high amid the Annamese Cordilleras, a rugged mountain range that ran up the spine of the Indo-Chinese peninsula. The scabby red earth of Lang Vei stood out like a raw canker sore on an otherwise unbroken sea of green. During the dry season it was a dust bowl. Now, at the height of the rainy season, it was frequently shrouded in fog. Because of the elevation, the weather could become surprisingly cool. Temperatures in the low fifties or even upper forties were not unusual. In fact, it was near that now, and I was freezing. I was glad that I had thought to pack my field jacket.

I peered north across the camp. The flagpole and fire arrow were located in a small central parade ground directly opposite the main gate. The yellow and red striped South Vietnamese flag overhead snapped in a brisk westerly wind. A .50 caliber machinegun sat just to the right of the clearing, mounted in the middle of a sandbagged emplacement. The big weapon was covered with a tarpaulin tied at both the breech and the muzzle. The gun's location puzzled me. From this position, it would be impossible to fire the heavy weapon toward the perimeter without shooting through at least one building. Then it dawned on me that this close to the DMZ we might have to be concerned about a North Vietnamese air attack. The .50 was an anti-aircraft weapon. That realization startled me. The possibility of an enemy air raid had never entered my mind before.

A 105mm howitzer position lay just thirty yards beyond our bunker. I frowned, imagining some sleepless nights ahead. I walked past the main gate toward the north side of camp where the ARVN quarters were located. A dozen or so troopers were engaged in a spirited volleyball game in the alleyway between two bunkers. Shrill hoots and laughter accompanied every play. They paused to eye me curiously as I passed.

I walked by the camp commander's bunker. I recalled something that Walsh had mentioned about Captain Lam during our ride in from Khe Sanh. Apparently there was little love lost between the two. Walsh had described his counterpart as a typical political appointee. He regarded Lam as something of a playboy who always wore sunglasses and favored carefully tailored camouflage fatigues. According to Walsh, Dai Uy Lam had never once been to the field. The big Marine made no secret of his disdain for the ARVN officer.

Circling back along the western perimeter, I passed the medical bunker and the ARVN radio room. Then I approached two structures that I hadn't noticed previously. One was a small thatched hut with a 55 gallon drum mounted on a log platform above it. A gasoline powered heater protruded from the open top of the barrel. I'll be damned, I thought. An honest-to-God shower! I glanced inside. A series of bamboo pipes ran from the drum to a crude shower head. One had only to lower a hinged conduit to produce a cascade of warm running water. How nice!

The second structure was a compact corrugated shed about five feet square. I opened the door. It was an outhouse! Inside was a sit-down platform with a toilet seat centered over a hole cut through the planks. The user could do his business in relative comfort, if he didn't mind risking a few splinters in the ass. Better than a bullet, I suppose. In any case, I was delighted. No more squatting over shit trenches! Thinking back now, it still amazes me that something so basic as an outhouse could seem like such a luxury. But I guess that was Vietnam in microcosm.

I gazed across the wire perimeter beyond the outhouse. The ground fell away sharply to the village below. From this height, I could look down on the thatched roofs of the montagnard hamlet. It was typical of most in the area, comprised of perhaps two dozen grass huts raised above ground level on six foot wooden poles. Smoke from several cooking fires swirled lazily overhead. The village seemed quite peaceful.

Having completed my brief survey, I returned to our bunker. A young ARVN soldier was sitting at the table inside, and scrutinized me as I came through the entrance. He had a pleasant pudgy face and was wearing a brown infantry beret. Walner was nearby, fiddling with a Coleman lantern. He looked up. "Hey, Oliveri... say hello to Troung. He's our jack-of-all-trades."

"Chao, Troung."

The young soldier grinned. "Chao, Ha Si (Corporal)." He dropped his gaze to my name tag and reached over to touch the print. "Oh-Lee-Ver-Ee." His pronunciation was slow and laborious. "Ha Si speak "V'etnamee?"

I held up my thumb and forefinger about an inch apart. "Ti-ti" (a little.)

Troung laughed. "Ahh, numbah one!" My CIB caught his eye. He placed his finger lightly on the blue and silver badge and then glanced up at me as if to ask: "What is that?"

Captain Walsh, who had been watching from his cot, chimed in, "That means he's a good soldier, Troung."

The cheerful Vietnamese peered up at me, and then down again at the CIB above my breast pocket. "OK! OK!"

I smiled. I was beginning to feel more at home with each passing minute.

The next morning, Walner and I drove back to Khe Sanh to pick up some supplies and mail coming in on a "Caribou", the flying workhorse of northern I Corps. Also aboard was Marine 1st Lt. George Kiesel, the final member of the team, who was returning from Dong Ha. After stowing our goodies in the jeep, Walner led me between two nung sentries toward the team house. The entrance was carefully sandbagged. A tiny squirrel monkey chirped atop the burlap and sand wall, tethered on a delicate aluminum chain. "Captain Allen's pet," muttered Walner as we entered the building. "Be careful. The little bastard will piss on you if you get too close."

Lieutenant Lukitsch, the Team A-323 second-in-command, and Sergeant Burris, the communications non-com, greeted us warmly. Waldman introduced me as a new member of the Lang Vei team. Upon hearing that I was a radio operator, Burris asked if I'd like to see the radio room. "Sure," I answered eagerly. I had often marveled at the logistical prowess of the Green Berets. They always seemed to have the best and latest equipment. Now I was anxious to see it for myself.

Burris didn't disappoint me. He had a powerful single-side-band radio capable of reaching Saigon, if necessary, 400 miles to the south. I examined the set with open admiration. It had a modern, streamlined appearance, quite unlike my ancient Angry/9. The casing was highly buffed aluminum. A metal hand mike about the size of a baseball hung from a bracket, its tightly-coiled black cable attached to a port in the rear of the set. There was a colorful decal on the front of the radio that depicted a grinning skull wearing a green beret. Beneath it was an inscription reading "Sinh Loi (Sorry about that) Victor Charlie!" I had seen that before, but it still brought a smile to my face.

Burris gave me a brief demonstration by running a quick commo check with Da Nang, headquarters for Special Forces in I Corps. The response was almost immediate and very strong. It was much like holding a conversation with someone sitting across the table. I was duly impressed.

We talked shop until Walner and Lukitsch came looking for us. Burris was a highly-skilled technician, so I appreciated the way he had treated me as an equal. I thanked him for his time and reluctantly got up to leave.

During the ride back to Lang Vei, I had a discussion with Walner regarding the state of our communications. I knew Walsh was concerned about escalating VC activity in northern I Corps. Just ten days before, the VC had bombarded Khe Sanh with twenty high-caliber mortar rounds. Until I arrived, Lang Vei had been without a radio operator for a week. It was easy to see that not having direct contact with the advisory team had grated on the nerves of my fellow advisors. I understood then why Walner had been so happy to see me the previous day.

Once back in camp, I set about evaluating the communications set-up. We had just the single Angry/9 in the bunker. Our jeep had mounts for a radio, but there was no spare equipment on hand. Since it appeared obvious to me that we would frequently be on the road between Lang Vei and Khe Sanh, I was determined to have mobile commo capability. I made a mental note to request another radio from Quang Tri.

Walsh, Walner, Kiesel and I began holding daily intelligence discussions, usually as we sat around the table after the evening meal. The allied presence in the area had given the local populace a false sense of security. It was an attitude the VC desperately needed to change. Several days after my arrival, they took the first step toward doing just that.

We later pieced together the following scenario. The market place in Khe Sanh village was still crowded even as dusk approached. Dozens of merchants frantically hawked their wares, hoping for one last sale before darkness closed them down. A bony, slant-eyed man emerged from the lengthening shadows. He was clad in loose-fitting black pajamas, the traditional garb associated with the Viet Cong. He attracted no attention, however, since many in the market place were dressed in a similar manner. Moving casually along the periphery of the square, he glanced to his left and right. No one seemed to notice him. He slipped a hand beneath his shirt and withdrew a green, egg-shaped object. Yanking the pin from the grenade, he lobbed it into a knot of chattering villagers.

The shattering blast created havoc in the cramped confines of the market place. A dozen Vietnamese, mostly women and children, writhed in agony on the ground, their bodies peppered with shrapnel wounds. Three others lay motionless. As the smoke cleared and the echoes of the explosion died away, the ruthless terrorist melted into the gathering gloom.

Word of the atrocity reached Lang Vei by nightfall. ARVN radio flashed the message to Hue. Headquarters, concerned about escalating VC terrorism, quickly ordered our battalion to conduct an offensive sweep along Highway 9.

Captain Walsh briefed us the following morning after meeting with Dai Uy Lam. "This will be a two day operation," he began. "We'll clear both sides of the road to Khe Sanh, stay overnight at Som Bai, then sweep back along the same route tomorrow morning. I doubt we'll find anything. The VC aren't stupid. But it might make the villagers feel better."

I spoke up. "Where's Som Bai, Dai Uy?"

Troung, who had been listening quietly, made an emphatic gesture toward the main gate. "Som Bai," he said, pointing a finger toward the east.

Walsh nodded. "It's an old French fort along Highway 9 on the way to Khe Sanh. Not a bad place to spend the night."

We loaded up the jeep and prepared to move out with the battalion. Walsh left Walner behind to monitor the Prick-10 that would serve as our only means of communication with the base camp. I put a fresh battery in the matching set in our jeep. I already regretted not having gotten a second Angry/9 from Quang Tri yet. The Prick-10 was an FM, or "line-of-sight" radio. If we got down into a valley, or behind a hill, we would lose all direct commo. I wasn't happy with that.

The sky was heavily overcast, and it was quite chilly when Walsh, Kiesel, Troung and I crammed into the jeep and drove out of camp. Not much rain had fallen, but a persistent mist lingered over the hills. In the distance, Tiger Tooth Mountain, the peak that would gain lasting notoriety several years later as the site of the battle for "Hamburger Hill", lay shrouded in fog. The ARVN infantry had departed Lang Vei about an hour earlier, flanking both sides of the highway as they slogged slowly toward Khe Sanh. Welch's orders were to move up to Som Bai and join the ARVN headquarters unit.

I was behind the wheel as our jeep bounced along Highway 9 headed east. The road was crowded with civilians. The previous night's incident had apparently done little to discourage business as usual. War or no war, the locals still had to sell their goods or buy food. Life went on.

We came to Som Bai, located on a slight rise overlooking a sharp bend in the road several miles outside Lang Vei. The old French fort looked much like a rural stone farmhouse. It had once served as the headquarters for the first contingent of Green Berets who arrived in the area during 1962. We drove up the modest incline leading to the site, and I parked the jeep in front of the building. We went inside.

ARVN radio men had already set up a commo center in the large main room. I stowed my gear beside a massive stone fireplace that made up the entire far wall. Someone had thoughtfully lighted a fire to help drive the dampness from the building. The crackle and hiss of the burning logs was quite soothing. Multi-colored sparks danced up the chimney. I was drawn to the cheerful sight, and crouched before the fire to warm myself.

After a few minutes, I tore myself away from the cozy fireplace just long enough to make a commo check with Lang Vei from the jeep. Walner responded immediately, reporting that he could hear me loud and clear. Before we left camp, I had given the Australian a crash course on operating the Angry/9. In an emergency, Walner knew enough to raise Quang Tri by voice. That made me feel a little better.

I retreated inside again, where Troung was brewing some tea over the open flames. He handed me a metal cup, and I sipped the steaming beverage with gusto. "Ahhh… Number one, Ha Si Troung!" The Vietnamese corporal flashed a boyish grin.

The day dragged on toward late afternoon, with ARVN patrols reporting no enemy contact, much as Walsh had suspected. By nightfall, we began staking out sleeping positions. I claimed a corner across from the fireplace where I could watch the darting flames and absorb their radiant heat. The warmth soon made me drowsy.

The ARVN commo team settled down nearby. Horrendous Vietnamese music blared from a transistor radio. I rolled my eyes in dismay at the vocalist's high-pitched wail, hoping it wouldn't go on all night.

The hard stone floor was uncomfortable, and I tossed fitfully until dawn. When I finally arose I felt not the least bit refreshed. There had been no activity during the night; no contacts, no suspects, nothing. The elusive VC had once again escaped the South Vietnamese net. I stretched, trying to work the kinks out of my limbs. Troung appeared with another cup of tea. I smiled. I was really beginning to appreciate the little Vietnamese. We returned to camp soon afterward, having accomplished nothing at all. In my experience it was not the first time; neither would it be the last.

When we got back to our bunker I said matter-of-factly to Walsh, "You know, Dai Uy, there's got to be a better way to win this war."

He glanced across at me with a devilish grin. "Well," he said. "You and I could attack Hanoi while Dave and George invade Laos. That should do it."

"OK," I dead-panned. "But I have to take a leak first."

We all shared a hearty laugh and another cup of tea, and that was the extent of our plan to end the war.

Several days later, we took part in the most unusual celebration I'd ever attended. The major holiday in Vietnam is Tet. To the Vietnamese, it is like Christmas, New Years and the Fourth of July all rolled into one. During the war, both sides generally observed an unwritten truce while the combatants returned to their homes to celebrate. Even westerners were swept up by the festive atmosphere. On the afternoon of January 31st, Walsh, Kiesel, Walner and I, plus the Green Beret officers at Khe Sanh, were invited to the villa of Monsieur Felix Poilane to observe Tet. Poilane was one of the third generation Frenchmen who owned the coffee plantations on the plateau.

Freshly shaven and wearing clean uniforms, we drove the short distance to Khe Sanh village, arriving just after 1500 hours. Madeline Poilane, the petite wife of the coffee grower, welcomed us at the entrance of the yellow cement villa. Inside, her husband greeted us warmly and offered small glasses of bright green crème de menthe.

It was beginning as a relaxing and enjoyable afternoon. I had heard rumors that Poilane paid off the local VC to keep them from disrupting his business. But no one had ever substantiated that charge. I regarded the sincere, friendly man seated across the table. The rumors were probably true. After all, this was his home and his livelihood. If he chose to steer a middle course between the two opposing sides, who could blame him?

I glanced down at the holiday table, heavily laden with a wide variety of French and Vietnamese delicacies. Chafing dishes filled with boiling vinegar bubbled merrily at either end. Platters of beef sliced paper thin sat beside each burner. Poilane showed us how to dip the meat into the hot liquid for just a few seconds, then roll it up like a cigarette and pop it steaming into our mouths. It was delicious. The table abounded with traditional Vietnamese dishes as well. There was a bowl of chicken chunks prepared in a hot, dark sauce with pieces of crushed bone. I had first tried this while dining with the ARVN at Ta Bat and found it quite good. I recommended it to the others. Captain Allen and Lieutenant Lukitsch tasted it, and their enthusiastic compliments delighted Mme. Poilane. Walsh proposed a toast to our generous hosts.

The couple's hospitality made us all feel very much at home, and helped to restore some of the holiday spirit we might have missed. I thought of my own family and friends back in the States as I surveyed the group enjoying the celebration. God, it would be great to go home. My own DEROS (Date Estimated Return Overseas) was just three months away. It was almost shocking to me that what had once seemed so impossibly distant was now practically within reach. That realization helped me to enjoy the party even more.

I was disappointed when Walsh finally announced that we had to leave. But it would be wise to get back to Lang Vei before dark. We extended our profuse thanks to the Poilanes, said good-bye to the Green Berets and then drove back along Highway 9 to our camp.

I never had occasion to see the Poilanes again. During the Tet offensive in 1968, Felix Poilane was killed in an aircraft accident at the Khe Sanh combat base. I have no idea what became of Madeline Poilane. But for one afternoon, at least, we had all enjoyed their generous hospitality while crossing yet another day off the calendar. I was now a legitimate short-timer, having broken the three month barrier.

ESCALATION

B EFORE DAWN ON FEBRUARY 7TH, Viet Cong infiltrators attacked the U.S. base at Pleiku in the central highlands. Under cover of a mortar barrage, the terrorists hurled satchel charges at the numerous American aircraft parked on the runway. Ten airplanes were destroyed in the onslaught. There could be no doubt that the assault was directed at American servicemen. The brief but violent confrontation took the lives of eight U.S. soldiers and wounded more than a hundred others including one I had met in Saigon.

President Lyndon Johnson was furious. This time the Communists had gone too far. Johnson quickly authorized Operation Flaming Dart, a retaliatory bombing mission against North Vietnam. This was to be a joint American-South Vietnamese effort. Within hours, allied aircraft took to the skies over Dong Hoi, a military installation fifty miles beyond the DMZ. A major escalation of the war was about to take place.

Ken Keller was relaxing on the roof of the advisors' hotel in Hue early on the morning of February 8th, taking advantage of an opportunity to absorb some sun through a rare break in the clouds. Armed Forces Radio had broadcast the details of the raid on Pleiku the previous evening. Now, as he worked on his tan, the sputter of many approaching aircraft caught his attention. Ken peered south down Highway 1, shielding his eyes with the palm of one hand. He was startled to see a flight of heavily armed VNAF Skyraider fighter-bombers roaring toward him at an altitude of just a few hundred feet.

The lead aircraft soared over the hotel, waggling its wings as it passed. Keller waved to the grinning pilot, who was wearing a purple scarf. Unknown to Ken at the time, this aviator was Air Marshal Nguyen Cao Ky, happily commanding his country's first air raid against the North. The plane was gone in a flash, continuing up Highway 1 toward its destination. Ken watched in wonder until the attackers disappeared from sight and the thrum of their engines faded away, then returned to working on his tan. Such unusual occurrences were nothing new in I Corps, and were met sometimes with a shrug.

Operation Flaming Dart, initiated by Ky's mission, proved largely ineffective. But a greater, more extensive bombing program loomed on the horizon – Rolling Thunder. For the moment, however, the allies were satisfied that they had delivered a clear and powerful message to "Uncle Ho."

We knew nothing about this at Lang Vei until several days later. The reserve Angry/9 had arrived from Quang Tri, and I wasted no time mounting it on our team jeep. When not in use, we usually parked the vehicle behind the bunker, so I decided to erect a second antenna back there in the event we wanted to transmit from the jeep. In truth, it would be much easier and quicker to do so, since the radio worked off the vehicle's battery, and I wouldn't have to crank up the generator to transmit. I also kept the original set in the bunker for emergencies, with the generator vented to the outside. If we ever came under attack, I would be able to broadcast without leaving the bunker, a far cry from the dangerously exposed conditions I had endured at Ta Bat. That seemed like a good idea to me, I can tell you.

I sought out the ARVN artillery officer. Since one of the antenna poles I planned to put up would be close to the 105mm howitzer pit, I wanted assurance from him that it wouldn't interfere with the big gun's line of fire. Troung acted as my interpreter and helped explain what I wanted to do. The lieutenant examined the site I had chosen. He walked back to the sandbagged gun pit and crouched down on the red clay, sighting toward the spot where I was going to put the pole. When he was satisfied that his shells would safely clear it, he nodded his approval.

Troung helped me to erect the poles and string the antenna wire. When we were finished, I hooked up the radio for a test. It worked beautifully.

Later that afternoon, Walsh told me about the raid on Dong Hoi. I was mildly surprised. "You know, Dai Uy," I said, "if the lid blows off, we could be one of the first targets."

"Yeah," he said, scratching his head thoughtfully. "That's been on my mind, believe me."

"Suppose we sandbag the area where we park the jeep," I suggested. "We could make a pretty good fighting position back there, and we'd have a radio right in there with us."

Walsh nodded. "That's a damn good idea. And I just re-membered something. The Vietnamese are tearing up an old compound near Som Bai. I saw a shit-load of sandbags lying around there when we drove over to Khe Sanh. See if Troung can borrow a trailer from ARVN, and we'll pick up as many as we can before someone else grabs them."

"Right." I went off to find the corporal.

The encampment near Som Bai had been well scavenged by the time we got there. The villagers had already removed everything useful, except for the sandbags. Walsh was right. There were hundreds of the dirt filled burlap sacks littering the area. Many were rotten and had burst open, spilling their dank contents into small red piles. But enough remained that we were able to haul six trailer loads back to Lang Vei. By the time we felt we had enough, our uniforms and the trailer were caked with thick red mud. We quit for the day, and I was looking forward to getting cleaned up.

After reporting back to Walsh, I grabbed a towel and headed for the primitive shower, clogs flapping against my bare feet. I reached the bamboo structure and swung the door open. Much to my surprise, a flock of ducks (Walsh called them "ARVN C-rations") had taken up residence inside. I guess it made sense. The tiny building provided shelter from the elements, and it was cool inside. The birds were probably attracted to the thin trickle of water from the crude shower.

I stomped my foot and bellowed, "Get the hell out of here!" I waved my arms wildly in an attempt to start them moving.

The ducks squawked and began to waddle away from me, but made no effort to leave. In exasperation, I pushed the door open and tried to shoo them outside. The birds honked and flapped their wings, moving from side to side across the aptly-named duckboard flooring. I managed to get behind the flock and chased them toward the door. They were outraged, and the noise was horrendous. I kept stomping my feet until they were all outside. The ducks bobbed and weaved in unison as they moved off across the compound. It was such a ridiculous sight that you could only laugh. I watched them for a few minutes, shaking my head in wonder. Finally I went back inside to take my shower, being careful not to step on any of the black and white cylinders of duck shit that littered the floor.

We began building our fighting position the next morning. There was already a thatched overhang above the spot. Following the general outline of the grass roof, I laid the first row of sandbags, using an interlocking pattern I had learned from the Vietnamese. Troung labored beside me until we had raised a chest-high wall.

I searched the camp and scrounged several lengths of heavy timber. With these as supports, we fashioned three gun ports in the sandbag walls. By the end of the day, Troung and I had a functional bunker in place. We couldn't find enough materials to construct overhead protection, but I was satisfied with what we'd done. We were still vulnerable to mortar fire, but the structure would shield us from small arms and shrapnel.

Walsh and Walner came by to inspect our work. Good-natured insults flew, and we shared some hearty laughter. Walner snapped a picture of Troung and me standing in front of the new bunker. Weeks later, when I finally had the film developed, I was amused to see Walsh in the background with his middle finger raised.

Several evenings later small arms fire broke out not far from camp. I snatched my carbine and raced outside to our new fighting position to man the radio. Once inside, I wasted no time cranking up the "Angry 9" in case we needed to call for help.

The firing had ceased, but I was assuming nothing. By now I had experienced enough enemy contact to know, as Yogi Berra supposedly said, "It ain't over 'til it's over." I felt fairly composed despite the fact that my heart was hammering in my chest. I thrust the carbine through one of the firing apertures and peered out. It was now dusk, and there was little to see in the gathering gloom. I laid my .45 carefully within reach on top of a sandbag and glanced warily at the entrance to the bunker. That side of the position was wide open to allow the jeep to get in and out. In a firefight it could be our Achilles heel. I stared intently in that direction, fervently hoping to see nothing.

Before long, an ARVN patrol entered the camp through the main gate, carrying what appeared to be several wounded soldiers. They passed by on their way to the medical bunker. Apparently the enemy had ambushed them in the coffee groves somewhere between Lang Vei and Khe Sanh. That news certainly got my attention.

I powered down the radio and made my way inside, where Kiesel and Walner waited with their weapons at the ready. From what we were able to piece together, an ARVN night patrol had been ambushed just outside the camp and taken several casualties. That was all we knew. Kiesel suggested that we head over to the medical bunker to find out more.

We covered the fifty yards quickly and clomped down the steps into the interior. Two dead soldiers lay on the floor, obviously having suffered some ghastly wounds. One had been shot through both thighs and the chest while the other had received a traumatic head wound. The Vietnamese medics were already cleaning and wrapping the bodies by the feeble light of a single Coleman lantern. They glanced up, and then paid us no further mind as they went about their work. I was glad that they hadn't asked for another lamp. I'm not sure that I would have complied given my painful and humiliating experience at Ta Bat. After a moment Kiesel jerked his head at me as if to say, "Let's go."

Once outside away from the stench of blood and gore he said, "I didn't particularly want to see that."

I nodded. "Neither did I. We probably shouldn't have gone in there now anyway."

We made our way back to the advisors' bunker and rejoined Walner. I boiled some water and made tea while we wound down from our adrenaline high. Outside the big 105 boomed belatedly as it spat out several rounds toward the ambush site. We stayed on alert, but there was no further excitement that night.

Barring the occasional contact, life at Lang Vei would have been terribly tedious without the madcap antics of the Australian and the two Marines. We played infantile tricks on Troung and on each other to help pass the time. Otherwise, every day of the rainy season was a rerun of the previous one:

clouds, fog, some drizzle, an occasional period of heavier rain. Only rarely did the sun appear, its sickly glow masked by the stubborn overcast.

By now I had discovered that Lang Vei had its own version of the "rat races." The nightly commotion within the corrugated overhead of our bunker nearly drove us to distraction. One evening, Walner, in a fit of annoyance, carefully tracked the progress of a particularly persistent rodent across the metal ceiling. When the rat halted, the Australian pressed the muzzle of his carbine against the roof and fired one round. There was a brief silence followed by the renewed scrambling of frantic rats. Walner threw up his hands in defeat while the rest of us roared with glee.

Meals were another problem. We existed mainly on K-rations, and kept an abundant supply of the big green cans on hand. However, the menu was somewhat limited. Sliced beef, franks and beans, and canned sausages warmed over a small gasoline stove constituted the bulk of our diet. Sometimes we augmented this with fresh potatoes. Dai Uy Lam had a weakness for the western vegetables, so he had assigned two privates to tend a compact garden near the perimeter. Sometimes we traded them some cigarettes for a handful of spuds. Once, Troung bought two live chickens in the marketplace, killed them outside the bunker, and carefully plucked their feathers. I fashioned a crude barbecue out of an old metal pail and started a fire with some odd pieces of wood that were left over from the construction of the bunker. Troung handled the cooking. The chicken turned out burnt and rubbery, but it was still a welcome change from K-rations.

I tried many times to get Troung to share a meal with us, but the young Vietnamese always turned me down. He couldn't stomach the thought of eating rich American food after subsisting most of his life on plain boiled rice and greens. But

I persisted. We laughed heartily each time Troung wrinkled up his nose at my latest offering. Sometimes when he did this, I would twist my face into a grotesque mask, raise my hands like claws, and pretend to stalk the young corporal with my "slowly I turned" routine. Troung would dash off with a nervous laugh, never quite sure whether I was serious or not. Something in the personality of the Vietnamese soldier touched my psyche. Perhaps it was because I saw much of myself in him.

The bombing of the North seemed to have little impact on enemy activity in our area. By the time I marked my first month at Lang Vei in mid-February, nothing much had happened since the firefight outside the camp. That was fine with me. I hoped it would stay like that for two more months until I was ready to go home.

We made frequent trips to the Special Forces camp, more out of boredom than necessity. Captain Allen and his Green Berets always made us feel welcome. We had a mutually comfortable relationship, aided by the knowledge that we could support one another in the event of an attack on either installation. But as much as I enjoyed visiting Khe Sanh, I disliked driving there. The main leg of the trip along Highway 9 was relatively safe, but after turning off onto the dirt road leading through Felix Poilane's coffee groves, things could get hairy. Thick brush grew right up to the sides of the road. Tall trees formed a living canopy overhead, shutting out what little sunlight filtered through the persistent overcast. It was a perfect spot for an ambush, as we had learned earlier. With that in mind, I had removed the top from a metal ammo box, and placed it between the jeep's two front seats with a couple of easily accessible grenades inside. I don't know what possible good I thought I could do by trying to toss grenades while driving, but having them there foolishly made me feel a bit more secure.

Troung and I made regular trips to a stone well in Lang Vei village to replenish our drinking supply. The water was relatively clean and safe to drink after we added a few iodine tablets to it. Our arrival always created a stir among the villagers, particularly the children. One morning, buoyed by a rare glimpse of the sun, we piled the water cans into the back of our jeep, backed out of our spanking new revetment, and drove down the hill to the village.

Along the way, Troung excitedly pointed out a man dragging a huge dead python along the side of the road. I was astonished. That thing had to be at least 16 feet long and a foot thick in the middle. The man had one end of the reptile slung over his shoulder with the rest trailing behind. I have to admit that I was a bit unsettled at the thought of such a fearsome snake so close to our camp. This one, however, was now on its way to some local's dinner table. I just shook my head in wonder and drove on.

As usual, we attracted a small crowd of laughing kids. Most of them wore only shorts despite the cool temperature. Their chests and feet were bare. One little girl of about eight years carried an infant—probably her younger brother—comfortably stashed on her hip. She eyed us quizzically as we unloaded the jerry cans. When I winked at her, she ran off.

Another group of three or four boys approached. They were better dressed than the others. One wore a pith helmet, while a second had on blue and white striped pajamas and a cap that resembled a railroad engineer's hat. They caught my eye and made smoking motions with their fingers. "You! You! Got cigarette-ee?"

I patted my pockets and raised my empty palms skyward. "No have," I said truthfully. "No smoke." I shrugged.

The boys grimaced. One of them raised his middle finger. "Fuck you!"

My jaw dropped. "Why, you little bastard..." I took a step as if to chase them. The urchins scattered, leaving me glaring helplessly after them.

Troung roared with glee and slapped his thigh. "Ah, Ha Si... you very funny!"

I frowned at him. "Yeah, a real riot."

Troung raised his hands in a half-assed imitation of my stalking act. "Ha Si... slow I turn!" He convulsed with laughter, and I threw my cap at him. When he finally composed himself, we filled the water cans and headed back up the hill to camp, with Troung still chuckling, much to my annoyance.

Corporal Troung outside the Lang Vei bunker.

As we drove out of Lang Vei village, we passed two young Vietnamese men walking in the opposite direction. One of them glared at us as we went by. Troung spun around in his seat to scrutinize the pair. His eyes were wide as saucers and he became quite agitated. "Ha Si," he hissed. "They VC!"

"What?" I exclaimed, turning to eyeball the men. "How do you know that?"

Troung just nodded emphatically. "They VC, Ha Si." He looked frightened.

I risked another peek at the two. The one who had initially eyed us shot a malevolent scowl at me, then turned and continued on toward the village. There was little we could do. They were obviously unarmed, so we had no clear reason to force an encounter, which was probably just as well. We drove on to camp with Troung watching our rear the whole way. I had no idea how he recognized them as the enemy, but I trusted his judgment. It would have been foolhardy not to do so.

If the two were indeed VC, they may have been going to Lang Vei village to purchase food or just to take a little "R&R". In either case, they hadn't been happy to see us, nor we them. Meeting the enemy in broad daylight at that stage of the conflict was highly unusual. I chalked it up to one of those strange incidents that sometimes occur during war. Later that afternoon Walsh decided to make a quick run to Khe Sanh. He planned to catch a flight to Quang Tri the next morning for a short break from the field. Captain Allen had invited him to spend the night at the Special Forces camp. Since there was no traffic on the net, I offered to drive him. "OK," said Walsh. "But you're gonna have to drive back alone, so don't hang around too long."

"No sweat, Dai Uy. I'll be back here long before dark."

I backed out the jeep from our new revetment and checked the gas gauge. There was only a quarter of a tank, so I pumped a few gallons from the drum behind our bunker. This is gonna be my next project, I thought. Got to get this gas below ground where it belongs. During an attack, it wouldn't go well for us if a tracer round found that drum while we were inside the bunker. I finished sloshing the fuel into the tank and then climbed in behind the wheel.

While I waited for Walsh I placed my carbine behind the driver's seat and checked to be sure that the two lethal-looking grenades were nestled securely in the bottom of the ammo can beside the gear shift. I patted my side out of habit to be sure that the .45 was in place.

Walsh emerged from the bunker and hopped into the jeep. He stowed a small overnight bag between his feet. I glanced at the sky as we pulled out past the 105 pit. It was a dreary, overcast day. There was virtually no traffic on the road, so we reached Khe Sanh in about fifteen minutes. Captain Allen was standing outside the team house when we arrived. I waved to him. The stocky Green Beret smiled and raised a hand in return.

Walsh eyed me mischievously. "Is that how you greet an officer – you wave to him?"

I grinned. "I'm just doing what you told me, Dai Uy. You said not to salute out here."

Walsh snorted and playfully tugged the bill of my cap over my eyes. We clambered out of the jeep and went inside. Allen tried to tell us a bad joke as we walked. Walsh and I both groaned.

Sergeant Burris was seated at the table. He glanced up and spotted us. "Hey, Oliveri… Sit down and have a beer."

I took off my cap and used it to slap the road dust from my uniform. "Aw, come on, Sarge. You know I'm not a beer drinker."

"Well then have a Coke." Burris got up and reached into the refrigerator for a can of soda. He opened it with two quick thrusts of a can opener and handed it to me.

"Thanks." I took a long swallow and belched softly. We sat at the table and quickly got into a discussion on the merits of a speed key. Burris was a font of communications knowledge, so I liked to pick his brain whenever I got the chance.

Twenty minutes later, Walsh called across the room. "Hey Ollie. You better move out before it gets dark."

I peeked at my watch. "OK, Dai Uy. I'll see you tomorrow." Walsh threw me a casual wave. I said good-bye to Burris and headed for the door.

The afternoon shadows had already grown long by the time I drove across the airstrip. I turned left and skirted the perimeter of the runway before plunging into the coffee groves to the west. Once inside, I quickly realized that I should have left sooner.

The road through the coffee plantation was almost like a tunnel. Branches from the trees on both sides criss-crossed overhead, effectively blocking what little daylight remained. Except for the steady whine of the jeep it was deathly quiet. I felt vaguely uneasy. I was dangerously exposed, and I wondered how I had been foolish enough to put myself in such a predicament. The road was now so dark that I considered putting the headlights on, but decided against it. No sense in advertising my presence. Besides, five minutes more and I would reach Highway 9 and comparative safety.

As the jeep bounced along, my skin was crawling and I began to feel real apprehension for the first time. Drops of perspiration from my underarms soaked through my uniform shirt. Damn! I considered how easy it would be for the enemy to ambush me. Or, if they were more ambitious, they could block the road and take me prisoner. That was not a very pleasant thought.

A movement in the shadows about twenty yards ahead caught my eye and with the incident at Lang Vei village still fresh in my mind I freaked out. I stomped on the accelerator as my pulse sky-rocketed. I didn't know what I had seen and I wasn't waiting around to find out. As the jeep lurched ahead, I drew my .45 and slipped it onto the seat between my legs. Somehow I had the good sense to point it away from my balls. There was no way I could reach the carbine on the back seat if trouble developed. I would have to depend on the pistol, not exactly my best option. I didn't even think about the grenades.

I kept the gas pedal floored and hurtled around a slight bend in the road. My back arched forward as if expecting a stream of bullets to rip through the seat any second. I've always had a good imagination, but this was definitely not an opportune time for it to shift into overdrive. My heart was beating wildly and my breath came in short gasps. I crouched behind the wheel until the jeep finally erupted from the darkness of the coffee groves onto Highway 9.

I breathed a deep sigh of relief and continued on through Khe Sanh Village until I reached the ARVN District Headquarters about half a kilometer west of the turnoff. Several Vietnamese soldiers were milling about outside the building. At the sight of friendlies, I took my foot off the gas and slowed down. Pulling abreast of the group, I waved and drove on at a more reasonable rate of speed. Five minutes later I pulled into Lang Vei, rolled quickly through camp and parked behind our bunker. I was surprised to find that my legs wobbled a bit as I stepped out of the jeep. I made a mental note to never drive to Khe Sanh by myself again.

Our campaign against the VC continued throughout the following week as ARVN mounted a series of search and clear operations aimed at the montagnard villages dotting the plateau. The hamlet of Lang Troi, a short distance south of Lang Vei, was the first target. Our team joined the early morning sweep.

Lang Troi was a typical montagnard village – a dozen thatched huts set in a tight cluster atop spindly support poles.

Huge hogs roamed freely in the open spaces beneath the primitive dwellings. Chickens cackled and flapped as our fifty man force swept into the hamlet. A bare-chested woman was husking rice in the central compound by pounding it on the hard ground with a rough wooden pestle. She eyed us suspiciously as we passed. I could scarcely conceal my wonder. It was a scene right out of National Geographic.

Kiesel and I scouted around while the ARVN lieutenant in charge of the operation sought out the village elder with Walsh. We gravitated toward an open fire in the middle of the compound. An old woman squatted behind it, casually minding a small child perhaps three years of age. The little boy was clad in a ragged shirt and sat barefoot in front of the fire. He was grimy and forlorn. Sensing that they were afraid of us, I greeted them cheerfully. The old woman nodded politely, but the child just huddled closer to his guardian. The reaction didn't surprise me. I understood how they thought. The ARVN and the Americans were here now, but the night belonged to the Viet Cong. The montagnards supported neither side, and wanted merely to be left alone.

It was a cool, damp day, so I warmed myself briefly by the fire until Kiesel called me away. The Vietnamese lieutenant had located the village elder and begun questioning him in the center of the hamlet. The ARVN officer directed a question to the ancient montagnard, who then smiled benignly and shook his head from side to side. He muttered something I couldn't understand.

I turned to Kiesel. "What's going on?"

Troung had been listening closely to the exchange. "He say no VC this village."

The lieutenant jabbered excitedly while the old man stroked his gray, wispy beard as he calmly examined us. He replied in a soft, even voice, his eyes never leaving us. "No VC. No VC."

Walsh turned to Kiesel. "He's just protecting his village. The VC would kill anyone they thought was giving us information."

At this point, a little girl appeared from a nearby hut and dashed to the old man. She threw her arms around his leg and peered shyly up at us. The youngster seemed to be about four years old and was probably his grandchild. The elder glanced down and for the first time flashed a sincere smile. The little girl was obviously his pride and joy.

I caught the child's eye and grinned at her. She ducked back behind the old man momentarily before risking a peep at me again. I crouched down and held out a C-ration chocolate bar that I had been carrying in my pocket. Much to my surprise, the little girl rushed to my side and wrapped her arms around my leg. I handed her the candy bar and her face lit up. I couldn't help laughing. I whisked her into my arms and she didn't seem to mind. I was amazed at how light she was – probably less than twenty pounds. The old man chuckled softly with delight. There was a lot of love in that laugh.

The ARVN lieutenant seemed annoyed that we had interrupted his interrogation and threw up his hands. I really didn't give a damn. I felt that we had finally found a way to connect with the villagers, something he had thus far been unable to accomplish.

The lieutenant ordered his men to search the village for weapons or supplies that might have been concealed by the enemy. Finding nothing, they formed up again and began to move off toward camp. I waved good-bye to the little girl, who was happily eating her chocolate bar.

It rained heavily that night. I stood for a few moments on the top step of the bunker, watching the drops splatter on the ground. There was something soothing about the steady rhythm of a good rainfall. Walner was heating water on the tiny stove When it came to a boil he poured us each a cup of tea. We sat at the table, comfortable and dry, sipping the hot brew and discussing the events of the day. "At least," said Walner, "this rain will keep Charlie quiet." He couldn't have been more wrong.

Early the next morning, while the others were all off somewhere, Troung burst into the bunker as I sat on my cot lacing up my boots. "Ha Si! VC! VC! Lang Troi!" He was so agitated that I had to put my hand on his shoulder to stop him from jumping up and down. This didn't look good.

"Calm down, Troung. What's wrong?"

Despite his limited English and my narrow grasp of Vietnamese, I was able to piece together the following story. Apparently the VC had gone into Lang Troi the previous evening after we left. They gathered all the montagnards into a group where they were forced to watch in horror as the Communists cravenly executed the village elder. They must have figured that he had told us something. Then, in a fit of barbarism, they cut the little girl's head off. The VC strung up the dead elder by his wrists and disemboweled him while the decapitated corpse of his granddaughter lay at his feet like a broken doll. Several montagnard women gathered in a loose circle around the bodies and wailed pathetically. The Communists had established a new level of depravity in creating an object lesson for the villagers.

I was devastated. The VC had delivered a powerful message to the montagnards: Cooperation with the ARVN or Americans in any form would be severely punished. It was ruthless and gruesome, but highly effective. Subsequent patrols found that the villagers refused to even acknowledge their presence. They simply stared straight ahead, never once looking at the Vietnamese troops.

I couldn't get my mind off the little girl. I hadn't even learned her name. She had been so delighted with the modest gift I had given her. Her grandfather had been so openly proud of her. Now they were both dead. The little girl's only crime was that she had been friendly to an American. They murdered her for accepting that goddamn piece of chocolate from me. Tears boiled up from my eyes and cascaded down my face. I pounded the table with a fury born of anguish. What a fucking country! What a fucking war! My feelings toward the enemy, which had been somewhat ambivalent to this point, now intensified to extreme hatred. I vowed that, if given the chance, I wouldn't hesitate to kill the animals who could slaughter an innocent little girl like that. There was something else that was painfully obvious. The VC had been very close while we were in that village, in fact close enough to see me holding that beautiful little child. It was a chilling thought. But my concern was no longer for myself. For the rest of my life I would curse not having had the opportunity to kill those barbaric bastards before they could do their worst. And I would spend many a sleepless night wondering if the suspected VC Troung and I had seen at Lang Vei village had taken part in the atrocity. To this day that possibility still weighs heavily on my heart, and I continue to punish myself for having taken no action against those two likely enemy soldiers.

I'm not sure that my fellow team members even knew about the hideous incident at Lang Troi. They never mentioned it, so neither did I. For me the topic was just too painful to discuss. But it was seared into my mind forever, a horrendous memory that would become a permanent part of my psyche even though I tried desperately to dismiss it. From that day forward, I would never look at life the same way again.

———

STRIFE

AFTER A PERIOD OF RELATIVE quiet following the horror at
Lang Troi, we began holding nightly poker games in a
vain attempt to combat boredom. Dai Uy Lam, who was
an avowed gambler, somehow found out about them. One
evening he swaggered into our bunker while we were playing,
accompanied by his subordinate, Thieu Uy Duc. Lam strutted
down the steps looking like a pompous ass in his signature
sunglasses. I wondered how the hell he managed to see where
he was going at night.

Walsh glanced up from the cards he was shuffling. The big
Marine was clad in shorts, a green T-shirt and clogs, and was
smoking a thick cigar. The corners of his mouth turned down
slightly when he spied Lam. "Hello, Dai Uy," he said in a cool
but civil tone. "Come on in."

Lam nodded and stepped into the cone of yellow light cast
by the Coleman lantern that hung over the playing table. Duc
was close behind. "Ah, you play poker?" he asked, feigning
surprise.

Walsh puffed on his stogie. "That's right. Would you like
to join us?"

Lam smiled. "I would like that."

Dai Uy Lam disliked Americans, particularly those who
attempted to give him advice. He especially loathed Walsh,
who had been pushing him hard to be a more aggressive commander. Believe me when I say that Lam was no military tactician, but he had a tremendous ego that would not permit

him to accept input from outsiders. Lam had sought out the card game to teach Walsh—and us—a lesson, and to humiliate us if possible. His strategy for accomplishing this soon became apparent.

Lam and Duc sat opposite each other at the narrow table, their knees almost touching. When either felt he had a strong hand, he would tap the other with his foot. That was the signal for both to begin raising in an effort to drive the rest of us out of the game. It worked at first, at least until we caught on to their scheme. I exchanged knowing glances with Walsh and Walner, but we kept quiet. Our relationship with the Vietnamese officers was already rather sour, and it wouldn't help matters to create an ugly incident. Besides, there was this macho thing about wanting to beat the pricks at their own game. I studied my companions. Walsh had a grim scowl on his face. Walner's eyes smoldered, but he said nothing.

I soon tired of this and made an excuse to throw in my hand, but Walsh and Walner played on. However, after several more hands, the big Marine lost his patience. Walsh slapped his cards onto the table. In an icy voice he said, "It looks like you're the big winner, Dai Uy. I think I've had enough for tonight." He chomped angrily on his cigar.

With a smug grin, Lam put his hands around the stack of piaster notes in the middle of the table and drew it toward him. "I think, Dai Uy Walsh, that you do not like to lose. What is it you Americans say, a 'bad sport'?"

Walsh shot him a smile that was anything but friendly. "It's not the losing that bothers me. I just don't like being cheated."

Lam lurched as though he had been stung. His voice was a shrill screech. "Cheat? You say I cheat?"

Walsh locked eyes with him. "That's right," he said, his voice a cool hiss. "That's exactly what I say."

Lam sprang to his feet, face contorted with rage. "Fuck you!" he howled. "Fuck you!" He was hopping up and down like a man on hot coals, all the while spewing obscenities at the Marine captain.

Walsh rose slowly and menacingly. Walner and I rushed to get between the two, not liking the look in our commander's eyes. "Hey, take it easy," rasped the Australian. Lam raved on. Suddenly he reached down as if to draw his pistol.

Walner was beside him in a flash with his bush knife drawn. He pressed the point to Lam's throat. "You rotten little bastard!" he snarled with barely controlled fury. "If you ever try that again, I'll gut you!"

Lam blanched. A tiny trickle of blood dribbled down the side of his neck where Walner's knife had pricked him. The Australian gave him a vicious shove toward the door, and Lam's momentum carried him up the steps and out of the bunker. He didn't return. Duc glared murderously at Walner, and then hastened after his superior.

Adrenaline was coursing through my veins as I turned back to my companions. Troung had been sitting wide-eyed throughout the incident and now appeared terror-stricken. Walsh struggled to regain his composure. "We better take turns standing guard tonight," he said at last. "That sonofabitch is just crazy enough to try something else." We agreed.

Fortunately, Lam had lost enough face for one night. There was no further trouble. Before the week was out, both Walsh and Lam were summoned to Hue. The Marine officer returned the next day—alone. ARVN command had transferred Lam to some other duty. Walsh had little to say about the matter, and we didn't press him. As long as Lam was gone, we didn't really care. A new camp commander was on his way to Lang Vei. He HAD to be better than his predecessor. I hoped that wasn't wishful thinking.

———

MENDING FENCES

D AI UY DINH, THE NEW commanding officer at Lang Vei, was a short, chubby-cheeked man with a pleasant, cherubic face. He seemed genuinely warm and friendly. I thought he looked a lot like one of the munchkins in the movie "The Wizard of Oz." Walsh punched me on the shoulder when I said that. But Dinh's accomplishments belied his innocuous appearance. Lacking political connections, the captain had earned his command by rising slowly through the ranks. A devout Catholic, Dinh had fought the French as an enlisted man. Following France's disaster at Dienbienphu, Dinh migrated south and subsequently joined the ARVN. He was an excellent soldier and a competent tactician. I Corps command had made a wise decision in sending him to Lang Vei. It didn't take long before we realized what a vast improvement he was over Lam.

Dai Uy Dinh immediately set to work strengthening the outpost's defenses. The mine field was broadened. Dinh installed new "tangle-foot" wire on three sides of the perimeter, and topped it with a double layer of "concertina" wire. Dozens of additional claymore mines were put into place. It would be a very determined enemy who tested Lang Vei's new defensive capabilities.

Dinh also established an ambitious program of regular patrols. ARVN infantry now made daily forays into the surrounding bush in search of the VC. Night ambushes were also set along trails likely to be used by the enemy. Walsh was delighted. This was the sort of strategy he had preached to Lam for months. But the former commander had always ignored him, preferring to keep himself and his men safely in camp unless ordered out by headquarters. Too bad Dinh hadn't replaced him sooner. Now maybe there would be no more enemy ambushes right outside the perimeter. In any case, Lang Vei had more eyes and ears in addition to its tough new shell.

Perhaps as a result of this aggressive new posture, Viet Cong activity slackened considerably during the latter part of February. We took advantage of the lull. With the height of the rainy season having passed, the sun began to make more frequent appearances. Walner strung a hammock between the bunker and one of my antenna poles. He removed his shirt and slid into the canvas with a bottle of beer clenched in his hand. Walsh resurrected an old beach chair he had picked up someplace, and joined the Australian. I looked at this scene and smiled. Just like a quiet Sunday back in the States. With only two months to go, my thoughts were turning more and more frequently to home.

When we weren't running operations, the time passed very slowly at Lang Vei. Days were remarkably similar except when punctuated by an occasional dramatic incident. One evening around 2100 I was sitting at the table in the bunker reading a book and monitoring the net, as I often did at night. The Angry/9 on the bench behind me hissed and crackled softly. Suddenly a carrier wave interrupted the static. I turned toward the radio in curiosity. Someone was preparing to send a message. There followed a series of "Vs" in Morse, and then the operator switched to voice. It was Lane at Cam Lo, one of our newer operators.

"Frost Weed Alpha, this is Frost Weed Golf. I have one operational immediate. Over."

That got my attention. In our scale of importance, an operational immediate message rated ahead of "routine" and "priority", and was surpassed only by the urgent "flash." I put down my book and stepped closer to the radio.

I couldn't hear net control's reply, but Lane evidently did. He responded, "Alpha, this is Golf. We have one, I say again, one advisor casualty. Request immediate medevac. Over." Normally we would never broadcast information like that in plain language. This was obviously an emergency.

It was very difficult to make out what Lane was saying, and now the VC began jamming as well. I picked up the black plastic headphones and put them on. I still couldn't hear Hue, but I managed to make out Lane's response. "Roger, Alpha. Will wait for further information. Out."

Several minutes later I heard Lane on the air again. "This is Golf. I roger no medevac possible until morning. Thank you. Golf out."

One problem with being isolated at an outpost like Lang Vei was that you could intercept a message like the one I had just heard, but seldom learn its disposition. Sometimes I would copy and decode messages sent to other stations just to pick up some information. I didn't learn what had actually happened at Cam Lo until my next trip to Quang Tri.

Apparently a young lieutenant, who was only in-country a week, had been assigned to Cam Lo as the new advisor there. On just his second day in camp, he went into the field, foolishly hanging two hand grenades from his breast pocket by their handles. Somehow the pin from one of them had worked loose, and the grenade exploded. Badly wounded, the lieutenant died before the medevac arrived the next morning. The incident simply bore home the obvious fact that guns, explosives and inexperience compounded by stupidity did not mix well. I certainly knew that. At Ta Bat I had kept a grenade beneath my bunk and each night unscrewed the fuse, thinking it was the safe thing to do. I didn't realize at the time how dangerous that actually was. It was only through the grace of God that I was not blown sky-high like the young lieutenant at Cam Lo. In truth, it was a dangerous game we played, and sometimes men died needlessly.

The Vietnamese challenged us to a volleyball game the afternoon after the tragedy at Cam Lo. We accepted immediately. Walsh welcomed the opportunity to promote some good will with the newly-confident ARVN. There was a noticeable improvement in our relationship with our allies now that Lam was gone.

The game began in a picnic-like atmosphere near the parade ground. At first glance it seemed like a gross mismatch. We were each a foot taller than most of our opponents. But the Vietnamese made up for their lack of height with speed and skill. We had never played together before, and lacked any degree of cohesion. As we started the game, a crowd of enthusiastic soldiers surrounded the crude court to watch the good-natured contest. They cheered or hooted with every shot.

It was a fun contest. Whenever the Vietnamese scored a point, we stopped to applaud them. The ARVN spectators loved it. This was the way it was supposed to be, but seldom was between us. Once, Walsh leaped to spike a shot over the net. His massive bulk collided with a defending Vietnamese and smashed him to the ground. The huge Marine reached beneath the net and lifted the tiny man to his feet with one big paw. Then he stepped back and bowed. The crowd roared with delight. We had decided earlier that if we took a lead we would deliberately go into the tank and lose the game. We didn't have to do that. The Vietnamese troopers won fair and square. Everyone went to bed happy on the last day of February, 1965. March dawned peacefully the following morning. And with its arrival, I was less than two months from my departure.

———

LAOS

LYNDON JOHNSON WAS FRUSTRATED. ENTERING the spring of 1965, ARVN forces had proven unable to stem the tide of Communist aggression against South Vietnam. The VC continued to strike boldly at installation after installation, often inflicting casualties on American support troops. The president had strong suspicions that ARVN was not up to the task of protecting "his boys," so on March 2nd, he authorized "Operation Rolling Thunder." In contrast to "Flaming Dart," which had plainly been just a retaliatory strike against North Vietnam, Rolling Thunder was a comprehensive program of continuous bombing designed to break the will of the aggressors. Originally slated for eight weeks duration, Rolling Thunder would persist for three long years. In the final analysis, it failed to curtail North Vietnamese military ambitions. But the one hundred American pilots who took to the air on March 2nd to successfully bomb an enemy ammunition dump had no way of knowing that their mission and the ones to follow would eventually conclude in failure.

Rolling Thunder briefly shifted the spotlight west to Laos again. During one of our regular trips to Khe Sanh (we were now always accompanied by a squad of ARVN soldiers), Captain Walsh and I found a Royal Lao Air Force cargo plane parked on the runway. The airplane's twin doors were wide open, revealing an empty interior. We paused to look inside the seemingly abandoned craft, wondering why it was on this side of the border.

Captain Allen greeted us outside the team house. "Hey, come here, you scumbags. I gotta show you something."

He led us around to the side of the team building, where the Green Berets had set up a small table in the shade. A Laotian major sat there in forlorn isolation, his face a mask of despair. He wore a faded green uniform and a battered fatigue hat. His ragged appearance was no surprise, considering that the Laotian army was a poor one. We knew that they got much of their equipment from the North Vietnamese. Compared to the Laotians, ARVN was a first class fighting machine. This officer ignored our presence and focused his gaze upon the mountains to the west.

Allen sneered. "You're looking at the former commander of the 33rd Laotian Elephant Battalion. His own men mutinied and planned to kill him. Someone tipped him off, and he managed to escape on that cargo plane. My guess is that he was stealing their pay. We've heard some rumors about stuff like that going on. Anyway, it must be hell on his ego to come crawling here." The Green Beret captain glanced back at his unwanted guest. "I bet the bastard understands every word I'm saying."

I peered curiously at the Laotian. "What are you gonna do with him, Dai Uy?"

Allen shrugged. "Nothing. The intelligence boys are on their way out here. They'll take care of it." He paused and studied the Laotian once again. "There's a goddamn Red as sure as I'm standing here."

Walsh seemed surprised. "Why do you say that?"

"Easy. His old battalion sits right on the Ho Chi Minh Trail. If he wanted to, he could have at least tried to stop some of that traffic we've been seeing. But he didn't. I'll wager he's been taking payoffs from the NVA as well as stealing from his own men. Oh, this sweetheart was doing quite well for himself. He's not happy about having to give it up, I can guarantee you that. And the Vietnamese won't exactly welcome him with open arms once they find out what he's been up to. He knows it, too. Right now this poor sombitch is probably wondering if he wasn't better off taking his chances in Laos."

I glanced back at the Laotian, who continued to study the mountains to our west. I almost felt sorry for the man. Almost. Allen turned back to us. "Come on. I'll buy you bums a beer."

Something was obviously happening across the border. Later that evening, after we returned to Lang Vei, I was reading a paperback at the table in the bunker. The Coleman lantern hissed softly overhead. I looked up as Troung clomped down the steps, eyes wide as saucers. "Ha Si... Come! Come!" The young corporal was quite agitated. Unable to find the words he needed, Troung raised his hands and made a gentle floating motion toward the ground.

I was perplexed. Now what the hell? I put down my book and followed Troung outside. The Vietnamese soldier was stabbing his finger into the night toward Laos. I took one look and felt a chill run down my spine.

Dozens of lights were drifting earthward near the western horizon. My first thought was that the VC were carrying torches as they came down a mountainside after us. That was an eerie notion, and I felt my pulse quicken. My fertile imagination was in creative mode again. The sight brought to mind a scene from the old film, *Gunga Din*, when the members of a killer cult had marched down a hillside in the darkness heading toward their temple. Quickly recovering from the initial sense of dread, my mind slipped back to a more rational state. The mountains in Laos were actually quite far off. A small hand-held torch couldn't possibly appear so bright at that distance. What we were looking at was an optical illusion. Those brilliant lights had to be flares. Troung and I stood transfixed, watching the lights as they continued to drift slowly down. As they reached the earth and burned out, new ones magically appeared in the dark sky above. The show went on for several minutes.

A series of blinding white explosions suddenly flashed in the distance. Bombs! I counted a string of more than twenty bursts within a matter of seconds. The blasts were so far off that no sound reached us. But the effect was awesome even from this distance. We watched in wonder until the final flares flickered out on the horizon and disappeared.

Some minutes later, I spotted the blinking navigation lights of several large aircraft passing high overhead. The planes were headed southeast at great speed. The Vietnamese Air Force had nothing like that; they had to be American, probably B-57s out of Da Nang.

Troung and I followed the flight until it vanished in the distance, then returned to the bunker. I scrabbled through a stack of newspapers and magazines near the radio until I found what I was seeking. I picked up a recent copy of *Stars and Stripes*, the military news. The headline blared:

NO BOMBING IN LAOS: U.S.

I scanned the article while a small smile crinkled the corners of my mouth. We had just witnessed a bombing mission that hadn't officially taken place. I tossed the paper back on the pile. Things were certainly getting interesting around here.

———

MISSION ALONG
THE BORDER

T HE AFTERNOON FOLLOWING THE BOMBING in Laos, I was busy in the bunker playing chef. I had taken some K-ration sausages and thrown them into a battered frying pan with a large can of tomato puree, then dumped in some spaghetti I had cooked earlier. The entire concoction was now bubbling softly atop our tiny gasoline stove. It looked like sewage and smelled like motor oil. I had often watched my grandmother prepare sauce, but never with ingredients like these. My first attempt at making a spaghetti dinner didn't seem all that promising at the moment. When I judged it to be done, I slopped the entire concoction into a large glass bowl. I held it out to Troung. "You want some?"

As usual, the Vietnamese corporal grimaced and shook his head. "Troung," I said. "This time I don't blame you."

A commotion at the top of the steps caught my attention. I put down my spoon as Walsh stuck his head into the doorway. "Hey, Ollie!" he shouted. "You finished cooking that mess yet? We have a guest for dinner." I had no idea who the hell he could be talking about.

Walsh clomped down the log steps followed by a stranger. "Say hello to 'Mister' Callison," said the big Marine, purposely stressing the 'Mister'.

Callison had short blond hair and pale, watery eyes. He was dressed in khaki civilian clothes that looked as though he had worn them for days. There was an unusual submachine gun slung across his shoulder. I recognized it as a Swedish "K", and immediately realized who our visitor was. Only the CIA carried the Swedish "K." But the most conspicuous feature of the man standing before me was a jagged scar extending from above his left eyebrow down across his cheek and under his chin.

I almost laughed. This was like something out of a grade "B" movie. What was next, a villain with a handlebar moustache and a trench coat? I guessed that Callison had somehow been involved with the previous evening's bombing mission, but the look on Walsh's face convinced me to say nothing.

The agent shook my hand and then glanced across at the table. "Say," he murmured, "is that spaghetti? It's been a while since I had a hot meal."

I grinned. "You must be hungry if you think this crap looks good. Pull up a chair. I've been waiting for someone with the nerve to try it."

Walsh and I joined him, and as we ate we talked about the war and what was happening in the area around Lang Vei. Callison said nothing about his mission, and neither of us questioned him. He was the only one who took seconds of the spaghetti. After the meal, he thanked us profusely and prepared to leave, hoping to get back to Khe Sanh before dark.

I was still curious about why Callison there, but thought it better to mind my own business. After more than ten months in Vietnam, I had already seen far too much. I suppose Callison's mission could have had something to do with the Laotian captain we had seen at Khe Sanh. Perhaps the intelligence boys had gotten some interesting information out of him—information important enough to attract the attention of the CIA. I'm sure there was a common thread running from the Laotian to Callison to the bombing mission we had witnessed, but I had neither the inclination nor the wherewithal to learn more. I had already seen too much. To be frank, I was more interested in thinking about going home.

Shortly after Callison's visit, Captain Allen sent his Green Berets on a brief patrol along the ill-defined boundary with Laos. In order to ensure their own security, the Special Forces troopers needed to know what was going on across the border. Allen assigned the job to Lieutenant Lukitsch and one of his strike force companies.

Captain Allen also solicited ARVN participation. Dai Uy Dinh, the camp commander, asked permission from his superiors to support the mission. They authorized him to transport a 105 howitzer to the border, but not to cross into Laos. Lukitsch's men stepped off just before dusk. The ARVN troops, accompanied by our advisory team, were scheduled to move out at first light.

A high, dark overcast and an intermittent drizzle ushered in the dawn. Dai Uy Dinh's artillery unit, protected by a company of infantry, rolled out of Lang Vei in a small convoy, pulling the big howitzer behind them. We rode in the middle of the column with Walner at the wheel of our jeep. I sat in the back with the radio and Corporal Troung, our Vietnamese aide. It was only a couple of miles to the border, but by the time we got there the rain had stopped and the skies were considerably brighter. I had often heard that the weather was always better in Laos than on the Khe Sanh Plateau. Apparently there was some truth to that rumor.

We arrived at a cement milepost that marked the border. On one side, painted in large red letters was: VIETNAM, DONG HA, 83km. An arrow pointed to the east. The other side indicated: LAO, SAVANNAKHET, 245km, with another arrow pointing in the opposite direction. Our convoy halted just short of the marker and began deploying into a small open field.

I had been here before. There was a tiny ARVN listening post about one click (kilometer) east of the border on the Vietnamese side. Squads of infantry manned it on a rotating basis. The position was badly exposed and very vulnerable to attack, but the occupants could give early warning of any trouble coming down Highway 9 from Laos. That was a big concern of ours. If the North Vietnamese decided to come across the frontier or down from the DMZ in force, they would sweep right over our little camp. Manning the outpost could be scary duty, but most of the time it was just boring and lonely. Very little traffic crossed the border at this point.

Two platoons of infantry fanned out to form a loose perimeter around the convoy. The gun crew quickly set to work manhandling the 105 into position, while another squad began uncrating ammunition. Before long, rows of heavy shells rested on wooden boxes within easy reach of the gunners.

I raised the jeep's whip antenna and picked up the handset dangling from the Prick-10 to make contact with the patrol. For this operation the Green Berets' call sign was "Boat Crane." If the patrol needed artillery support, Lukitsch would contact me, and I in turn would relay the necessary information to the gun crew through an interpreter provided by Dai Uy Dinh. It was a cumbersome arrangement, but Lieutenant Lukitsch felt more comfortable with an American on the radio. I squeezed my mike. "Boat Crane, Boat Crane, this is Frost Weed Delta. How do you hear me? Over."

The response was almost immediate. ""Delta, this is Boat Crane. I hear you 5 by (loud and clear). How me? Over." Judging by the strength of the signal, I guessed they were no more than a couple of kilometers away. Considering how ill-defined the border was at this point and how close we were to it, I figured that they had to be INSIDE Laos. That would have been illegal, but I'm sure it wasn't their first concern. They were more worried about what the enemy was doing across the border where the NVA could operate free from the threat of the Allies.

"Roger, Boat Crane. I hear you the same. Be advised that we are setting up now. Over."

"This is Boat Crane. Request you call again when 'Long Tom' is ready. We may want some markers. Over."

"That's affirmative, Boat Crane. Frost Weed Delta standing by. Out."

I put the handset down and walked over to where Walsh, Walner, Kiesel and Troung were watching the gun crew prepare the howitzer. I told them what Lukitsch wanted. Walsh nodded and turned back to the 105.

An ARVN crewman had removed the breech-block from the gun and was sighting it in by aiming through the barrel at a tree on the distant hillside. A second soldier peered through a device resembling a periscope that was attached to the top of the weapon's armor shield. When the images coincided, they replaced the breech-block. Other soldiers were busy embedding the twin spade-like braces on the rear of the carriage into the heavy clay earth. The entire procedure took almost half an hour before the artillery lieutenant finally signaled that they were ready.

I strode back to the jeep accompanied by the interpreter, and called Lukitsch again. "Boat Crane, this is Frost Weed Delta. 'Long Tom' is ready. What's your pleasure? Over."

There was a brief delay before Lukitsch broke squelch. "Roger, Delta. Give us three 'Willy-Peters' (white phosphorous) at coordinates Yankee Delta three-six-niner, seven-eight-two. Let me know as each round is out. Over."

"Roger, Boat Crane. Three 'Willy-Peters' on the way. Stand by."

Author *(left)* with Vietnamese officers at the
Vietnam/Laos border, Spring 1965.

I turned to watch as the interpreter shouted instructions
to the gun crew, reading the coordinates from notes he
had scrawled in a small memo book. Two computers—soldiers trained to calculate the information needed to aim the
gun—worked feverishly beside the tube, then called out their
numbers to the firing crew. One man slid a shell into the
breech while loaders stood by with two more rounds. Another
soldier adjusted the elevation and direction. When all this
was done, the lieutenant raised his arm and then yanked it
sharply downward. "Ban!"

The howitzer recoiled violently as the shell rocketed out of the barrel. I could actually see the round silhouetted against the slate gray overcast as it soared skyward. I clicked the handset. "Boat Crane, this is Delta. Number one fired. Over."

I turned to watch the 105. The crew inserted another shell into the breech. The big gun bucked. I shouted into the mike. "Two fired!"

"Roger," replied Boat Crane.

The gunners repeated the sequence. "Three fired!" I said. Lukitsch rogered again. The howitzer crew stepped back momentarily and waited.

The sudden quiet seemed greatly magnified. I could hear a large insect humming in the distance. Then squelch broke again. "Delta, we see them. Come right 300 and add 200. Over."

"Roger. Stand by."

The interpreter relayed the new instructions. The gun barked and I bellowed into the mike. "On its way!"

I imagined the round arcing toward the target. Contrary to popular belief, an incoming shell doesn't arrive with a high-pitched and descending whistle as portrayed by Hollywood. Rather, I knew from experience that the sound is more like the rushing noise of an approaching freight train, gradually increasing in volume as it draws closer. That had happened at Ta Bat when the gunners at A Luoi fired some marker rounds near our camp. Lt. Mowrey and I had raced to the nearest trench as the first big shell came howling in. It's not a pleasant thing to hear, I can tell you, particularly if you're on the receiving end.

After another short pause, Lukitsch came back on the air. "Delta, that one was right on. Please stand by for further instructions. Out."

I put down the handset and climbed into the front passenger seat to wait.

The afternoon dragged by at an agonizing snail's pace. All was quiet except for the soft whooshing sound emanating from the Prick-10. I hadn't heard from Lukitsch since we fired the last marker round several hours ago, but didn't bother with a commo check. I knew he'd call if he needed us.

I waited expectantly, hoping to hear a contact message from Boat Crane. This was weird. It was almost like some Saturday football game except that instead of getting ready to score touchdowns, we were preparing to kill people. Yet, I found it strangely exhilarating. Maybe we would even get a chance to take out those bastards who had killed the little girl at Lang Troi. Payback, as they say, is a bitch.

While I waited, I thought back to a story I had heard recently. ARVN artillery had caught some VC in the open up near Con Thien, resulting in six KIAs. When a patrol brought the bodies back to camp, American advisors examined them. The dead Communists were heavily caked with mud, but that didn't mask the gruesome efficiency of the artillery. One victim had lost both his legs below mid-thigh. The entire chest area of another had been shredded and blown out as if someone had blasted him with a shotgun at close range. A third had evidently been killed by concussion. Congealed blood radiated from his nose and ears and matted his thick dark hair. Flies were already settling on the stiffened corpses.

One of the advisors leaned over to look more closely at yet another body. There was a small black hole behind the man's right ear, but no evidence of any bleeding. Someone had given this poor bastard the "coup de grace" after he was already dead. Apparently brutality wasn't limited to the other side. But I couldn't work up a whole lot of negative sentiment over that story. In fact, I found myself hoping our mission would produce similar results. That's how strong my hatred for the VC had become. I'm not proud to admit it, but that was just the reality of what I was feeling at the moment and I make no apologies for that. I sat quietly in the jeep, battling my conflicting emotions.

The ARVN soldiers set about building small fires nearby to cook their mid-day rice. It was extremely humid but not, thankfully, very hot. I sat absently watching them go about their business. Walsh and the others had gone off somewhere with Dai Uy Dinh and his entourage. The soft whooshing sound from the Prick-10 remained uninterrupted by any calls from Lukitsch. In spite of my best efforts to stay alert, the gentle drone from the radio made my eyelids droop. I stepped out of the jeep and walked around a bit to clear my head, being careful to stay within earshot of the radio. This went on for several hours. There was still no word from "Boat Crane."

Finally I spotted Walsh walking toward me and perked up. "We're gonna call it a day," said the big Marine. "Lukitsch will head back this way at dawn, and the artillery will cover him. Dai Uy Dinh wants to keep the gun here tonight instead of doing this all over again in the morning. His troops will camp here and stand guard. We're gonna stay at the listening post."

I nodded. It was now late afternoon. Troung and I packed up the jeep as the veiled sun began to dip behind the mountains. When the others returned, Walner drove us the short distance to the tiny outpost and parked inside the single roll of barbed wire that surrounded the narrow compound.

The ARVN garrison had cleared out one of the crude bunkers for us. It was dingy and stank of stale urine. There were no cots. Troung busied himself in the bunker while I built a small fire near the jeep and heated some C-rations. As dusk fell, we sat around the fire on two logs and ate from the stubby green cans with plastic forks. Walsh glanced at me with a mischievous look in his eye. "Hey, Ollie," he needled. "Your cooking still sucks!"

I glared at him. "So don't eat it if you don't like it," I growled.

We all chuckled, including Walsh. Back in Saigon, or even in Quang Tri, I would never have talked to an officer like that. But out here we were equals, within reason, of course. I liked that. In fact, we all did.

It was already dark by the time we finished the spartan meal. The overcast had thickened once again, effectively shutting out what little light the stars might have provided. I shuddered to think what it must be like for the squad of ARVN who had to stay out here alone night after night. In the deepening blackness, it would be too dangerous to use a lantern. Walsh ducked into the bunker and prepared to turn in. The roof was so low that he had to hunch over or risk cracking his skull on a crossbar. The others soon followed.

I waited until they were all inside, and then kicked dirt onto the fire. Settling into the front seat of the jeep, I reached over and switched on the Prick-10. Boat Crane's frequency was quiet. I monitored the radio for a while, rehashing the events of the day. Now and then I glanced down at the dying coals glowing red in the darkness. The jungle was still except for the occasional buzz of an insect, or an isolated shrill outburst from some goddamn Communist bird. Tiring of this eventually, I shut down the radio and made my way into the bunker. Troung had left me a space in a corner. I stretched out on the floor, careful not to disturb the others. I unlaced my boots and yanked them off. As I settled back, I wondered what the hell the next day would bring.

It was a long and uncomfortable night. Every time I finally dozed off, something would scuttle about in the darkness and startle me to wakefulness. It gave me the creeps. I slept little and was quite happy to see the first pale light of dawn seeping into the open bunker. I reached across and nudged each of my companions. "Hey... wake up, you guys." Snorts and grunts and a loud fart rewarded my efforts.

I reached down and shook out my boots. There were big ugly bugs in Vietnam—foot long centipedes, some scorpions. You never put your boots on in the morning without first turning them upside down in case an uninvited guest had taken up residence inside during the night. To say nothing of snakes. I hated snakes. I smiled wryly, recalling the time a colorful banded snake had slithered down the steps of our bunker, sending three heavily-armed advisors racing outside while Troung and another soldier cornered the reptile and killed it. That sucker probably ended up in somebody's cooking pot. And Troung laughed about the incident for weeks, much to our annoyance.

We boiled some water and made C-ration coffee. I called Boat Crane while the others collected their gear. Lukitsch and his men were already en route. They planned to meet up with us at the 105 position. When everyone was ready, we crammed into the jeep again and scooted back up Highway 9.

The ARVN emplacement was a beehive of activity as Dinh's men prepared to break camp. Walsh conferred briefly with his counterpart and then returned. "Dai Uy Dinh's men will wait here for Lukitsch. We're going back to camp."

I had mixed emotions about that. We weren't going to get the chance for revenge that I craved, but I was glad to be heading back to Lang Vei. I didn't know it yet, but this was to be our last trip to the border. However, a new chapter in the expanding war was about to unfold.

———

THE BUILD-UP BEGINS

ENERAL WILLIAM C. WESTMORELAND WAS concerned. Intelligence indicated that there were some six thousand Viet Cong in the area immediately surrounding the huge U.S. airbase at Da Nang. Westmoreland, lacking faith in the ability of the ARVN to protect this vital installation, asked the president for two Marine battalions to deploy around the facility. Over the objections of some of his advisors, Lyndon Johnson approved the request. On March 8, 1965, more than three thousand Marines arrived off Da Nang on board ship. They stormed ashore in a combat assault, and were met not by enemy fire, but by laughing Vietnamese who threw tropical flowers to the heavily-armed American troops.

Newspaper headlines trumpeted: 1st US COMBAT TROOPS LAND IN VIETNAM! Walsh snorted derisively when he read that. "What the hell do they think we've been doing," he griped, "playing ping-pong with the VC?" In any case, the floodgates had been thrown open and the pent-up military might of the United States was about to be unleashed upon what at first consideration may have seemed to be a far inferior opponent. The first trickle would quickly become a flood.

Enemy activity in I Corps slackened to practically nothing after the Marines arrived, as if the Communists had deliberately pulled back in order to assess this new development. The Americans took full advantage of the lull to land a second force at Hue near the Nguyen Hoang Bridge. I later heard that a number of advisors from the hotel were waiting nearby to see the show seated in beach chairs. That didn't mean much to me at Lang Vei. I welcomed the break. In less than a month I would be out of the field and preparing to go home. If I never hear another shot again, I thought, I'll be very happy.

It was so quiet in our operational area that Walsh organized a target practice session. That was probably a good idea, since I hadn't fired my weapon in quite a while. We set up a makeshift range on the western perimeter of camp facing the mountains of Laos. There was a stiff breeze blowing. The yellow and red-striped ARVN pennant atop the flagpole was snapping sharply in the wind. As it turned out, I realized too late that we would be shooting directly into the teeth of a near gale.

I drew my .45, cranked a round into the chamber and took aim at a coconut we had thrown across the wire. I squeezed the trigger. As the heavy pistol bucked in my hand, the whistling wind blew the muzzle blast back into my face. I hadn't thought to use earplugs, so the effect was like that of a shot fired next to my head. I was momentarily deafened by the concussion. There was an intense ringing in my right ear. Kiesel said something to me and I was surprised that I could scarcely hear him. The Marine lieutenant's voice sounded hollow and far off, something like what you hear when you hold a seashell to your ear.

I switched to my carbine and fired that instead. After half an hour we returned to the bunker. My hearing problem improved slightly after several hours, but the constant ringing persisted. It was extremely irritating, almost maddening. During a quick visit to Khe Sanh the next day, I had Sergeant Brady, one of the medics there, take a look at the ear. Brady found a perforated ear drum. He said that it should heal by itself, but there was no way to know if there would be any permanent damage. Wonderful.

It was very difficult to sleep with that horrendous ringing in my ear. I was concerned the next morning that it hadn't improved much, if at all. Little did I know at the time that it would never go away. But for now it was a dangerous condition, because I couldn't hear any sound originating from my right.

I went out to the jeep to make my morning commo check feeling extremely irritable. Two Vietnamese signalmen sat nearby outside their communications bunker. As they often did when I went to my radio, they strolled over to the jeep, chattering happily.

The Angry/9 had an adjustable tone control. Since I was having difficulty hearing the bass tone, I twirled the knob all the way to the right. Then, as I began tapping out Frost Weed's call sign, the radio emitted a weird-sounding sequence of high-pitched squeaks. The ARVN radiomen burst into laughter.

I exploded. "Get the hell out of here!" I roared, slamming down the key. "Go on, beat it!"

The little soldiers recoiled in shock. One of the radiomen held up his hands and said, "OK, OK," hurt clearly etched on his face. They turned and walked slowly back to their bunker, occasionally risking astonished glances at me.

I regretted my outburst immediately and swore softly, angry at myself for my lack of composure. I had always had a good relationship with the ARVN commo men. In fact, we had helped each other with signal problems previously. Now it seemed likely that I had ruined that good will. I knew then that I had spent too much time at Lang Vei. Extended field duty had a way of rendering you quick-tempered and overly sensitive. The ear problem had exacerbated that. There was no doubt that I was now wrapped a bit too tight.

After completing the commo check I returned to the bunker and borrowed several packs of cigarettes from Walner. I then walked sheepishly into the ARVN radio bunker and approached the two signalmen. "Sinh loi" (Sorry about that), I said. I could feel my cheeks burning with embarrassment. I handed a pack of cigarettes to each of the perplexed soldiers. They thanked me civilly, but were uncharacteristically cool. And they never again approached me when I was on the radio. I felt very badly about that then and still do.

Thompson and Keller went home at the end of March. They rang me up on the radio before they left to say good-bye. It was a somewhat emotional conversation, considering the circumstances. I was overjoyed for my friends. They had, after all, survived a year in a combat zone and were finally returning safely to their families. But I knew that I would miss them sorely. You cannot live through what we had shared and not feel the loss of parting. My one consolation was that Doug and I were scheduled to follow them within a matter of weeks.

Some time later I heard from home that Tony had contacted my parents when he arrived back in the States. He told them some of what we had experienced, but not too much, and assured them that I would be returning soon. It was a kindness that my family never forgot. I also learned that Thompson had taken a Bronze Star with him, the only one of our team to receive that prized decoration. I was proud of my friend. He deserved it.

———

HOMEWARD BOUND

LEFT LANG VEI IN THE middle of April, 1965. That gave me enough time to get back to Quang Tri to gather up my gear and check out of my now one-man room. Then it was down to Hue for a couple of weeks to unwind before departing for Saigon where out-processing for the journey back to the States would begin. On the morning of my departure, I awoke to find a going-away gift from Troung. The Vietnamese corporal had constructed a magnificent wooden steamer trunk for me. I couldn't believe what fine work he had done with just the crude tools and materials to be found at the outpost. It must have taken him countless hours to finish. I was deeply touched.

I shared a last breakfast with Walsh and Walner. As fate would have it, they were both going to follow me in a few days once a new advisory team arrived. Lieutenant Kiesel had already left several weeks previously. When it was time to go, I shook hands with Walner and vowed to see him back in Hue. Walsh carried my trunk to the jeep. He had offered to drive me to Khe Sanh so that I could catch a ride on an incoming Huey.

I turned hesitantly to Troung, who looked forlorn sitting on a wooden box beside the steps. I had grown quite fond of him, and patted his shoulder gently. "Chao, Troung," I said. "You take good care of Lang Vei."

The despondent corporal hung his head. "Lang Vei numbah ten thousan'," he mumbled.

I swallowed hard, trying to banish the lump in my throat. Walner looked away. On an impulse, I reached inside my fatigue shirt and unclasped the Combat Infantry Badge that Troung had always admired. I pressed the medal gently into the young soldier's palm. "Here, Troung... you keep this until I see you again."

I immediately regretted my choice of words. There wasn't one chance in ten million that we would ever meet again, and we both knew it. But the corporal's face brightened as he looked down at the CIB. He turned it over and over in his hands. "Cam anh (thank you), Ha Si," he murmured. A weak smile crossed his face. "Chao."

I turned and quickly sprinted up the steps, feeling too much emotion to speak further. Walsh was waiting in the jeep with the engine running. For the first time in many weeks, some feeble sunshine was filtering through the clouds. The rainy season would soon be past. I paused to take one last look around the camp where I had experienced so much during the previous four months, then climbed in beside the captain. We roared off scattering a cloud of red dirt.

Neither of us spoke during the brief ride through the coffee groves to Khe Sanh. Upon reaching the Special Forces camp, we went into the team house where I said good-bye to Captain Allen and the handful of his men who were present. We wished each other good luck. Within minutes, the distinct pudda-pudda-pudda of an incoming Huey thrummed in the distance.

Walsh walked me to the helicopter as it touched down. The rotors continued to spin at full power. We ducked our heads beneath the whirling blades as a helmeted machine gunner peered curiously at us through the open door. I turned to the big Marine. "Dai Uy, I..."

Walsh cut me short. He practically had to scream to be heard above the roar of the engine. "Shut up and get your ass out of here! You were a fucked-up radio operator anyway!" He smiled and grasped my hand warmly. "I'll see you back in Hue."

I tossed him a snappy salute and then hopped aboard the vibrating aircraft. Welsh handed up my trunk with a grunt. The Huey lifted off with an accelerating whine and a swirl of dust and debris. I waved to the grinning Walsh as we gained altitude and Khe Sanh began to recede below. The door gunner tapped me on the shoulder. "Hey, man... You goin' home?"

I glanced back at the now distant Special Forces camp. "Yeah," I shouted through the wind whistling in my face. "I'm going home."

———

GOLD TOOTH

LATE ONE AFTERNOON AFTER CHECKING out of Quang Tri, I was sitting at the bar in the Hue enlisted men's club. A master sergeant I recognized as having served as an advisor to the ARVN 3rd Regiment came in. I'm unable to remember his name, so I'll call him Sergeant Hanlon. He pulled up a stool and sat beside me. After engaging in some small talk, he began to tell me a remarkable story.

Hanlon had been on an operation somewhere in Quang Tri Province, and was waiting at a landing zone for pickup by an ARVN H-34 helicopter. Two VC suspects captured by the strike force during a sweep of a nearby village stood sullenly nearby, hands tied behind their backs and under guard. One was a short, wiry man who appeared to be in his middle forties. The other was a slim youngster perhaps nineteen or twenty. Both were clad in black pajamas.

As the helicopter settled to the ground, the group turned away from the sudden blast of dust and debris thrown up by the rotors. The guards practically carried the two suspects to the chopper and lifted them roughly aboard. Hanlon scrambled in after them and found a seat as far from the others as he could get.

A grizzled Vietnamese non-com with a gold front tooth took charge of the two prisoners. He nodded to Hanlon, unable to conceal his irritation at having an American aboard. Then he shoved his captives against the fuselage and kicked their feet out from under them. The helicopter lifted off with a roar. "Gold Tooth" stood beside the open door and eyed the suspects coldly. The two prisoners fidgeted uneasily as he removed a small notepad from his pocket. It was apparent that "Gold Tooth" was an interrogator.

The sergeant crooked a finger at the older prisoner, and one of his men yanked the man to his feet. The interrogator made a great show of opening his notepad and writing a brief notation in it. Then he said something to the suspect. Engine noise and the wind whipping through the open door of the helicopter prevented Hanlon from hearing what was said. But he was able to read the prisoner's lips as he answered, "Khong biet" (I don't understand.) "Gold Tooth" repeated his question. The man shook his head.

The sergeant lashed out suddenly and slapped the prisoner viciously across the face. The younger suspect, who had been watching closely, cringed and began to perspire. "Gold Tooth" asked another question and received the same response. It was becoming obvious that he would get no information from the man. He then braced himself and kicked the prisoner as hard as he could, propelling him through the open door. The captive's blood-curdling scream carried above the roar of the engine as he dropped like a stone toward the ground a thousand feet below.

The younger suspect was terror-stricken. Urine bubbled through his trousers, collecting in a yellow pool that sloshed back and forth with the motion of the aircraft. He began to wail hysterically. "Gold Tooth" knelt beside him and said something.

Information gushed from the panic-stricken youngster like an open faucet. "Gold Tooth" recorded everything in his notepad, pausing occasionally to mutter, "Lam... Tot Lam" (Good... Very good.) When the sergeant was satisfied that he had all he was going to get he snapped the notepad shut and stood up. Two guards jerked the weeping prisoner to his feet. "Gold Tooth" spoke some soothing words to the frightened wretch. Then, with a lunge, he shoved the tightly-bound boy through the door. A horrible screech erupted from the captive's lips.

Hanlon was shocked but said nothing. This was not his show. "Gold Tooth" turned and glared at him as if to say, "This is how WE do things, American. You're just an intruder here." When the helicopter landed, "Gold Tooth" and his guards disembarked without so much as a glance at Hanlon.

At first I was skeptical. Soldiers, after all, have a talent for contriving bullshit stories. But Hanlon had told his tale with such detail that it had an air of authenticity to it. If true, I wondered how "Gold Tooth" managed to explain the loss of the two prisoners, or if he even had to. I couldn't imagine that ARVN command would care much about what happened to them as long as they got the information they wanted. I suppose Hanlon should have done something to prevent the atrocity, but I understood why he hadn't tried. This was their war; we were merely observers. The two suspects were obviously VC. It was hard for me to work up much sympathy for them. A year earlier, such a story would have disturbed me. But since the horror at Lang Troi, I had developed such a blatant hatred for the enemy that now I couldn't care less that those two had met such a fate. I still didn't believe in the murder of helpless prisoners, mind you, but certainly wasn't as indignant about it as I might have been previously. Later in life, during the quiet moments while awaiting sleep, I sometimes reflected on that and wondered how I had become so crass. Even now I occasionally experience a pang of guilt for feeling as I did, at least until I think about the atrocity at Lang Troi, and then it usually vanishes. However, that day in Hue I simply chalked it up as a questionable story that couldn't be verified, but was probably true. That was the extent of my emotional involvement. I had grown fairly callous about the treatment of the enemy I now hated so much.

———

WINDING DOWN

I T WAS A HOT SUNNY morning in Hue. The mosquito netting surrounding my bed billowed silently in the gentle breeze generated by a softly-whirring fan nearby. I had just completed a midnight to 0800 radio shift and fallen asleep almost immediately, not even bothering with breakfast when Doug relieved me. After months of the cool Lang Vei weather, I was finding the heat of Hue City somewhat tiring.

The radio room had been relocated to the Citadel near ARVN headquarters while I was gone. I was now back at the hotel in the same room I had shared with the others so long ago. The door swung open slowly and a shadowy figure crept quietly into the room. The intruder halted beside my bed and cautiously raised a portion of the white netting. As he bent over me, my tired mind registered a soft hissing sound. The mysterious interloper released the netting and quickly re-treated. As he left the room, his all too familiar cackle brought me to full wakefulness.

I glanced about in confusion, wondering what the hell was going on. My hand touched something wet and warm on my chest. I looked down. Shaving cream! Mounds and mounds of white foam covered my body from neck to waist. Chop... That sonofabitch! I bolted from the bed, grabbed a towel and wiped off the soapy mess. On impulse, I threw open the shutters and stepped out onto the balcony.

Sergeant Kane was scurrying across the parking lot toward a jeep waiting to take him to the Citadel. He was going home.

He glanced back and spotted me on the balcony. "So long, Ollie!" he laughed. "That's for the shorts!"

I had to chuckle in spite of myself. I hadn't realized that he even knew who was responsible for getting his underwear starched. I gave the departing Chief Operator the finger and then called out, "Good luck, Chop!" The jeep lurched out onto the road and ground off toward the airfield with Kane seated proudly in the passenger seat, the self-satisfied grin of a Cheshire cat plastered on his face.

Potter guffawed when I told him of the incident. "So he finally got even after all you did to him." I didn't think it was quite as amusing as he did, but, as they say, "If you want to dish it out, you've got to be able to take it." And besides, with just two weeks left in my tour, I wasn't about to let anything short of a catastrophe spoil my good humor. And today I sometimes wonder what became of old Chop.

LEAVING ON A
JET PLANE

O UR LAST FEW WEEKS IN Vietnam were quite uneventful. With the arrival of U.S. Marine combat units in March, the North Vietnamese Army and local Viet Cong seemed to draw back to assess this new situation. I Corps was very quiet. Not that we were complaining, mind you. I was quite happy to be away from the dangers of the field. It's just that, well, things were really boring. We went through the motions of manning the radio net, but nothing much was happening. The days passed very slowly.

Doug and I began to feel mildly euphoric now that we knew we were so close to going home. With four radio operators in Hue, our flexible schedule allowed us plenty of free time. We used it to take care of some personal business.

I ordered three custom-made suits from the Indian, choosing colorful and outlandish linings for each of them. Wait 'til they see these back home, I mused. It wasn't until months later, when the thread began to disintegrate and the suits fell apart that I realized how I had been taken. The Indian was shrewd. What was I going to do, bring them back?

I also bought some souvenirs for my family as I remembered Lansing having done almost a year earlier. That seemed like a lifetime ago. So much had happened since then – things that would change my life forever.

I Corps remained extremely quiet. The arrival of the Marines probably helped keep it that way, although the gyrenes had yet to be tested in battle. The units based near Phu Bai occasionally came to the hotel for hot showers, hot meals and a few hours rest. Doug and I watched one afternoon as a platoon marched in close order up the street and into the parking lot. "They've got a lot to learn," I concluded. "One grenade would get the whole gang." Doug nodded.

We made several trips to the river to watch the Marine landing craft bringing ashore a modest stream of supplies. Little did we imagine what a torrent would soon follow. But for now, the tiny boats flew the only American flags in Hue. It had been almost a year since we had seen the stars and stripes. The sight drew us back again and again.

Time seemed to move more slowly as we approached DEROS. Sergeant Schwamborn, Kane's replacement, did his best to make life more pleasant for the veteran operators. The new "chop" was a good-natured, middle-aged man whose first concern was "his boys." After what we had been through with Kane, Schwamborn was a breath of fresh air. He even organized a pool party for us at the Cercle Sportiff.

It was a luxurious way to use up a day. We swam in the crystal clear water, soaked up the re-emerging sunshine and later ate steaks grilled over open coals in the club's restaurant. When it was over, we thanked Schwamborn profusely. "Are you kidding?" he said. "Who deserves it more than you guys?" Doug and I just smiled in appreciation. "Oh, by the way," continued Schwamborn. "I'm recommending both of you for the Army Commendation Medal. Just make sure you get the hell out of here in one piece." We weren't about to argue with that.

All this lavish comfort was in such stark contrast to what we had known in the field as to be almost impossible to process.

Only scant miles away, Americans were living in primitive conditions and dying in filth. But that was the nature of war in Vietnam during 1965. I suppose during the previous eleven and a half months we had done enough to earn a little slack.

Around the middle of April, Doug and I brought our hold baggage to the supply room to be examined. Returning soldiers always sent their excess belongings home prior to their actual departures. The sealed containers usually arrived back in the States just before their owners did.

We presented our trunks to the young second lieutenant who was waiting to examine them. The officer opened my trunk first, and ran his hand admiringly along the lid. "Say, this is nice work."

I beamed. "Yeah, I know. A friend of mine made it."

The lieutenant rummaged through my paraphernalia until he came across a carbine magazine I had placed in the bottom of the trunk. He held it up and said, "For a minute there I thought I found some contraband narcotics."

I knitted my brows. Drugs? Of course. We had just spent a year in one of the most prolific narcotics producing regions on earth, yet I had never once seen any. That seemed rather incongruous, considering the widespread drug abuse among our troops later in the war. We had many problems in I Corps during 1965, but that wasn't one of them.

Several days later, Doug and I were down to the single digits on our "short-timers" calendars. Almost every American had one of these drawings of a well-endowed woman with her body delineated into segments numbered in reverse order from 100 down to 1. The last three numbers, appropriately enough, were on the two breasts and the crotch. A soon-to-depart soldier simply crossed out the body part corresponding to the number of days he had remaining until he finally reached number 1, his ultimate reward. We chuckled over the

prospects of soon becoming "breast men." It was a crude but
highly effective means of tracking our time in-country.

There was a flurry of activity the following morning. The
VC had ended their self-imposed stand-down by mortaring
Quang Tri during the night. The advisors compound there
took several direct hits. Five or six Americans had been slightly wounded by shrapnel including my replacement, a tall slim
black youth named Danzy. I just shook my head when I heard
the news. I always seemed to be just one step ahead of or
one behind those VC bastards. At this point in my tour I was
quite grateful for that.

Since there was no dispensary at Quang Tri, the injured
men were brought to Hue for treatment. None of them had
serious wounds, but the victims didn't seem particularly grat-
ified at the prospect of a relatively easy Purple Heart. "Man,"
said a clearly worried Danzy. "I've only been here three weeks
and I'm wounded already. What's gonna happen to me in the
next eleven months?" I could certainly sympathize with him.
I understood that kind of thinking.

Doug and I had orders to fly down to Saigon three days
before leaving for the States. In our detachment it was cus-
tomary for departing team members to join the Senior Advisor
for dinner the night before leaving. We found mimeographed
invitations from the adjutant in our mail slots inviting us to
dine with Colonel Bissett the following evening.

That afternoon, I took a last walk across the bridge. Banners
hanging from the overhead girders blared: LONG LIVE VIET-
NAMESE-AMERICAN FRIEND-SHIP and WELCOME 3RD
U.S. MARINE BATTALION. Unfortunately, the political atmosphere represented by those two banners would not be as
long-lived as all concerned would have hoped.

On my way back to the hotel, I stopped to buy a bunch
of finger-sized bananas in the crowded market place. One of

the first things we learned at our initial orientation sessions was to avoid locally produced fruits and vegetables. The Vietnamese were notorious for fertilizing their crops with human waste. I don't know what I was thinking, but I ate several of the bananas. I guess I figured they were safe since you had to peel them. Big mistake.

Severe cramps struck me during the night. I vaulted from bed and raced to the bathroom clutching my stomach. Waves of nausea swept over me as violent diarrhea tore at my innards. The agonizing bouts of illness continued throughout the night and were so debilitating that I could scarcely crawl back and forth to the toilet.

Whatever bug had invaded my intestines was obviously a Communist one. I was still deathly ill the following morning. Except for a quick trip to the dispensary for some medicine, I didn't get out of bed all day. Doug came by to check on me in the afternoon. The expression on his face was a mixture of concern and amusement. "How you doing, partner?"

I looked up at him with bloodshot eyes and a ferocious headache. "Not too good. Do you believe this shit the day before we leave?"

Doug scratched his head. "You gonna be able to make the Colonel's dinner?"

I winced at the thought. "No way. I couldn't handle it."

"I'll tell him you're sick. Listen, when I get back I'll help you pack."

"Roger. I'll see you later." I had already packed most of my gear so I just rolled over and closed my eyes in a desperate effort to will away the unrelenting misery.

I felt somewhat better the following morning. The uproar in my intestinal tract had subsided, yet I was still feeling weak and washed out. I was struck by the irony that I had been deathly sick just before arriving in Vietnam, and now equally ill as I was about to depart. But nothing was going to stop me from making the trip to Saigon. I gathered up my bags while Doug went downstairs for breakfast. I shuddered at the thought.

The hotel was practically deserted when we left. An American sergeant waited in a jeep to drive us to Phu Bai for our flight. We hurled some last insults at Yniguez, who was watching from the balcony above much as I had done when Kane left two weeks earlier. Doug and I shared a last look at the compound as we pulled out of the parking lot and turned the corner onto Highway 1. So much had happened to us here, both good and bad. We gazed back at the hotel in silence until it disappeared from sight.

A C-123 sat on the runway at Phu Bai, its engines already beginning to sputter. I clambered apprehensively aboard behind Doug. I had been worrying about getting the runs during the flight, but then I spied a tiny lavatory across the aisle from my seat. I can chuckle about it now, but that sight really boosted my spirits. Now there was no reason to miss our scheduled flight home.

It was a long, non-stop trip to Saigon. Doug and I were the only Americans on board, sharing space with a platoon of combat-ready ARVN soldiers. Why in the world they were going to the capital was beyond me. And to tell the truth, I was too wrapped up in my own physical problems to care much about that. I napped fitfully throughout the flight. Thankfully, I had no need to visit the john.

By the time we landed at Tan Son Nhut, I was feeling almost normal. After not eating for two days, I was experiencing some robust hunger pangs. "Man, I'm starved," I griped to Doug. He just snickered.

We boarded a bus that transported us to the Capital Hotel, of all places, where we had begun our assignment a year before. We were so green then! It was easy to laugh at the memory, but we had paid dearly for our inexperience. This time we got a room on the second floor of the hotel. In twelve months we had gained two ranks and three floors. We actually felt like VIPs.

We enjoyed a leisurely meal that evening in the hotel cafeteria. Doug downed several glasses of fresh, cold milk, while I opted for pizza. We had seen neither since we went north to Hue. "Hey this is great," said Doug. "Maybe we should extend."

I just glared at him.

We turned in our weapons at the MACV compound the following morning. All I had left was the .45, having given my carbine and the Thompson to Walner. A pudgy sergeant stood inside the same supply room where we had drawn our handguns the previous May from the corporal who had told us we probably weren't coming back. Doug deposited his pistol belt atop the divider shelf and glanced around. "Say, Sarge... where's that wise-guy corporal who used to work here?"

The non-com looked up from his clipboard. "You must mean Gilliam."

"Yeah," said Doug. "I think that was his name."

"He went home a couple of months ago."

I tossed my pistol belt onto the shelf in disgust. "Too bad," I said, feigning disappointment. "We wanted to kick his ass."

Doug erupted into laughter while the supply sergeant simply stared, wondering what he had missed. As for me, I was on a personal high. We had not only survived our year in spite of Gilliam's grim prediction, but I was beginning to think that the damn bad dream that had been tormenting my nights for so long might soon be a thing of the past.

We spent our last full day in Vietnam snoozing through one briefing after another. Junior officers in crisply-starched fatigues spoke at length about the problems we might encounter when we re-entered the normal world. They offered suggestions on how to cope with the sudden and extreme transition from war zone to home. Most of us ignored them. We had our own ideas about how to handle it, and were anxious to test them.

At the conclusion of the briefings, medics gave each of us a small supply of anti-malaria pills to take after arriving home. There was also a wallet-sized card embossed with the MACV emblem. It had a personal message from General Westmoreland thanking us for a job well done. As we filed out of the room, a lieutenant admonished us from the podium. "Don't forget, you can't take more than a thousand piasters out of the country. If you've got more than that, make sure to convert it before boarding your aircraft, or it will be confiscated." Charming.

When we got back to the hotel, a cute young maid was working in our room. I struck up a conversation with her. "You number one co," I teased. "You have boyfriend?"

The girl giggled and nodded her head. "Ha' boy frien' in a'my. He in Dak To."

I extracted a twenty dollar bill from my wallet and held it up. "Maybe you like boom-boom?"

The girl scowled. "Numbah ten! Boy frien' no like!"

Leave it to me to find one with scruples. I laughed and put the money back in my pocket. What the hell, in another couple of days I'd be back among "round-eye" women. I decided to take a cold shower, which was the type most readily available at the hotel anyway.

Doug and I returned to the Saigon Enlisted Men's Club that evening to celebrate our last night in Vietnam. A group billing themselves as "The Chinese Beatles" was performing a full array of current American hit songs. We enjoyed the show until midnight and then made our way back to the hotel. I looked for the two "VC" who had transported us a year ago, but they were nowhere to be seen.

"Well, partner," said Doug as he prepared to climb into bed, "we're just about out of here."

I lay on my back watching a gecko lizard creep across the ceiling, much as I had done a year previously when we first arrived at the Capital Hotel. "I'll believe it when the plane takes off," I answered.

Something was gnawing at the back of my mind as I waited for the sleep that would close out my last night in Vietnam. Despite my burgeoning desire to go home I was troubled by a nagging suspicion that I was leaving without having finished my job. Had I done what I could to ensure that those who followed us were better prepared than I had been when Doug and I arrived in-country? Not really. Sadly, we never got the opportunity to meet our replacements or to pass on the knowledge and experience that we had acquired. I realized that I hadn't handled some things very well, but I now knew what I could have done better. Yet I was uncomfortable with my status as a now-competent soldier to be leaving, replaced by someone with minimal qualifications. That person would have to earn his knowledge and experience, probably at great cost, much as I had gained mine during the preceding twelve months. Little did I realize that this very problem would plague the American effort in Vietnam for years to come after I went home. Sleep did not come easily that night.

We arose early the following morning, our last day in-country. Our flight was scheduled to depart Tan Son Nhut Airport at 1100, and we fully intended to be there in plenty of time. Neither of us had much of an appetite for breakfast; we were far too excited for that. Our bus left the hotel just after 0900. By the time we arrived at the airport, checked in, and handed over our baggage, there was less than an hour to boarding.

To kill some time, I offered to buy Doug a Coke. There was a small outdoor café nearby where we found a vacant umbrella table on the veranda and ordered drinks. When the sodas arrived, we both sipped quietly, lost in thought. Doug finally broke the silence. "What do you think, Jim… did we accomplish anything here?"

I put down my drink and thought for a moment. "I'll tell you this… I think we did the best we could under the circumstances. This is a crazy place."

Doug nodded. "Yeah. It's pretty tough to help people who don't want your help. Or don't want to help themselves."

I studied his face. "Maybe. But I think our intentions were good. You know—stop Communism, help guarantee a free South Vietnam. Problem is we Americans are a little too idealistic—me more so than you. I don't really know if we can do any of those things. This place is just too damn complicated."

Doug stared into his glass. "I hope we did some good."

I looked up. It was unusual to hear him talk that way. "You know what?" I said. "For the most part, I feel pretty damn good about what we did here. Oh, there were a couple of things I'm not too proud of and would change if I could. But overall, I think we did OK."

Doug continued to study his glass. "Was it worth Foster's life? Or Sergeant Patience? Or any of the others?"

I lowered my gaze and grimaced. "Oh, hell, Doug… I don't know. I was only talking about my personal feelings. Maybe none of this was worth even one life. I just want to go home and let somebody else sort it all out. Now it's time to find a job, maybe a good woman. Start a family…" My voice trailed off. "There's one thing, though. I hope no son of mine ever has to go through something like this."

Doug nodded. "Amen to that."

We sat quietly for several minutes. I checked my watch, wondering when they would call our flight. Suddenly a tremendous explosion on the far side of the perimeter sent us diving reflexively beneath the table. When we raised our heads again, somewhat sheepishly, I pointed to a billowing cloud of black smoke rising beyond the runway. Some unfortunate truck driver must have triggered a big mine. "Jesus," I said. "For a minute there I thought we'd had it."

Doug chuckled nervously. "Yeah. Wouldn't that be a bitch? We make it through a whole year here and then get creamed waiting for the plane. Christ."

Sirens sounded, and several fire trucks raced to the site of the explosion. We were both a little uneasy at this point, so it was a relief when our flight number was posted soon after. There must have been huge grins on our faces as we hurried through the terminal, carrying only overnight bags. We passed through the gate and out onto the tarmac where a gleaming Pan Am 707 waited on the runway, just like the one that had brought us here a year ago. For all we knew, it might have been the same one. By the time we reached the aircraft, we were practically running. I paused just long enough to snap a photo of the plane, and then continued up the loading ramp.

We chose seats on the left side of the aisle, and then gaped in astonishment at the smiling stewardesses. It had been a long time since we'd seen "round-eye" women. The crew wasted no time. As soon as everyone was safely seated and the doors were sealed, the engines began to whine. The aircraft vibrated, and then bobbed slightly as it started to roll out onto the runway. When we received our final clearance, the engine noise rose to a piercing shriek.

The 707 hurtled down the runway until it reached takeoff speed. As we lifted off, the rumble of the wheels ceased. I glanced forward. The aircraft was canted upward at a severe angle. Doug and I turned to the window for our last view of Vietnam. The rice paddies surrounding the airfield were receding rapidly into the distance. As we gained altitude, the terrain below took on a brown and green patchwork appearance. That soon vanished beneath the clouds as if a curtain had symbolically been drawn, bringing a close to the chronology of my war and punctuating my final image of South Vietnam with a flourish.

When the jetliner was obviously beyond the range of any potential hostile ground fire, the passengers erupted in spontaneous cheering and applause. Some clapped each other on the back and hooted with joy. Others sat quietly, tears of relief streaming down their cheeks. Doug turned to me, extended his hand, and said softly, "We made it."

I clasped my friend's hand. "Damn right," I replied, choking back my emotions. "Feels good, doesn't it?"

Doug nodded.

The plane nosed out over the South China Sea, headed east—toward home.

EPILOGUE

M ORE THAN FORTY-EIGHT YEARS HAVE passed since I returned home from Vietnam. Hard to believe it's been that long. Not many people, other than fellow veterans, have ever asked me about the war or my small role in it. When they do I reply that Vietnam was actually two distinct conflicts. The early years (my war) were characterized by frequent incidents of small unit actions punctuated by the occasional big battle. That began to change in November of 1965 when the 1st Air Cavalry took on the North Vietnamese Army in the Ia Drang Valley. At that point the Vietnam War started to evolve from a counter-insurgency effort into a larger, more traditional conflict.

I was fortunate to avoid most of the heavy fighting. I always seemed to arrive someplace right after a fight, or leave just before one. The Special Forces camp at A Shau was overrun in March of 1966, forcing the closure of the other outposts in the valley, Ta Bat and A Luoi. A Shau was the first Green Beret camp lost to the Communists, and as a result became a very sore point of discussion for General Westmoreland. Once the A Shau Valley was abandoned, it quickly became a North Vietnamese stronghold. The enemy used it as a primary infiltration route from the "Ho Chi Minh Trail" into South Vietnam. During the Tet Offensive in early 1968, the valley served as a staging area for the NVA assault on Hue. Many more engagements were to be fought in the A Shau, including the infamous battle for Hamburger Hill. But the allies were never again able to establish control of the valley.

Last view of Vietnam, May 1965.

In 1967, Lang Vei was briefly seized by the Communists, and both American officers in camp were killed. The outpost was later accidentally bombed by allied aircraft. As a result, the decision was made to relocate the camp about one kilometer west along Highway 9 closer to the Laotian border. When the Marines assumed operational control of Khe Sanh, the Green Berets moved over to the new camp. In 1968 "new" Lang Vei was demolished by the North Vietnamese, who used tanks for the first time on the battlefield. Seven armored vehicles drove right through the wire perimeter and rolled over the bunkers, crushing them with their great weight. The defenders managed to knock out several of the tanks, but paid a heavy price. More than three hundred of the ARVN soldiers in camp were killed. Ten of the twenty-four Americans were lost. During the battle, frantic requests for help were sent to the

Marines at Khe Sanh, just a few miles away. But Marine commanders, fearing an ambush, refused to send aid. For years afterward, the Army bitterly resented their lack of action.

Shortly thereafter, Khe Sanh itself came under siege by twenty thousand North Vietnamese soldiers. For more than two months, the camp was bombarded daily by enemy artillery. But the anticipated major battle never materialized. The siege resulted in extreme damage to the camp and the rich coffee groves surrounding it. The stronghold there was finally abandoned in mid-1968. Many military tacticians now regard the encounter at Khe Sanh as an enemy diversion designed to draw attention away from the North Vietnamese general offensive beginning in late January that was aimed at the major cities of South Vietnam.

The beautiful city of Hue was virtually obliterated during the Tet Offensive as seven thousand North Vietnamese and Viet Cong troops occupied the former imperial capital. U.S. Marines and ARVN forces rooted out the enemy in vicious house-to-house fighting that lasted for three weeks. Most of the Communist attackers were eventually wiped out. The Hue Citadel and the revered Palace of Peace were heavily damaged during the battle. Viet Cong sappers blasted the Nguyen Hoang Bridge into the Perfume River. The MACV compound, where I was first quartered upon arrival in Vietnam, survived a direct enemy assault and held out through the fight. However, our former communications house, one block from the MACV hotel, was demolished. Allied forces finally retook the city, but the toll was enormous. More than three thousand civilians were executed by the North Vietnamese, many of them buried alive. Eighty percent of the structures in Hue were destroyed, leaving roughly one hundred thousand people homeless. It was a victory for the Allies, but one that eventually proved irrelevant as U.S. forces withdrew from the country in 1973 and South Vietnam finally fell to the Communists in 1975.

I spent my last three months in the Army back at Fort Dix again, serving, if you can believe it, as a clerk/typist. Doug Potter and I were assigned to the 86th Engineer Battalion, which was headquartered in a brick building very close to where we had attended ISROC. The facilities, in fact, were almost identical. It was here, unfortunately, that I ran afoul of the commanding officer, a reserve colonel. For some reason he took an instant dislike to me. At the core of the problem, in my opinion, was the fact that he may have resented a junior enlisted man possessing combat decorations when he had none. Doug and I had certainly experienced that type of behavior before. It probably didn't help that I had a bad attitude and a chip on my shoulder, since I didn't want to be there. In any case, he did his best to make life miserable for me. Admittedly, I brought some of that upon myself. I sometimes conducted myself with behavior bordering on insolence, especially after I learned that the colonel had ordered the battalion adjutant to pull my personnel file and verify that I was actually entitled to wear my awards. I'm sorry, but after experiencing what I had in Vietnam, I found all this garrison "chicken shit" difficult to accept. In my mind, our commander compared poorly to Colonel Collins, who had earned my utmost respect. Same rank, same army, but different species.

I spent much of my time with the Engineers preparing citations for the CO. "...2nd Lieutenant Lance T. Snotnose performed admirably during his assignment as Battalion Laundry Officer..." I apologize for being flippant, but after serving with true soldiers like Walsh, Collins, Crittenden and Mowrey, it was hard for me to take any of this stuff seriously. Anyway, the colonel mellowed somewhat as I approached my separation date. In fact, toward the end, he actually told me,

"You type more accurately than I write." It was the only compliment he ever gave me. Thankfully, we had finally reached something of a civil understanding in a one-sided clash that I had no chance of winning. All in all, my stint at the 86th Engineers did not represent my finest hour in the military.

Both Doug Potter and I had a brief brush with the real Army again. The 1st Cavalry Division (Airmobile) was being formed that summer, and the scuttlebutt was that this innovative new combat outfit was critically short of experienced personnel, radio operators in particular. Lieutenant Berman, the battalion adjutant, told me that both our names initially came up for assignment, but neither of us had the 90 days of service time left that was a prime requisite. That was certainly good luck for us, since the Cav was slated for shipment to Vietnam where it would fight many tough battles against the North Vietnamese Army. I'm not sure that we realized at the time just how fortunate we had been.

At the end of September, 1965, I packed my gear into the new Pontiac Catalina that I had purchased with the combat pay I'd accumulated and drove up the Jersey Turnpike to Long Island for the last time. I haven't been back to Fort Dix since.

Ken Keller, Tony Thompson, Doug Potter and I had a reunion in 1984 at a resort in the Catskills along with our growing families. I have never been able to contact any of the other Americans or Australians who served with us. I have no information on the fate of Corporal Nguyen Troung. I only hope he survived the war and lived to eventually teach his children the "slowly I turned" routine.

In March of 1988, the family "torch" of military service passed to my son. Jim Jr. enlisted in the Army and took his basic and advanced training at Fort McClellan, Alabama. My wife and I flew down to attend his graduation. When American boys once again took the field during "Operation Desert

Storm" in 1991, we agonized every day wondering if the call would come for our son. Fortunately it never did. For that I am eternally grateful.

But someday that call will come again. Almost fifty years after I landed in Vietnam, world peace continues to elude us, and I see no real prospects for it in the near future. Unfortunately, man is essentially a warlike creature, so conflict is a normal part of his behavior. One need not be clairvoyant to know that Americans are sure to take up arms once again. When that happens, "Uncle Sam" will summon his "nephews" and perhaps even his "nieces." That torch may pass to yet other members of my family. For them I offer this simple advice. The power of the torch can be very seductive indeed. It can change your life forever if you accept it, but by doing so, you can never let it go. Once the torch comes your way, you will never be the same again.

Today the war is still with me. And perhaps surprisingly it isn't the terrifying moments when bullets were flying that dominate my memories. It's the nights I sat alone at some isolated and vulnerable outpost, wondering if someone was coming at me from out of the darkness, that still occasionally haunt my dreams. Those unsettling shadows sometimes awaken me from otherwise quiet and peaceful sleep, forcing my conscious mind back through the many intervening years to that strange, far-off land I visited in my youth. When that happens, I'll often get out of bed to sit silently in the stillness of the early hours contemplating memories of what I experienced there. Some of the images of people, places and events are still so incredibly vivid, especially the disturbing ones. Those shadows may never fully disappear, but I think at long last that I'm finally learning to live with them. However, the medical conditions related to my exposure to Agent Orange are likely here to stay. Thankfully, I have long since bid farewell to my guilt regarding why I lived and some others died. Somewhere along the line I accepted that it was simply the luck of the draw and let it go at that. I think that may have spared me many sleepless nights. There's one thing I do know for certain, though. I was a far different person when I left Vietnam than I was when I arrived there.

One final thought. I envy veterans who have made return trips to Vietnam, and I can't help but speculate what it would be like to see that beautiful land again without having to worry about getting shot. I, too, would like to make a cathartic visit and walk once more along the paths I followed such a long time ago. But time is growing short now and the chances of that happening seem very remote. So I'm left with just the memories of my one great adventure in life. I suppose that will have to be enough.

———

THE SOLDIERS
OF THE SKY

I knew when you became my wife
The Lord gave me his best.
So when I reach the end of life
I have but one request.

Please bury me where soldiers lie,
In earth that's rich and warm,
Where veterans guard the distant sky
Through wind and rain and storm.

For I was once a soldier too,
So young and filled with pride.
I grasped the torch of war and drew
My strength from those who'd died.

For God and flag we went abroad,
The Yankee was the stranger.
We met the cruel and deadly horde,
And faced the guns of danger.

We bore the heat, the blood and tears,
Endured the shot and shell.
We silently concealed our fears,
And plumbed the depths of hell.

When at last our time was done,
We left the land of fire,
Changed forever having known
The bones upon the pyre.

Wiser, stronger, sadder men,
No gratitude we knew.
We felt unloved, but gladly, then
The good Lord sent me you.

And soon came children of our own,
Through sickness and in health.
What they've become and how they've grown
Means more to me than wealth.

My comrades met the final call,
The years have whispered by,
Their names upon a marble wall,
Now soldiers of the sky.

And when it's time for me to rest,
My duty here well done,
Please let me lie among the best,
Their battles fought and won.

Find for me a sacred garden
Sown with boots and caps,
Where none within has need for pardon,
And buglers still play "Taps."

Names and faces matter not,
Nor heritage, not color.
We'll share the honor of our lot,
Our strength and deeds of valor.

If I should come to God's right hand,
Perhaps he'll pause to tell
Why he permitted me to stand
While those around me fell.

I'll be with you as I am now,
No man could ask for more,
Eternal love my silent vow,
The guardian at your door.

And so, my love, we'll meet again,
Of that you can be certain.
Perhaps you'll lie beside me then,
When God brings down the curtain.

For on that day we'll be together
As bright flags snap nearby.
We'll rest in peace, protected ever
By the soldiers of the sky.

———

Jim Oliveri
1995

ABOUT THE AUTHOR

photo by Mike Spinelli Photography

JAMES OLIVERI is a native Long Islander who graduated from Lawrence High School in New York with a Regents scholarship. He attended New York University prior to entering service with the United States Army. He is a Vietnam combat veteran who earned eight decorations, including the Combat Infantry Badge and Army Commendation Medal, during his assignment to Southeast Asia.

Following his separation from the military, James embarked on a forty year career as a banking and financial professional, eventually retiring with the title of Vice President. He has been a member of Kiwanis International since 1969, served two terms as a club president and holds a Hixson Fellowship, one of the most prestigious awards available to a Kiwanian. He is a past commander of an American Legion post, a member of the Veterans of Foreign Wars and the Vietnam Veterans of America, and is currently the publicity chairman for the Daisy Mountain Veterans Day Parade, the largest in the state of Arizona. In addition, he has been a regular contributing writer for several Arizona-based magazines.

James Oliveri provides editing and proofreading services for authors from his home in Anthem, Arizona. He also administers a blog at Familyshadows.com. James and his wife, Maureen, have four children and eight grandchildren. For more information, contact him at Yeeditor@cox.net.

———